COME NORTH
WITH ME

BERNT BALCHEN

COME
NORTH
WITH
ME

An Autobiography by

Bernt Balchen

HODDER AND STOUGHTON

CONTENTS

1 RACE FOR THE POLE, *1926*   13

2. ANOTHER WORLD, *1926–1927*   50

3. RIM OF THE ARCTIC, *1927*   68

4. THE GREAT NEW YORK TO PARIS AIR
    DERBY, *1927*   87

5. THE LAST VIKING, *1927–1928*   123

6. ANTARCTICA, *1928–1930*   148

7. NEW HORIZONS, *1931–1941*   193

8. BLUIE WEST EIGHT, *1941–1943*   215

9. VE DO IT, *1943–1945*   257

10. TRUE NORTH   298

MAPS

Antarctica, from Little America to the South Pole   150
Greenland   217
The Scandinavian countries   259

PHOTOGRAPHS

Bernt Balchen   *Frontispiece*

                                                                 Facing page

At Advent Bay, Spitsbergen: Bernt Balchen starting up the
motor of the Amundsen-Ellsworth Relief Expedition plane
in 1925   28

Commander Richard E. Byrd's plane, the *Josephine Ford*, and
the hangar for the *Norge*, the airship in which Amundsen
flew over the Pole   28

Roald Amundsen   29

Commander Richard E. Byrd and his pilot, Floyd Bennett,
just after their North Pole flight   29

The *Josephine Ford*, then the biggest passenger airplane in the
world, at Mitchel Field, 1926   32

Operations office of Western Canada Airways at Hudson, Ontario   32

The *America*, Commander Byrd's trimotor Fokker, and Bernt
Balchen at Roosevelt Field before the transatlantic flight in
1927   33

The *America* on the ramp from which it took off for France   33

The *America* after ditching on the French coast   64

PHOTOGRAPHS 9

Commander Byrd signing the Golden Register of the City of
Paris 64

Floyd Bennett, Bernt Balchen and Charles Murphy shortly
before the start of the Greenly Island relief expedition 65

Test-flying the *Floyd Bennett* for the South Pole flight 65

Fitting skis on the *Floyd Bennett* at Le Pas, Manitoba 96

The first survey party setting out from the *City of New York*
to locate a site for Little America 97

Camp at Ver-sur-Mer Inlet, housing men setting up Little
America 97

The beginning of the blow at the Rockefeller Mountains 128

The situation at the camp at the Rockefeller Mountains after
the blizzard 129

The *Floyd Bennett* emerging from its snow hangar 160

Building the sledge to carry the survival gear 160

The survival equipment we took on the South Pole flight 161

We are warmly welcomed at Little America on returning from
the South Pole 161

The Queen Maud Range in Antarctica, photographed from
the *Floyd Bennett* 192

At the Fokker factory, Teterboro, N.J., in 1930: Eddie Ricken-
backer, Bernt Balchen; the three members of Kingsford
Smith's crew, Van Dyke, Stanaghe and Saul; Kingsford
Smith and Tony Fokker 193

Dr. James H. Kimball, then head of the New York office of the
U.S. Weather Bureau, and friends at the testimonial dinner
given for him by transatlantic fliers   193

Lincoln Ellsworth and Bernt Balchen in the *Polar Star*   224

A view of the Antarctic pack ice from the *Wyatt Earp* during
the Ellsworth Expedition   224

Returning four years later to the drifted-over camp at Little
America, I find only the tail of the *Floyd Bennett* rising
above the snow   225

The wreck of the Lincoln Ellsworth Expedition plane *Polar
Star*   225

The belly landing of the PBY on the Greenland Icecap during
rescue operations there   256

After our long journey across the Greenland ice fields following the rescue of the B-17 fliers   256

General "Hap" Arnold visits us in Iceland   256

Watercolor by Bernt Balchen of a USAAF plane delivering an
air drop to underground forces in occupied Norway   257

Opening a container of American-made sabotage equipment
dropped by Operation Sonnie to Norway's freedom fighters   264

A container drop is received by Norwegian resistance forces   264

Supplies and equipment stacked high on the beach at Thule,
Greenland, during construction work on the airfield in 1951,
and ships at anchor in the iceberg-filled harbor   265

USAF troop transports getting ready to drop paratroopers in
the vicinity of Thule during Operation Windchill, March,
1954   280

Pack ice at the North Pole   281

Presentation of the Harmon International Trophy by President Eisenhower to Colonel Balchen   281

COME NORTH
WITH ME

ONE

RACE FOR THE POLE

1926

"29 April. S.S. Chantier arr. Kings Bay, 1600."

We have been watching the smudge on the horizon since ten o'clock this morning. The sailors on the *Heimdal* spotted it first, and they called to the workers uncrating supplies on the coal dock below; and the men cupped their hands and yelled to the mechanics on the hill, riveting the upper sections of the dirigible mooring mast, and the word spread quickly through our whole camp. I was in the machine shop when I heard my name shouted, and I answered "Ja, I come," and hurried out and shaded my eyes and looked seaward where everyone was pointing.

The feather of smoke was floating in a thin layer of sunlight, sandwiched between the sea itself and the grayish blue reflection of the ocean on the low overcast that we call in Norwegian the "water sky." Sometimes the smoke-plume seemed very near, sometimes far away. This is a trick of the Arctic, where there are no dust particles in the clear air and distances are hard to estimate. East of our expedition's base the mountains named the Three Crowns stick up through the glacier. These nunataks look almost near enough at times to reach out and touch. The other Sunday I put on skis and started toward them; but after ten miles they were as distant as ever, and I turned back to camp.

All morning long we have paused now and then in our work, and glanced at the smoking funnel on the horizon, and muttered uneasily to each other. We are not sure yet. It could be a supply ship for the mine, or a sealer headed for the ice pack. We look over the tar-paper roofs of the mining camp, toward the superintendent's house on the hill where Captain Amundsen is living. Has he heard yet, does he know? We shake our heads and look back again at the strange vessel, holding a straight course for Kings Bay.

We are in Kings Bay, on the west coast of Spitsbergen, to set up the advance base for the Amundsen-Ellsworth-Nobile Transpolar Flight. Here is only a small Norwegian coal-mining operation, running with a reduced staff of about fifty people—the northernmost human habitation in the world. It is 500 nautical miles north of Norway, and almost 700 miles from the North Pole. From this base Captain Amundsen will attempt to fly by dirigible from the old world to the new, the first flight in history over the northern axis of the earth.

It is the biggest and most carefully planned air assault on the polar regions yet. Since last October, construction crews have worked through the long Arctic night to pour the concrete foundation for the mast and to erect a huge open-roofed hangar which will house the dirigible *Norge* when it arrives. At the edge of the flat, towering above the fjord, is the 130-foot metal mooring mast, the highest structure north of the Arctic Circle. Already the *Norge* is standing by at Leningrad, waiting for the signal to pick up Captain Amundsen at Kings Bay and carry him across the Pole.

Eight days ago, on April 21st, we landed here with Amundsen from the supply ship *Knut Skaaluren,* and we unloaded our 1500 tons of equipment and began moving it up the hill and across the mile and a half of snow-swept flats to the hangar site. There is a narrow-gauge railroad running from the coal pier to the mine; but shortly after we landed came a tremendous two-day snowfall, with winds up to fifty miles an hour, burying the buildings of the mining camp up to the second story. The tracks were blocked with drifts as solid as the mountain side itself, and since then everything has had to be hauled by hand sleds. There was one lone horse belonging to the mine—a short-maned pony of the Nordfjord breed used in Norway since the times of the ancient Vikings—and also a tractor which nobody could run. Fortunately I had tinkered with mechanics in the Norwegian Air Force, and I managed to get it started. I checked out a couple of crewmen from the gunboat *Heimdal,* which had come to assist us, and day after day the tractor and the pony moved up and down the slope past each other, the tractor back-firing and the horse snorting in answer, and the *Heimdal* sailors in their round blue caps and sea boots slipping and sliding in the snow as they panted behind the heavy uphill loads.

In the continuous daylight of the early northern spring, we have been laboring in shifts around the clock to make everything ready for the arrival of the *Norge.* Today the weather forecast calls for the passing of a warm front and a gradual clearing, with favorable flight conditions predicted over the entire route to Alaska. We have another reason for haste. We have known for a month that a rival expedition from America is coming here to Kings Bay in an attempt to beat us to the Pole.

At noon the operator from the Kings Bay radio station hurries past us, bound for the headquarters building on the hill. He has just picked up a signal from the approaching ship. It is the American vessel *Chantier,* bringing Lieutenant Commander Richard Evelyn Byrd and his party. His airplane is on board, ready to fly and with almost twice the speed of our dirigible. Now we know it is a race, and the odds are against us.

At two P.M. the *Chantier* rounds the point and moves into the mouth of the fjord, and we can see its black outline clearly against a glistening white iceberg. It is ten miles from the fjord's entrance to our camp, and the ship is making about six knots, feeling its way through the floating debris of blue and iridescent green ice-cakes which have been calved by the crumbling glacier at the head of the bay. The sharp bow of the ship throws a white wave on either side, like a pair of fangs, and I think of a husky dog baring its teeth at the sight of a rival pack.

All work at our base has halted, and the men of the Amundsen expedition stand in silent groups along the bluff. We resent this foreign ship coming here to our own country to snatch the prize which we feel belongs to Captain Amundsen alone. We of his party are loyal to him to the point of worship, and any one of us would lay down his life without question for one of the greatest of all living explorers. In 1905 Amundsen had sailed a small fishing smack, the *Gjoa*, through the churning ice of the Northwest Passage, making the first successful voyage from Greenland to the Bering Sea over the route where Sir John Franklin's expedition had perished in a previous attempt. On this trip he had discovered the vacillation of the Magnetic Pole. Six years later, traveling on skis and dog sled, he had planted the Norwegian flag at the South Pole. In 1918–1920 he had brought his own ship, the *Maud*, around the Arctic rim of Scandinavia and Siberia through the Northeast Passage to the Bering Sea, the first man in history to circumnavigate the globe above the Arctic Circle. He had made two unsuccessful attempts to reach the North Pole by air—one a valiant effort with Lieutenant Oskar Omdahl in a single-engine Junkers airplane from Wainwright, Alaska, and the other a year ago when he and Lincoln Ellsworth set out from this very base at Kings Bay in a pair of Dornier Wal flying boats. Of all the challenges of the icy unknown, only the North Pole has eluded him until now. His flight over it would be the climax of a dedicated career, and more than any other man in the world, we feel, he has earned the right to this final honor.

One of the men turns, and nudges another, and we all look up at a lone figure on the hill behind us. People always turn to look at Roald Amundsen, as their eyes would be drawn to the tallest mountain. He stands at rest on his ski poles, still very straight in his middle fifties, as hard-muscled and vigorous as a young athlete. With his hand he slowly pushes back the visor of his ski cap to view the rival expedition.

His face is expressionless and we cannot read it. Beneath the thick tufts of his eyebrows, white as hoarfrost, his eyes in their deep sockets are hidden in shadow. His cheeks are leathery and folded into hard creases, with a fine network of wrinkles spreading out from the corners of his eyes like a map of all the dog trails he has run. The most prominent feature of his face is the thin and arched nose, which gives him the look of an eagle. It is a face carved in a cliff, the face of a Viking.

We wait for him to speak, but he pivots on his skis without a word and strides back to the headquarters building.

When I was about twelve years old, back in Norway, Captain Amundsen came once to my stepfather's house in Kristiansand. This was in 1912, the year after he reached the South Pole, and he was the national hero of Norway. He was the idol of every small boy my age, so when my mother told me the greatest of all explorers was coming to our own home for dinner, and I should see him in person, there was no limit to my excitement.

Every day the newspapers carried his picture, with the stone face and the unmistakable eagle's beak, and I lived over his adventures every night. I had even been taken to see some of the dogs which were to haul his sled across the Pole, and which had

been kenneled in Kristiansand. Sometimes I would put on my
skis and pick out a fence post in the field behind our house, and
say "There is the South Pole" and cross the snow toward it, past
imaginary penguins and seals lurking behind the woodshed,
making believe that I was the first person to discover that fence
post in all history.

My mother said I should be allowed to come into the front
parlor, where the menfolk would be sipping their champagne
before dinner, and shake hands with Captain Amundsen; but I
was not to speak unless spoken to, and was to leave at once. You
see, back in those days there was the strictest discipline in Norwegian families, and children did not have their meals with
their elders but ate at a separate table with the servants. Whenever my stepfather came into the room, I would jump to my
feet and click my heels at attention.

My stepfather, Olaf Harlem, was a captain in the Field Artillery, and my uncle was Major General Oluf Dietrichson, later
in command of the garrison at Kristiansand. Six times a general
named Dietrichson commanded the local garrison. In 1888 my
uncle had crossed the Greenland Icecap with Dr. Nansen, and
through him Captain Amundsen had come to know my family.

General Dietrichson was fighting in the Balkans at the time
of the visit, but my stepfather was there, and all the ranking
officers in Kristiansand were sitting in the front parlor when I
was brought in. It was a large paneled room, as I remember,
with pine beams from which hung old-fashioned copper lan-
terns that had only recently been wired for electricity. The walls
were hung with guns and crossed sabers and dueling swords, and
fans made of bayonets; and over the fireplace were lances and
hellebards with curved ax heads, and small boarding hatchets
used in the old navy to scale the wooden sides of an enemy man-
of-war.

There were twenty or thirty guests in the room, the commanders of the army and navy units and all the military schools,

for Kristiansand was a big garrison town. They wore full-dress navy uniforms with gold braid in loops on the sleeves, and double-breasted army uniforms of deep blue with red trim and gold epaulettes, scarlet sashes around their waists and red-striped trousers, and long black riding boots with parade spurs clicking across the sand-scoured pine floor.

Only one man in the room was in civilian clothes. He was sitting very straight in a chair of Spanish leather, so erect that at first glance it seemed as though he were being held up by his high starched collar. He wore a tight-fitting blue suit and a green tie that had a metal sheen, and a heavy watch chain across his vest. My mother led me to him, and I stood at attention, trembling all over.

"Captain Amundsen, this is Bernt," she said. "He likes skiing and the outdoors."

All I could do was stare at the heavy weathered face, the arched nose, the chilling blue eyes beneath shaggy brows. His expression did not change, but his eyes grew warmer, and little crow's-feet formed at their corners. He seemed to be smiling with his eyes alone.

"Well, Bernt," he said, "what do you want to do when you grow up?"

I blurted out boldly: "I want to be an explorer and go on an expedition with you, and hunt seals and maybe polar bears."

I heard my mother gasp, and my stepfather's face grew red, but Captain Amundsen's eyes were amused. They seemed to melt his stern face like a winter morning sun thawing the snow. "Then you must keep on skiing," he said, "and get in real good trim, and prepare yourself. In the Arctic you must always be prepared for the worst, and then whatever happens will be easier."

My mother was tugging at my sleeve, and I could hear my stepfather harrumph in his throat, but Captain Amundsen held

me with his smiling eyes and I could not move. It was as though
we had a secret between us. I had forgotten my trembling.

"It is never easy, the life of an explorer,' he said. His voice
reminded me of water running under ice. "You go places where
no one has ever been before, and you do not know what year
you will come home."

My mother gripped my arm hard, and I clicked my heels and
bowed, and she hustled me from the room. She closed the door,
and murmured the old Norwegian saying: "Han er den siste
Viking. He is the last of the Vikings."

Our next meeting was thirteen years later. I was by that time
a lieutenant in the Royal Norwegian Naval Air Force, assigned
to the naval aircraft factory at Horten. On June 1, 1925, I received a phone call from my commanding officer. Captain
Amundsen and Ellsworth and their expedition had disappeared
ten days ago on an attempted flight from Spitsbergen to the
North Pole, and I had been recommended as a pilot to serve
with the government search party.

We arrived in Kings Bay on June 17th with two Norwegian-
built Hansa-Brandenburg twin-float seaplanes, single-engined,
and of less than moderate performance; but we determined to
get the most out of them. It was clear right away that we should
have to operate from the edge of the ice pack to get maximum
coverage of the ice fields. A depot ship was sent ahead, and
we planned to catch up with it by plane at the edge of the pack.
Meantime we camped aboard the *Hobby*, Captain Amundsen's
supply ship.

I was on the deck of the *Hobby*, pulling on my flying cover-
alls ready to go out to my aircraft moored in the bay, when the
Norwegian sealer *Sjöliv* came alongside and a familiar voice
shouted: "What are you doing here, Bernt?" It was my friend
Lieutenant Oskar Omdal, a member of the Amundsen party.
The group on the *Sjöliv*'s deck were covered with dirt and

grime, their faces almost unrecognizable behind a month's growth of whiskers; but there was no mistaking the tallest figure, the hawklike nose and the piercing blue eyes.

Later on the *Hobby* they told us what had happened. When they were only 120 miles from the Pole, one of their two Dornier Wals developed engine trouble and had to make a forced landing on the pack ice. The other aircraft landed near-by, and the six members of the expedition began an epic fight against starvation and slow death. On the ever-shifting floes, using the few inadequate tools they had in the plane, they hacked out six successive landing strips before one runway held long enough to let them escape, just as the ice crumbled and broke beneath them. The masterly piloting of Hjalmar Riiser-Larsen, who was to command the Royal Norwegian Air Force during World War II, got them back to the north shore of Spitsbergen, where they sat down safely and were picked up by the *Sjöliv* and brought here to Kings Bay.

That night, at dinner, Captain Amundsen showed up again freshly clothed and shaved. The sun and the wind and the years had aged his seamed face, but his eyes had the same warm light as he shook my hand.

"I remember you," he said. I could not believe that he would remember me after twelve long years, but he added: "It was at your stepfather's house in Kristiansand, and you told me you wanted to be an explorer and go on an expedition with me." His eyes twinkled. "You see, I do not forget."

He did not forget. The following April he was back at Kings Bay for his third attempt to fly across the North Pole; and I was a reserve member of the expedition, on leave from the Air Force, to assist with the technical preparations.

At four P.M. the *Chantier* glides within hailing distance of the gunboat *Heimdal*, which is berthed in the only available space at the narrow coal dock, and asks permission to tie alongside. Captain Tank-Nielsen replies that it is not possible, because he has not yet finished taking on coal and water, and in addition the *Heimdal* must be ready for departure at a moment's notice in case the *Norge* is forced down on its flight over 500 miles of open ocean from the mainland.

Even to this day it is still argued that Tank-Nielsen deliberately sought to hamper the rival expedition. But the fact is that he was under strict orders from the Norwegian government to be on twenty-four-hour standby for possible rescue work, and, as it turned out, it proved to be a fortunate decision for Commander Byrd himself, since his airplane could not have been brought ashore on the narrow rail beneath the coal chutes on the pier.

The *Chantier* pulls on past the pier and moves to a spot in the bay, indicated by Captain Tank-Nielsen, and drops anchor there, three hundred yards from shore. Looking out from the window of the machine shop, I can see a lifeboat being lowered, and four tiny figures descend the ladder and are rowed ashore. The bay ice has gone out, leaving an accumulation of glacial fragments called an ice foot, which lines the whole beach. They find a break in the jagged barrier, and leap out of the boat and cross the treacherous ice foot to solid ground.

I watch the party work its way around the bay to the dock. A few curious families from the coal-mining village have hurried down to the water's edge, and they step back as the strangers pass. The barking of several sled dogs chained behind the houses is the only sound of greeting. They start across the long flat toward our camp, and the workers hauling supplies give them hostile glances and make way in sullen silence. I step out of the machine shop as they approach, and the leader of the group calls: "I'm Commander Byrd. Can you tell me where I'll find Captain Amundsen?"

I am full of interest at meeting this explorer of whom we have heard so much. He is in navy uniform, every button of his blue overcoat carefully fastened, the bottoms of his trouser legs stuffed into sturdy buckled galoshes. Commander Byrd is in his late thirties. His face is clean-shaven and very handsome, with small, regular features and a firm mouth. He reminds me at first of a young high-school principal, but there is an unquestioned air of authority as well as competence about him. He is in command, and the three other men in the party stand respectfully in his shadow.

I wipe the grease from my hands with a ball of waste, and lead the way up the hill, over the thawing snow. Commander Byrd's eyes are busy, darting from left to right as we cross the camp area, and he is taking in every detail. He observes the commissary and the hospital and the distant hangar, loaded with equipment, and his quick glance climbs the framework of the mooring mast to the gin pole at the top, ready to hoist the cone into place. A couple of cooks peer out of the mess hall and mutter something in Norwegian as we pass, but if he is aware of tension he shows no sign.

I am always a fast walker, but he lengthens his stride and keeps up with me, and I can see he is in fine physical trim. We halt before the manager's building, and I knock on the door. Amundsen answers: "Come in."

Captain Amundsen rises from behind a table strewn with charts, and holds out his hand to Commander Byrd. "Glad you're here safe, Commander," he says. "Welcome to Spitsbergen."

Byrd's manner at first is reserved. The *Heimdal*'s refusal is still not forgotten, I suspect, and he is politely formal as he introduces the other members of his party. "Lieutenant George Noville, my executive officer, and Lieutenant Robb Oertell, who is handling the fuel supplies." He indicates a rawboned, reticent figure lingering in the doorway. "And my pilot, Floyd Bennett."

Lincoln Ellsworth edges unobtrusively in from the kitchen. He and Amundsen had met Byrd in New York three months earlier, and they shake hands briefly. I am curious to see these fellow countrymen greet each other. They are courteous, of course, but there is no real warmth in their greeting; and a couple of times, glancing at Ellsworth as he slips into the background, I detect a trace of annoyance in his face, as though he is piqued at the fact that he is no longer the only American explorer in Kings Bay.

Amundsen remarks genially that he is sorry he could not keep the promise he made to Byrd in New York: "I told you the bay would still be frozen over in May," he says, "and you would have an ice surface to take off on skis. But there's one thing we should never say up here—that a certain thing will happen at a certain time in the polar regions. This has been an early spring, so I have not been able to keep my word."

I cannot help but notice the striking contrast between the two leaders: Amundsen, shaggy-haired and rugged and seasoned as an oak mast; Byrd, immaculately groomed and slender and every inch the cultured gentleman. He is half a head shorter than Amundsen, and must look up as they talk. Amundsen senses that this makes him uncomfortable, and motions to everybody to be seated.

Noville and Oertell move over to the sofa and talk together in low tones, so as not to disturb the heads of the two expeditions, and I borrow a chair from the kitchen and straddle it, while Amundsen and Byrd unroll maps and discuss their mutual problems. A persistent question crosses my mind, which I have asked myself many times since as I have sat alone in the cockpit flying the Arctic wastes. What makes an explorer? What driving force causes a man to leave comfort and security, and risk hunger and privation and even death in search of something he cannot keep even when he finds it? At times in Captain Amundsen's face I have detected a haunting look of infinite sadness. I know he is unmarried, a lonely and somber man, always restless to be going. Is he seeking something when he sets out for the ends of the earth, or is he escaping from something? I wonder if he himself knows the answer.

Or take Ellsworth, seated in the corner of the room unnoticed by the rest. A man of wealth, he has given generously to make Amundsen's explorations possible. He is thrilled to be associated with an expedition and with Captain Amundsen, and is unhesitatingly sacrificing a great deal of his time for the sake of polar exploration. Why doesn't he stay home with his family, and let others face the actual dangers? Must he prove something to them, or even to himself? A year ago he almost lost his life in a try for the Pole. What odd courage brings him back to Kings Bay to try again?

Or Commander Byrd here, an ambitious young naval officer who seems better fitted to sit at the head of a conference table or grace a drawing room. What has impelled him to leave a certain and safe career and come here to risk the unknown? I study his face, as he talks with Amundsen, and note the serious look in his eyes, and his set lips. Is it ambition that urges him on, I wonder? Or is he too, like Amundsen, haunted and ceaselessly driven?

Or Floyd Bennett, Byrd's pilot, a gawky country boy lounging against the doorjamb with his hands in the pockets of his navy warrant officer's pea jacket, saying nothing. Of all the men in the room, I think I can understand Bennett best. He is, like me, a flier, who is at home anywhere behind the controls of an airplane. He earned his wings in the United States Navy, he tells me quietly while the leaders are talking, and last year he flew Commander Byrd from Etah in northwest Greenland on the Donald MacMillan Arctic Expedition—the first flying, in fact, that had ever been done in the high Canadian arctic. It does not matter where he flies, so long as he is flying. We are almost the same age, and he impresses me as simple and straightforward and direct. I have a feeling that some day we shall be flying together.

Commander Byrd pushes back the maps on the table, and shakes his head. "That's the route, yes, but how will I ever get my plane in the air?"

"There is a flat area in front of this house," Amundsen says, "running north through the center of the camp to the very edge of the fjord. You can tramp it level and use it for your take-off strip."

Byrd looks at him curiously. "You are being very generous to a rival."

"But we are not competitors," Amundsen corrects him. "We are collaborators in a joint assault on the polar regions, an attack by two vehicles, one lighter and one heavier than air." He stands up and faces Byrd across the table. "We are partners in this venture together."

"30 April. Mooring mast finished; Jo. Ford ashore, 1530."

Today we are ready to raise the cone of the mooring mast at last. A swinging gin pole has been erected at the top of the slender 130-foot structure of crisscrossed steel girders, as fantastic against the sky line as a little Eiffel Tower standing on a glacier. A cable feeds through the pulley at the end of this gin pole, and one end is wound around the drum of a Diesel-powered winch anchored to the foundation. The other end is hooked to the eight-ton steel cone, twelve feet in diameter and painted a bright red. The winch begins to groan and shudder as the cable takes the strain and the cone rises slowly into the air.

An excited crowd has gathered to watch this final operation. It breaks into cheers as the massive steel cap reaches the tip of the gin pole, and the derrick swings around with its load, and the winch lowers the cone into the prepared slots. Steelworkers swarm up the ladder inside the open-work tower and crawl out on the narrow plank catwalk, balancing in dizzy space high above the bay as they bolt the cap securely. Now finally the mooring mast is ready to anchor the *Norge*.

The brilliant red ball shining in the sky is like a warning beacon to the other expedition. This sign of our own readiness spurs increased activity on the deck of the *Chantier*. The dismounted sections of their airplane were uncrated yesterday, and the lashing ropes untied. Early this morning we saw four lifeboats lowered overside and fastened together with planks; then a wooden platform was built on top of them to form a raft. We watched this ingenious solution with great interest, and not a little respect. Ferrying the airplane ashore through surging water and drifting ice cakes was a problem the Byrd party had not anticipated; but they did not hesitate to tackle it. These Americans are not to be discouraged by any new difficulty, I think; they never worry about a problem beforehand, but when it develops, that is the time to take care of it. This is the pioneer spirit of America that I have heard so much about; it is the quality that will open up the whole Arctic to air commerce some day, and it is the quality that I admire most in men.

I was already impressed by the eager members of Commander Byrd's expedition when, with Captain Amundsen, I paid a courtesy visit to the *Chantier* last night. A boisterous group lined the rail as we climbed the Jacob's ladder. They were almost all volunteers, from every walk of life; some were merchants and doctors and lawyers, some were officers in the American armed forces, some were college lads who had signed on for the adventure and who were sprouting their first scraggly beards. They wore all kinds of makeshift cold-weather apparel: padded down-filled jackets, lumberjack shirts, college sweaters, parts of navy uniforms, ski boots and high-laced pacs and moccasins and even tennis sneakers, white sailor hats and skating

caps and knitted toques with ear flaps—no two clad alike. It was
a strange contrast to our own men, all dressed in the same drab
winter garments we always wear in Norway. Many of them were
seeing glaciers and icebergs for the first time in their lives, but
they were imbued with only one thought, to make sure that
Commander Byrd's plane got off as soon as possible and won
the race.

Now puffs of steam suddenly mushroom from the winches on
the *Chantier*, and the fuselage of the airplane is lowered onto
the floating platform, and the single cantilever plywood wing
set in place across it. The volunteer sailors start sculling the
raft toward shore. It is snowing, not heavily yet but enough to
make the heaving planks slippery and dangerous to move
around on, and the fjord is full of milling ice cakes that bump
and grind against the sides of the supporting lifeboats. We
hold our breath: at any moment the running tide, or a squall
springing up suddenly, as they often do here in Spitsbergen,
could jam the ice floes around the raft and crush it. But these
American novices show no sign of panic, and work as a team
together to move their precious cargo across the treacherous
quarter-mile to the beach.

Already, with hand axes, they have hacked an incline in the
shore ice down to the water. The raft lines up with this, slides
onto it, and grates to a stop. Ropes are cast to a group of Americans waiting on shore, and they haul the airplane safely up the
ice ramp and onto the level snow. I step onto my skis and speed
down to the beach for my first close look at the *Josephine Ford*.

It is a trimotored Fokker, built in Holland the year before
and taken over to the United States by the designer, Anthony
Fokker. It has just won the Ford reliability tour, and I see here
before my eyes the latest thing in design and aerodynamic
efficiency, a trim and beautiful machine. Its wing span is 63
feet, and it is the largest passenger airplane yet, capable of
carrying eighteen people. The engines are Wright Whirlwinds,

At Advent Bay, Spitsbergen: Bernt Balchen starting up the motor of the Amundsen-Ellsworth Relief Expedition plane in 1925.

The race for the North Pole, 1926; Commander Richard E. Byrd's plane, the *Josephine Ford,* and the hangar for the *Norge,* the airship in which Amundsen flew over the Pole.

Roald Amundsen.

Commander Richard E. Byrd (*left*) and his pilot, Floyd Bennett,
just after their North Pole flight.

air-cooled, of 200 horsepower each, the brand-new radial air-cooled type.

Doc Kinkaid of the Wright Aeronautical Corporation, the motor expert of the expedition, tells me that two engines should be able to sustain level flight when the plane is not too heavily loaded—an important safety factor. The plane has been converted for cold-weather operations at the factory, but there was little time for extensive tests before leaving the States. They will have to rely more or less on the manufacturer's word and the printed manual, he tells me, to estimate what they may expect out of it. In order to give it additional range, they have installed two fuel tanks in the fuselage, each holding more than a hundred gallons, and there are of course the two standard tanks in the wings, of a hundred gallons each. If more fuel is needed they will have to carry it in five-gallon cans and dump it into the fuselage tanks during the flight.

Looking the plane all over, I can see that the Wright engineers have gone into the problem of cold weather very thoroughly; and the arrangements for heating the engines and shielding them against the extreme cold during flight seem adequate. What worries me is the design of the skis. They are to my way of thinking entirely too rigid, not large or strong enough, and I have a private hunch there may be trouble.

"2 May, Climb Mt. Z., 2,700 ft., 2 hrs."

Today is Sunday, and no work is ever done in Captain Amundsen's camp on the Sabbath, so I strap on my skis and set off alone for the white hills. I skirt the rim of the fjord and look down into the silent water, its deep blue mirrored in the undercut sides of the bergs. Here and there a ringed seal, spotted like a leopard, pops to the surface for a breathing spell in his hunt for cod and shrimp, looking around curiously with coal-black eyes.

Sea gulls are the only waterfowl around Kings Bay in early
May, but soon the great flocks of sea birds will be migrating
north—the auks and eider ducks and terns and horned puffins.
A year ago when I was here the cliffs echoed with their nesting
chatter, and every ledge at the mouth of the fjord was alive
with bobbing heads. Barnacle geese and graylags stalked over
the bare tundra, and the Alpine slopes were loud with the
whistles of plovers and snow buntings and tawny pipits. But
now there is only the muted white silence as I leave the bay
and head for the nearby ridge of mountains south of the mining camp.

The tallest mountain was named by some German explorers
for Count Zeppelin, and it seems to me to be a lucky omen for
our expedition, so I make for it. The front drops off steeply,
but as I circle it the slopes to the rear are gentler, and I jam
my poles into the drifts and wind my way upwards around the
contours of the ravines. Now and then a flock of rock ptarmigan
cackle and roar up from behind the rocks, and ahead of me,
almost invisible except for the black tips of their tails, I catch
sight of three white foxes following a fresh track in the snow.
A few minutes later I cross the huge paw-prints of a polar bear,
which the foxes have been trailing to pick up any bits of food
it might drop. I look for a sign of the tiny wild reindeer that
inhabit the east coast of Spitsbergen, but they are not to be
seen on this side of the island.

I fill my lungs with the fine, clean air, and lean forward to
speed down a dip in the ravine and up the other side. This is
what I love best. I have always been a friend of the boards, as
we say in Norway, where it is as natural to ski as to walk. Just
before coming to Spitsbergen, I was selected for the 50-kilo-
meter cross-country race in the International Ski Derby at Holmenkollen, the highest ambition for a Norwegian. Without
effort I make five or six miles an hour up the mountain side,

and in little more than two hours I am standing on the highest
peak.

From Mt. Zeppelin, I look directly down on the mining settlement of Kings Bay, known to Norwegians as Ny Aalesund,
on the south side of Kings Fjord. The fjord runs from the
glacier north and west for about fifteen miles to the open sea.
It is only a tiny indentation in the coast line of this great archipelago which covers about 24,000 square miles altogether, a
fifth the size of Norway itself. Straight to the north, eighty miles
away, the high mountains of upper Spitsbergen form a jagged
horizon, like a pressure ridge of jumbled ice cakes pushed
against the sky. They glitter with every color of the spectrum
in the crystal-clear sunshine.

I take out the small water-color box which I always carry
in the pocket of my ski jacket, and try to set down the scene
on my sketch pad, dipping the brush in my mouth for moisture.
I choose a French blue, with some black added, to make the
deep shadows of the crevasses. Now comes a little orange mixed
with brown to catch the streaks of sandstone that show here and
there, where the slopes are too steep to hold the snow. This
bright emerald is the color of the cracks in the timeless rivers
of ice, locked in the canyons between the nunataks. Behind
them I wash green and lavender-gray together for the open
ocean, and I leave a few spaces bare to indicate the white belts
of drifting pack ice. I select my lightest yellow, almost lemon,
to shade the sky as it thins away into the pale blue of infinity.

Below me, as I paint, the panorama of ice caps and glaciers
all around me is suggestive of the earth back in the ice age. I
remember learning in geology that all these mountains were
elevated during the Caledonian folding in late Silurian times,
a prehistoric upheaval which extended from Scotland along the
Scandinavian Peninsula north to Spitsbergen and all the way
to northern Greenland. Later sinkings formed the oceans and
seas which separate these lands today. The mountains are of a

sedimentary type, which explains their coal seams and other mineral deposits. At Kings Bay the miners have shown me fossils they have found, indicating that once, many millions of years ago, this was all a torrid zone with large ferns and other tropical plants growing here, a lush jungle vegetation. They have described extensive lava beds on the island, proof of active volcanoes, and even warm springs they have seen bubbling up through the snow over toward the east coast.

My mind keeps going back to how man first came here. It was the same as with the discovery of the Arctic islands north of Canada, the search for short routes to the riches of the Far East. The very earliest ones to see Spitsbergen were the Norsemen, long before anyone else, but the first to land were the Dutch whalers, in 1600. After the whalers, in the eighteenth century, came the fur trappers for fox and polar bear and seal pelts. Outcroppings of black coal had been noted as early as 1610, but it was not until the beginning of this century that mining began. An English company was the first to start, in 1904, and then Longyear brought an American expedition and staked some mine claims in 1905. Over on the Ice Fjord, forty-five miles by dog sled from Kings Bay across the large glacier called Kings Highway, is Longyear City, which the American company founded, the largest settlement in Spitsbergen today. There are also some small Swedish and Dutch operations, and even the remnants of a Russian coal mine.

But it is not in coal or fur or fish that Spitsbergen's future lies, I think to myself. It is in the air. Kings Bay is at 78° 50′ North Latitude. The tip of Norway is 71° 30′, and Point Barrow in Alaska is only 71° 20′. This position on the very rim of the polar basin has made it the logical starting point for numerous transpolar attempts. Way back in 1897, Andrée set out from here in his balloon, and Wellman with his crude dirigible tried it unsuccessfully in 1907, and again in 1909.

I slip the sketch pad into my pocket, and stand looking to the

The *Josephine Ford*, then the biggest passenger airplane in the world, at Mitchel Field before the start of the round-the-States air tour in 1926.

Operations office of Western Canada Airways at Hudson, Ontario, in the spring of 1927.

The *America*, Commander Byrd's trimotor Fokker, and Bernt Balchen at Roosevelt Field, before the transatlantic flight in 1927.

The *America* on the ramp from which it took off for France.

north horizon, and beyond the horizon to the future. Perhaps, when the secret of the Pole has been unlocked and the Arctic is opened to commercial travel over the top of the world, this strategically located archipelago may have a new importance. In many places around its shore line are wide coastal plains and forelands, a safe six miles from the foot of the mountains, which could be developed for flying fields. Some of them are big enough to accommodate even the largest aircraft of tomorrow. One day Kings Bay could be the gateway of the new Air Age.

That secret may be unlocked any moment now. Looking down, I see the oblong dirigible hangar and the red dot on the mooring mast, from which the *Norge* will make its try. Between the camp and the hangar, on the take-off strip that Captain Amundsen has turned over to the Byrd Expedition, the *Josephine Ford* is already parked at the end of the runway, like a crouched falcon. The antlike figures of the Americans have been moving up and down the strip all day, tramping the snow to pack it firmly in readiness. I wonder which of us will win the race, a race that will never be run again. Only once in history can anyone be the first to fly across the Pole.

Below me the mooring mast, like the arm of a sundial, throws a long shadow that reads a couple of degrees north of east. It is almost six o'clock. I start back to camp, down the steep foreside of the mountain. The snow whips in clouds in my wake as I gain speed, and the patches of dwarf birches rush uphill past me faster and faster. I shout aloud, "Jevlar, dette er livet!" but the wind snatches the sound away from my lips. This is the life, from adventure to adventure, always the cold and the flashing skis and the white unknown.

I reach the bottom of the mountain in fourteen minutes, and telemark to a halt in a cloud of flying powder snow. Captain Amundsen is angry that I have risked my neck traveling at such useless speed, and I make up my mind never to do it again—at least when he is looking.

"3 May, 1200. Jo. Ford first test-hop, fails."

A little war has broken out here in camp. Not between the members of the rival expeditions, for it is the policy of both commanders that we shall remain on friendly terms, and if there is any resentment among the men it is beneath the surface. But between the rival reporters and cameramen there are open hostilities now.

Each expedition has sold the exclusive rights to its story to a different newspaper syndicate in the States, and the syndicates have solemnly agreed not to take any unauthorized pictures or try to scoop each other. This is all very well on paper back home, but here in practice it doesn't work out. In the confined area of Kings Bay, the two expeditions are all intermeshed together. It is almost impossible to photograph our camp, for instance, without getting in part of the Byrd landing strip which runs right through the middle; and our own hangar and mooring mast are completely visible from the *Chantier,* where a cameraman with a telephoto lens can snap everything we are doing.

It is a kind of guerrilla warfare, with undercover operations and secret infiltrations. Scouts from the rival syndicates creep past each other, the Amundsen raiders disguised in American sailor hats, and the Byrd snipers wearing Norwegian ski caps, each seeking a vantage point to take pot shots at the enemy. Movie cameras whir suddenly like machine guns, and flash guns explode sporadically all day over the battlefield. A skulking still photographer pops up out of an empty crate to click a close-up of the *Josephine Ford,* or as we enter the dirigible hangar we see a pair of heels disappearing out the other end, the scurrying figure staggering bowlegged under a heavy camera and tripod. So intent are they on each other's business that they sometimes neglect their own. Actually it is a photographer from the syndicate covering the Amundsen expedition, Berge, who snaps the only picture of the accident to Commander Byrd's plane today.

The accident occurs on the first test hop. Earlier this morning, as I crossed the landing strip on my way to the coal dock, I noticed the *Josephine Ford* parked ready for its initial flight, and Lieutenant Oertell on his knees with a can of wax and a brush, polishing the skis. I asked him what in the world he was doing. He explained that he was waxing the bottoms so that they would slide on the snow surface. Now in the Arctic if there is one thing we know it is this: that the hard, crystalline snow, at this time of year, acts like sandpaper, and even if wax gave a sliding surface, it wouldn't last long. Our experience in Norway with both racing skis and airplane skis has taught us to use an entirely different preparation, a mixture of pine tar and resin burned into the wood with a blowtorch. I described this to Oertell, but he said there was no time to change, because the test hop was due at noon.

Down at the coal dock, when I arrived, I found the men wrestling with the last item of our own equipment, an enormous wooden crate on which was printed in Italian "Handle with care! Fragile!" This mysterious box had been sent all the way from Rome by Colonel Umberto Nobile, designer and pilot of the *Norge,* who is the Italian partner of Amundsen and Ellsworth in the expedition. It must have weighed two tons, and it was all we could do to skid it the length of the pier and hitch it to the tractor in order to haul it on a sled to the hangar. Halfway across the flat the drive shaft of the tractor broke, and we had to unhitch the crate again and push it by main strength the rest of the way. It has taken us most of the forenoon to get it to the hangar, and the exhausted workers mop their brows and watch curiously as we pry open the packing case to see what is so heavy. Inside is a giant searchlight, to guide the *Norge* on night landings. Inasmuch as the sun rises in Spitsbergen on the 7th of April, and does not set again

until the 10th of September, it is about as useful as an icebox
is to a Laplander.

In the back of my mind, all morning long, my hunch about
the undersized skis on the *Josephine Ford* has kept nagging me.
Back in the naval aircraft factory in Horten, I had experimented with various types of ski landing gear, and I know
what is required both in strength and in flexibility to stand up
under a heavy trimotor plane. I realize that any delay to Byrd
will better Amundsen's own chances, but at the same time I
feel a kinship with the American party that is hard to explain.
I had the same feeling a couple of years earlier when I was
fighting for the amateur heavyweight title of eastern Norway:
I wanted to defeat the defending champion, of course, but
there was no enmity between us, only admiration for each
other's skill, and we embraced after I won the bout. The ring-
side crowd could not understand, but the fact that we were
fighting each other brought us closer together. Deep inside me
today as I watched these spirited youngsters of the rival camp
double-timing up and down the landing strip to pack the snow
flat with their feet, roughhousing as they worked and making
fun of every new hardship, I knew I should be happy to belong
to such a team myself. If Captain Amundsen is not first over the
Pole, I shall be glad to see the honor go to these Americans.

At noon, in the machine shop making a new drive shaft for
the tractor, I hear above the sputter of my welding torch the
full-throttled roar of an airplane's motors. In the next second
all three engines snarl and choke off abruptly, and there is
dead silence. I yank off my dark goggles and run to the window,
but cannot see the landing strip. As I head for the door, it is
flung open and Captain Amundsen shoulders his way in:
"Balchen, there's been an accident. The Fokker's broken a ski.
Go see what you can do to help."

At the strip I realize at once what has happened. The waxed
skis stuck tight to the snow as they started their test hop,

Floyd Bennett tells me, and suddenly one of the skis ripped
loose, the plane slewed around, and the ski hit a hard drift and
shattered. The ground crew is gazing bleakly at the crippled
aircraft, canted at an angle against the snowbank. There is a
spare set of skis on the *Chantier;* but they are of the same specifications as the ones which broke, Bennett says gloomily, realizing that they are too fragile to stand the strain.

"I'm a float-plane pilot," he admits. "I don't know anything
about skis."

"Maybe we could shore up the spares with strips of hard-
wood," I suggest

"But where are we going to find any ash or hickory in
camp?"

I scratch my tow head for a moment. "How about the lifeboat oars on the *Chantier?"*

The ship's captain, Mike Brennan, protests vehemently at
first, but Bennett's grin wins him over. An armload of heavy
lifeboat oars is brought ashore and carried to our machine
shop. There the ship's carpenter, Chips Gould, and our own
woodworkers start to square the long shafts and drill holes for
the bolts. I watch with mixed feelings. Once again we have
turned the odds against ourselves in the race.

The race is getting hotter, we learn this evening. A message
received at the Kings Bay radio station from Point Barrow,
Alaska, reports that Hubert Wilkins and his pilot, Ben Eielson,
are about to attempt a flight from Barrow to Spitsbergen in a
single-engine Fokker. They have been waiting since the 23rd
of April, pinned down by storms and constant fog, and they
want to know about landing conditions at Kings Bay, the terminus of their flight.

Our meteorologist radios back to Wilkins that the weather
here has been developing slowly but steadily into what he be-
lieves will be a favorable synoptic situation. A high-pressure
area is building over the Arctic Ocean, with a very flat gradient.

The increasing distance between the isobars (the lines of equal pressure) indicates that there will be only light winds over the whole region, rather cold, but with clear skies to the North Pole and beyond. Only the weather in Alaska remains foul.

Now it is a three-way contest. Hubert Wilkins is poised at the starting line in Barrow; Commander Byrd's plane needs only the reenforced skis to be roaring on its way; and the *Norge* is straining at its mooring mast in Leningrad, still waiting for our signal.

"7 May, 0600. Norge arr. Kings Bay, Nobile and R-L pilots."

Yesterday we sent word to Nobile that the weather was right at last for him to proceed here, completing the last leg of his four-thousand-mile voyage from Rome. The *Norge* left Italy on the 29th of March, flying first to a mooring mast at Pulham, England, for refueling. From there it went to another mooring tower at Oslo, Norway, and then to Gatchina Field at Leningrad, Russia. Already it has traveled more than twice the distance it will have to cover on its final flight from Spitsbergen over the top of the world to Alaska.

Originally the big dirigible was designed by Nobile for the Italian Air Force and was christened *Italia*. When Amundsen and Ellsworth were seeking transportation for their polar crossing, Mussolini offered to furnish the airship, with the sly provision that the expedition would of course fly under the Italian flag. After much dickering, he agreed to a joint enterprise. Nobile and an Italian crew would operate the ship, but it would be renamed *Norge* and fly the Norwegian flag. Hjalmar Riiser-Larsen of the Royal Norwegian Air Force would be navigator and second in command.

After receiving our message, the *Norge* left Leningrad at 0930 yesterday morning, touched down at Vadsö, Norway, for a couple of hours, and then started across the remaining five hundred miles of open ocean to Kings Bay. At 0600 this morning we sight a tiny dot in the far sky, growing bigger and steadily bigger as it approaches from the south across the barren lands. At first it is a tiny minnow swimming over the tops of the distant nunataks; then it is a silver salmon gliding through the blue pool of the sky; now at last it is a great white whale as it comes floating directly overhead. It sinks into our camp, and is taken right into the hangar, leaving the red cone of the mooring mast empty.

The shackles are engaged, the ropes are tossed out, and the captive whale is hauled cautiously to the ground. A sudden gust of wind catches it and it leaps aloft again like a living thing, the ground crew clinging to the ropes as they are yanked helplessly into the air. Slowly it settles once more, and is held steady while Colonel Umberto Nobile steps out. He is greeted by Amundsen and Ellsworth, and they head for the manager's building while the rest of us walk the *Norge* to the hangar.

I gaze with interest at the sloping fabric underbelly of this beached monster, lashed down with ropes, flabby and helpless out of its natural element. The gas-filled bag is 350 feet long, with a lifting capacity of approximately 20 tons. The lift is influenced by temperature and barometric pressure, Riiser-Larsen explains. For each Fahrenheit degree that the thermometer goes up or down, the *Norge* loses or gains 80 pounds of pay load. A rise of one-tenth inch in the barometric pressure increases its lifting power another 140 pounds. Not only does it need clear weather and favorable winds, but it must have the lowest possible temperature and a high barometer to achieve maximum efficiency. Normally it carries a crew of eighteen, and has an average speed of fifty to fifty-five miles an hour. Its nonstop range is thirty-six hundred miles, almost three times that of the *Josephine Ford*.

Colonel Nobile is in excited debate with Captain Amundsen when we arrive at the superintendent's building to report that the *Norge* is safely inside the hangar. His high forehead is creased with anxiety. He has seen the American plane on the landing strip, and he insists there is no time to lose. He admits having had some motor trouble on the way up from Italy; however, replacing the engine and installing more fuel tanks as an added safety factor would take about three days. Naturally he would not waste time on such details now. The *Norge* must be off at once.

Captain Amundsen shakes his head. "We will not be rushed," he says calmly. "We will take every necessary precaution, and we will leave only when the ship and the weather are right."

Nobile flings both hands aloft, and the gold braid on the sleeves of his uniform crackles. He argues passionately, as though he could feel the hot breath of Il Duce on his neck; and Ellsworth and even Riiser-Larsen add their pleas to be first in the race. But Captain Amundsen is not to be swayed. Amid the rapid-fire conversation around him, his voice is as remote and measured as the rumble of a far-off glacier.

"Our flight is not a race. Its purpose is bigger than that. We're trying to chart a shorter route to the New World, and the North Pole is just a point we shall cross on the way."

The room is silent as he finishes speaking. Outside is the sound of airplane engines revving up. The *Josephine Ford* with its new skis is ready for the test hop.

"8 May. Jo. Ford attempts take-off Pole, 1210."

Today Commander Byrd receives the report from the meteorologist that he has been waiting for. The high-pressure area has continued to develop over the entire polar basin, with Spitsbergen on the western boundary of a stable zone which extends from Novaya Zemlya in Siberia clear across to southwest Canada. This unusual situation can be expected to last for at least forty-eight hours. There will be following winds

all the way from Kings Bay to the North Pole. Based on this, he
will have to reckon with a headwind on his return flight.

No announcement is made, but everyone senses that the
moment is at hand. Toward noon little groups from the *Chantier* begin moving up the hill and gathering around the *Josephine Ford,* which has been taxied up onto a slight snow ramp
at the head of the landing strip. Our own camp is idle, for this
is Sunday, and our men join the swelling crowd. The sun is at
its highest peak in the south, the temperature is in the thirties,
and some of us are in shirt-sleeves in the pleasant midday
warmth. Our ski boots churn the melting snow into slush as
we mill around the plane, watching the ground crews top the
tanks and give the controls and the electric wiring system a
last-minute check.

A murmur runs through the crowd when Byrd and Bennett
come across the flats. Bennett is red-faced and perspiring in his
heavy flying suit, Byrd is trim, immaculate and handsome. Bennett waves carelessly to the crowd as he mounts the metal steps;
Byrd halts and returns a crisp salute to his staff and climbs
inside. The door slams.

The middle engine coughs a cloud of smoke, and the propellers whirl. The left and right engines catch in turn, and run
up to full power, the props vanishing to be replaced by three
shining discs in the sunlight. The airplane seems to shudder,
but it does not move. The vibrating increases, the whole plane
bucks violently, and suddenly it jerks loose and moves down
the runway at a slow speed and then halts. Bennett turns and
taxis back up the slope. The engines are cut, and the spinning
props rotate jerkily to a halt.

The door opens again, and Byrd climbs out, his lips pressed
tight. Bennett hops down to the ground behind him, walks
forward to one of the skis, and squats beside it, puzzled. Byrd
beckons to me, and asks me what is wrong. I think I know the
reason; it happens here during the spring break-up period, I

tell him, when the temperature rises just above freezing and
the snow becomes sticky. There is only one thing to do: wait
until the snow freezes hard again during the small hours of the
night, and then the icy surface will make a take-off possible.
The disappointed crowd disperses slowly, and Byrd and Bennett walk back to the *Chantier* to catch a few hours' rest.

I stretch out on my bunk that night, but I am restless and
cannot sleep. The sun has dipped toward the northern horizon,
and the warmth has gone out of it, but the light streaming
through my window is almost as bright as that of noon. I can see
everything in the room clearly: the calendar on the wall with
the days crossed out to May 9th; even the minute hand of my
wrist watch on the table beside me, standing at a little after
twelve.

I pull on my ski boots and stroll through the silent camp.
The ball of the midnight sun is molten gold, and an eerie
glow tints the snowdrifts, and flickers like firelight in the windows of the sleeping barracks. The *Josephine Ford* throws a
long black shadow at the far end of the landing strip, and the
padded figures of the ground crew look like creatures from
another planet as they swarm over the plane. Their voices ring
out hollowly in the stillness of the deserted camp area, and I
sense tension. There is the sudden crunch of dry snow under
boot soles, and Byrd and Bennett stride swiftly across the snow
flat toward the airplane. In low tones they exchange a last few
words with the crew chief. Then they nod and climb inside.

The backfire of the first engine is like the report of a starting
gun. A few surprised faces appear in the windows of the barracks, and several men in long underwear pop out of the door-
ways. The other engines explode into life and build to a roar,
and cameramen start running toward the strip. The airplane
lurches, jerking the skis free, slides down the snow ramp, and
begins to pick up speed. Berge, of the Amundsen syndicate,

cranks his movie camera on its tripod, catching the actual take-off on film.

The *Josephine Ford* lifts smoothly off the end of the runway and is airborne, its roar fading to a steady drone as it climbs into the northern sky. Its wings glint as it levels off, and then it melts into the fiery white ball of the midnight sun. I take out my diary, and make an entry in pencil:

"9 May. Jo. Ford, B and B, depart Kings Bay, 0037."

All the rest of the night and the following day we try to carry on our duties as usual around the camp, but there is only one thought in our minds. We do not mention it to each other, but the anxiety of every man is apparent in the strange silence as we work, and in the occasional pauses to scan the empty northern sky. There is no way of communicating with the plane. All we can do is wonder. As the afternoon drags on Nobile pulls Amundsen to one side and suggests that perhaps something has happened. Amundsen's probing eyes regard his partner for a moment, and he replies that we'd better all pray they will be back safely. If anything happens, we must abandon our own plans for the transpolar flight. Only the *Norge* has the cruising range and facilities to conduct a search.

I am looking for something to keep me busy during the long wait, and I decide this is a good time to check out the Italian members of the *Norge* crew on arctic survival. Amundsen has insisted that every member of the expedition must have a knowledge of skiing, against the possibility of being forced down, and he himself sets an example by skiing ten or fifteen miles every day to keep in top physical condition. There is a gentle slope behind the hospital of the mining camp, about twenty feet high, with an easy turn at the bottom; and I lead the reluctant Italian crew members to the top of the little hill, and show them how to strap the boards on their feet. Most of them are from southern Italy, and have never seen snow before, and it is all they can do to balance themselves upright. When they start sliding, they cross their arms in front of their faces and close their eyes, forgetting all about the turn and usually winding up with a thud against the side of the hospital. No matter which way their skis are pointed, the building seems to draw them like a magnet, and as the steady bombardment goes on the patients inside must begin to wonder if a small avalanche has started. I think to myself that it might be easier to tie the skis on their stomachs, and let them make belly whoppers down the hill.

The poor fellows are homesick, I guess, for sunny Napoli. They have tried on the heavy woolen underclothing they are supposed to wear on the arctic flight; but the long drawers sag around their ankles, and they wriggle and scratch themselves miserably. They cannot get used to Norwegian food, and when we serve them a heaping platter of boiled fish with the heads on they push it away and turn a little green. Luckily they have brought along some dry spaghetti, and one of their crew is elected as cook. Tonight at supper he winds a dish towel around his head like a white chef's hat and enters the mess hall triumphantly, bearing aloft a steaming bowl of spaghetti and tomatoes. It is the first time the Italians have felt at home since they landed at Kings Bay.

We are in the middle of dinner when we hear shouts outside, and one of the Italian soldiers comes bounding into the mess hall, out of breath. He chatters in broken English, "She come— a motor!" and our chairs clatter backward to the floor as we stampede out of the building. We can hear the far-off hum of engines, and in the northern sky, at almost the exact spot where I had seen it vanish a little more than fifteen hours ago, a bright speck appears, approaching over the peaks. Men come boiling

out of the buildings, heading for the landing strip, and below
in the fjord I see loaded lifeboats putting out from the *Chantier*, pulling hard for shore.

The speck rapidly grows larger, coming toward us in a direct
line. The excited crowd has swarmed over the field, and the
plane has to circle Kings Bay while the runway is cleared. It
lines up with the strip, touches skis lightly at the far end, and
glides to a halt at the foot of the snow ramp. The mob surges
forward as the engines cut.

Amundsen is the first to greet Byrd as he steps out. I have
never seen him display so much emotion. He cannot speak. His
stern Viking face has broken into a rare and wonderful smile,
and the tears run from his eyes as he puts his arms around Byrd
and Bennett, drawing them both to him in a giant embrace,
and kisses them on each cheek.

The men of the Byrd expedition are charging up over the
hill, and Amundsen steps back as they surround their leader,
yelling and cheering, pounding each other on the back, wild
with victory. Two pairs of husky lads hoist Byrd and Bennett
onto their shoulders, and the others follow as if in a football
snake dance as they carry the conquering heroes down the hill
to the *Chantier*. In all the excitement no one has asked about
the operational difficulties and details of the flight. Tonight the
waiting world will hear in Byrd's own words that he has done
what no man in history has ever done before. He has flown over
the North Pole.

The swaying figures of Byrd and Bennett disappear over the
hill, jolting up and down on the shoulders of their crewmen,
and the cheers of the following crowd grow fainter. I take the
diary from my pocket, and make another pencilled entry:

"9 May. Jo. Ford returns King's Bay 1607."

*"11 May, 0855. Norge departs transpolar flight, A E and N, 16
men on board. 3 left behind."*

Still the weather in Alaska is sour, with Hubert Wilkins at
Point Barrow reporting violent sleet storms and turbulence
along the entire coast; and now at Kings Bay there are signs
that our own good weather may be drawing to an end. This
gives added force to Nobile's plea that we take off at once. Wilkins has indicated that an improvement may be expected at
Barrow shortly; and Nobile urges that we take advantage of the
present favorable winds that prevail at least as far as the Pole.
What will happen on the other side is a gamble, but if Kings
Bay closes in, he warns, we may have to cancel the whole expedition. At last Amundsen gives the command.

All night long we have been stowing the scientific instruments aboard the dirigible, including the sun compass presented to Amundsen by Commander Byrd after his return. It is
my responsibility to keep tally of every pound, because our
weight problem is critical. I count out the personal equipment
and survival gear, one sleeping bag each and a hand sled for
every two men, and carefully weigh the food supplies. Our
mainstay is pemmican, prepared in Denmark from Amundsen's
own formula of concentrated beef suet, yellow peas and steer
blood, packed sixteen slabs to a two-kilo can. The Italians take
a sniff and wrinkle their noses, and I catch one of them
smuggling a package of dry spaghetti aboard. He pleads that it
weighs even less than pemmican, and that I cannot deny. On
one point, however, Amundsen is adamant. Nobile has brought
along from Rome a complete set of full-dress uniforms for his
soldiers and himself to wear for the welcoming committee, but
Amundsen orders them removed from the ship. Only absolute
necessities can be carried on the trip.

Even some of our spare instruments must be unloaded at the
last minute, but still the weight is too great. Captain Amundsen

makes a hard decision. Three members of the flight crew will have to stay behind. Two are assistant engineers. The third is myself.

I try to hide my disappointment as I watch the others file aboard the *Norge*. All the men from our camp have assembled on the field, and a few members of the Byrd party have wandered up the hill to watch the take-off. Floyd Bennett is standing beside me, and his hand is on my shoulder; I think he knows what I am feeling. The crowd watches with a detached interest, curious to see how a dirigible is launched into flight. A few sailors from the *Chantier* snap souvenir pictures with their box cameras, but the photographers from the syndicate no longer object. The excitement of the race is over, and this is all an anticlimax now.

Amundsen is the last to reach the *Norge*. He comes down the hill from the manager's building alone, with a roll of charts under his arm, like a scientist quietly entering his laboratory. He wears a light blue windbreaker, a blue flying helmet, and his familiar canvas-topped mukluks, stuffed with a fine Lapland hay called sennegrass. He pauses at the foot of the steps, and the meteorologist hands him a final weather reading. He studies it, and lifts his carved face for a moment to the sky, weighing his decision. It is a face that lived a thousand years ago, and will live a thousand years from now. I continue to see it in my mind long after the *Norge* becomes only a silver dot in the north.

Bennett nudges my arm to bring me back to the present. "Commander Byrd would like to speak to you, Bernt. He's down on the *Chantier*."

Commander Byrd is seated at his desk as we enter the cabin, working on some of his reports. The worried look is gone from his eyes, and a smile plays over his fine features as he writes. He looks so young to have done so much—already, I think, he is a famous explorer, with the eyes of all the world on him at this very moment. He looks up from his notes and rises to greet me courteously. He comes right to the point with military precision.

"Lieutenant Balchen, I'm planning another expedition to the Arctic, and I can use your experience with skis and cold-weather flying. How about requesting a year's leave of absence, and sailing back with us on the *Chantier?*"

I hesitate. There is a little grin on Floyd Bennett's face; I know where the suggestion has come from. I want this more than anything in my life, to see the big new country across the ocean, to pioneer the new skies, best of all to be a member of the team I have grown to admire so much. But one thing holds me back.

"Can I give you my answer in a couple of days, sir," I reply, "when I have the word Captain Amundsen has reached Alaska?"

"14 May. Norge lands Teller. All safe."

The word comes three days later. This evening we pick up a brief message from the Norwegian press: *"Norge* arrived Teller, Alaska, elapsed time 71 hours, completing first crossing over Pole, Europe to America." It is not until several weeks afterward that I learn all the details of the flight. Amundsen and Ellsworth and Nobile dropped the three lead-weighted flags of their respective countries at the North Pole while the *Norge* hovered over the top of the world. As they approached Alaska, they ran into ice storms and turbulence. Despite Amundsen's advice, Nobile refused to climb above the bad weather, and insisted on trying to maintain visual contact with the ground. They crossed the coast line near Point Barrow, where Wilkins was still pinned down by the blizzard. As they fought to clear the coastal peaks, sleet froze on the braces and wires of the engine nacelles. Chunks of ice broke free and were hurled back by the propellers, the sharp fragments puncturing the hydrogen gas bags. Long ragged gashes were torn in the fabric and they patched them with frantic haste to keep the ship from collapsing, and sought to lighten their load by jettisoning every last item of loose equipment. As they approached the Eskimo village of Teller, seventy miles up the Bering Sea coast from Nome, their destination, the blizzard grew so violent that Amundsen gave the order to land. As they set out again in native umiaks for the rest of the trip to Nome, they could see the Eskimos swarming over the abandoned airship, salvaging bits of fabric and metal to fashion into knives. Already the *Norge* was melting away like the snow itself.

There is a last ironic touch to the story. When their ship finally arrived in Seattle, Nobile appeared at the gangplank in his full-dress commander's uniform, which he had kept hidden from Amundsen during the trip. Despite his gold braid, the welcoming committee ignored him, and rushed to greet the stern old man in his weather-beaten ski jacket and grass-filled mukluks, standing quietly in the background.

Meanwhile the first news of the safe arrival has set me free to sail with Commander Byrd, and I start to pack my meager equipment. It is not much: one Naval Air Force uniform, some winter clothing, a rifle. With a rucksack on my back and my skis over a shoulder, I embark for my future home.

TWO

ANOTHER WORLD

1926–1927

Captain Mike Brennan looms at the head of the ladder as I come aboard the *Chantier*. His face is lobster-red and weathered, and he has the martyred expression of a man constantly being picked on by Fate. His skeptical eyes take in my rucksack and the skis on my back. "Another of these goddam landlubbers, I suppose," he says resignedly.

I draw myself up stiffly. "I am an officer in the Royal Norwegian Naval Air Force."

"Naval, huh?" He brightens a little. "Well, that's something, even if it's only air. How the hell do they expect me to steer a ship with a crew of thirty-day wonders?" he complains. "Most of them couldn't find their own stern with both hands." He challenges me. "You know what a compass is?"

"You bet."

"Can you hold a wheel?"

"*Ja*, sure."

"That's good enough for me. Go below and sign on. You're the new quartermaster."

I have the first watch as we weigh anchor. The *Chantier* gropes its way through the floating ice of the bay under slow

50

bell. Gradually the bergs thin out at the fjord's mouth, and I begin to feel the pulse of the heaving ocean as we sail southward. Great flocks of migrating birds meet us on their way north to the nesting cliffs, streaming across our bow and both sides of the masts. Puffins and dovekies buzz by like bumblebees, and overhead the ragged skeins of snow geese trail across the sky, bringing spring to Spitsbergen. Mt. Zeppelin dwindles smaller and smaller in the distance, and the dark specks of our camp have already disappeared. The mooring mast stands alone on the bluff, an abandoned monument to our polar flight. Slowly the horizon pulls a white sheet up over the spindly tower, and drapes the red cone from sight. Kings Bay is put away behind me. Now I am on the way to a new adventure.

I am sharing a cabin with two others, one a cadet from West Point, the other a middle-aged reserve officer, a stockbroker from Wall Street, he tells me. They adopt me at once as a shipmate, and introduce me to all their friends at mess. They are always laughing good-naturedly at my clumsy Norwegian English, and when I say "Ve do it," or "*Ja, ja,* you bet," they slap their knees and ask me to say it again. Soon the whole ship is saying "Ve do it, *ja.*" I have much trouble with American slang, I have studied only Oxford English, and this is like trying to understand Lapp, almost. But I learn pretty quick to say "Get out the lead from your pants" just like an American, and I teach them in turn to say "Skaal!" when they lift their glasses and to clink the rims together.

We all stand regular watches, eight hours on and two watches off; and when we are not on duty we keep busy at chores around the ship, such as painting and chipping rust and swabbing decks, while Captain Brennan glowers down from the bridge. Sometimes he slams his hat on the deck and tugs at his hair with both fists as he watches a greenhorn trying to coil a hawser or clinging awkwardly to the rail as he empties a pail of slops into the wind. These volunteer sailors are eager to please, and one afternoon my bunkmate, the Wall Street broker, decides to surprise the captain by shining the brass binnacle.

For an hour he polishes the metal top of the compass while the helmsman, a college professor from Kansas, is steering the ship. I have noticed that when my bunkmate started, the *Chantier* was bucking a rolling swell, but now, as he rubs the brass, the swell comes from the side, and the sun, which was on our port side goes astern. As the sun swings full around to starboard, Captain Brennan bursts out of his cabin with the look of a man who had taken about all he can stand.

"What the goddam's going on here?" he roars to the helmsman. "Where the hell do you think you're going?"

The college professor replies timidly: "I'm right on course, sir."

"Then why are we heading back to Kings Bay?" the captain chokes. "Look at our own wake in front of us. We've made a circle."

The stockbroker is shining away busily, glad that he is not the object of the captain's wrath. He stoops over to polish the bottom of the compass stand, trying to make himself as inconspicuous as possible, and Captain Brennan's eye comes to rest on a steel marlinspike, sticking out of his back pocket. As he moves around the compass, the magnetized compass needle follows the steel spike, and the helmsman obediently follows the needle. There is a moment of dead silence, as Captain Brennan fills his lungs, and then he lets out a blast of seagoing oaths that rocks the ship and sends the stockbroker scurrying below. He is still cowering under the blankets when I go back to our cabin that evening.

The sun grows warmer as we head into the Gulf Stream, and after our watches we strip off our shirts and tan ourselves on the afterdeck, out of the wind. I have had to work hard to achieve a good build, but all these Americans seem to come naturally by a fine body, strong and healthy. They string a net on deck and get up a game of volley ball in which I have much trouble following the rules, until the ball solves it by bumping against my naked chest and bouncing over the rail into the ocean. So we spread a canvas on the hatch, over a padding of blankets, and my West Point bunkmate challenges me to a wrestling match, the onlookers cheering us both as we roll and grapple on the mat. It strikes me suddenly that this is the very thing I envied when I watched the Americans roughhousing on the packed snow of the landing strip. I belong to the team now, and all at once my heart is filled with something beyond expression in words, a feeling of oneness with them and a love for their land that I have not yet seen.

I am at the wheel about two o'clock one morning when we sight the coast of Norway, ten miles to the east. I can make out the snowcapped mountains, shimmering in the first dawn, and I know it is green in the valleys now, and the capercailzie on the slopes are sounding their strange mating call like rain dripping, and in the streams along the coast the salmon are leaping the rapids. The oily Atlantic rolls lazily, and the sky is afire with the new day, and I take a last long look at my home country and wonder when I shall see it again.

Our first stop is London. As we approach the mouth of the Thames, Captain Brennan barges into the wheelhouse. He recoils as he spots the helmsman, the same college professor from Kansas and emits a stifled cry of pain. "Balchen, take that goddam wheel," he moans, "or this ship will wind up in the courtyard of Buckingham Palace." I have to stay at the wheel for ten solid hours, steering through the crisscross traffic of fishing smacks and excursion boats and tooting ferries, until we toss our heaving-lines onto the dock at Shadwell Basin.

In London we have our first taste of the international excitement which Byrd's conquest of the Pole has aroused. While Commander Byrd is being dined and fêted, the rest of us wan-

der through the historic old city, greeted everywhere we go
with Cockney shouts of "Blimey, Yanks, ye done it!" We have
been given guest privileges at the Royal Aero Club, and that
night, as we are sitting in the bar, a British flier lifts his glass
of ale and proposes a toast: "To the Americans!" I hesitate in
the background, but my shipmates grab me and haul me into
the center of the group, and we all link arms and respond with
a chorus of "Skaal!"

There is only one sour note. At the Aero Club we read in
the London papers that the Italians have assailed the validity
of Byrd's claim to having been at the North Pole. The rest of
us laugh this off as mere jealousy on the part of the Mussolini
press, but Floyd Bennett reads every word carefully, and then
crumples the newspaper in his fist and hurls it to the floor. He
is a navy officer, as loyal to his commander as I am to Amundsen.

Now the *Chantier* leaves London and sets course for New
York. Commander Byrd is seldom seen, working alone in his
cabin where he reads the sheaves of congratulatory messages and
prepares his acceptance speeches. The active reserve officers
brush the wrinkles from the uniforms hanging in their lockers,
and the other members of the crew break out business suits
and neckties and shine their dress shoes. I feel out of place in
my rough woolens, and wander out on deck by myself and
lean against the rail, watching for sight of land.

It is our last night at sea. Tomorrow will start all the parades
and banquets and civic receptions, and I am beginning to get
cold feet already. I am never easy in a city or with crowds. I am
at home only in my aviator's helmet and flying coveralls behind
the controls of an airplane, and my spirits sink as I think of
the mob staring at me curiously, making fun of my thick accent
maybe. Much as I long to see America, I would be willing at
this moment to jump overboard and swim back to Norway,
skis and all.

Someone jostles my elbow, and Floyd Bennett is against the rail beside me. He has become, and will remain until the day of his death, my closest friend. He is no more eager than I am to face the crowds, and we talk of other things that interest us more: airplanes and airplane performance, wing loading and icing, and the problems of cold-weather flight. Like myself he belongs to the empty spaces of the sky, flying over the horizon to still new horizons beyond. The northern horizon is the one that calls us most loudly, and his big hand closes on my shoulder, and he makes a solemn vow.

"Some day we'll fly back to the Arctic together."

He goes below at last, and again I stand alone at the rail, looking westward, as the dawn behind me touches the tips of the *Chantier*'s masts, and slowly lights the whole sky. In the far distance I see a dark streak, darker than the ocean. It is the coast of America.

Despite head winds all the way, the *Chantier* has made the crossing in thirteen days, ahead of schedule. For the first time Captain Brennan's dour face is wreathed in smiles as he proudly notifies Commander Byrd that we are off Sandy Hook, about to enter the Lower New York Bay. Once more Fate deals the long-suffering captain an underhand blow. Byrd informs him that our premature arrival has caught the welcoming committee flat-footed, and they have radioed us to stand offshore until they send word the reception is ready. Captain Brennan, unable to trust himself to speak, yanks the lever to stop engines and stalks into his cabin with an outraged slam of the door.

Two mornings later the captain himself shakes me awake in my bunk, and I feel the ship throbbing. "Balchen, we're moving in," he growls. "Take the goddam wheel before we hit the Statue of Liberty or something."

I am the only one aboard who has never seen New York. I have my first glimpse of the city between the turning spokes as, following the orders of the Sandy Hook pilot, I steer through the Narrows and into the tumultuous confusion of the harbor. Airplanes zoom overhead and buzz our ship as we approach, tugs and small craft are blasting their whistles in endless toots and shrieks, and red fireboats are pumping streams of water aloft. All the yachts are strung with pennants and signal flags, and the Stars and Stripes are flying everywhere. Directly ahead, glinting in the sun, is the bronze Liberty with her torch, the shining symbol of the new world to all of us from the old; and in the distance, as I peer through the pilot-house window, I see Manhattan's towering skyscrapers, looking as high as the jagged nunataks of Spitsbergen. I have an overpowering first impression of the United States, the tremendous vitality it puts into its greeting of a new national hero.

A siren slices the steady din, and the press tug weaves toward us through the armada. The reporters and photographers aboard far outnumber the members of the expedition itself. Harry Bruno, who is handling public relations for Byrd, chats with me as the *Chantier* moves slowly across the harbor toward the Battery—and it is the beginning of my association with a man whose loyalty and wise advice have meant much to me ever since. The walks of Battery Park are black with massed humanity as we approach, and the cheers curl upward in wave after wave of deafening sound, surging to the tops of the office buildings, along the waterfront, and shattering like breakers in a white foam of ticker tape and torn newspapers that float downward to the streets below. I feel my lungs tighten; I cannot breathe. America is bigger than I ever dreamed, more overwhelming, more wonderful.

The gangplank is down, and a tall figure in a cutaway with a white carnation in his buttonhole hurries aboard. It is Grover Whalen, Bennett whispers, the city's official greeter. Behind him a smaller and even more dapper figure mounts the gangplank and grasps Commander Byrd's hand and everyone within hearing laughs at something he says. There is no need for

Bennett to tell me who he is. I recognize the world-famous smile of Jimmy Walker, the Mayor of New York.

The parade to City Hall is ready to start at noon. Mayor Walker and Byrd, the Mayor natty in his formal clothes and Byrd trim in his naval uniform, lead the way down the gangplank. Grover Whalen follows with Floyd Bennett; he turns to wave to me as he descends. The rest of my shipmates troop after them, and some of them glance up in surprise, as I lean over the rail above them and beckon to me to join them; but I am not invited to take part in the ceremonies—it has been explained to me that I am not a member of the Byrd Arctic Expedition.

Captain Brennan is the last to stride down the gangway. "Balchen, you've got the watch," he calls over his shoulder, gives a final hitch to his pants, and hurries to join the procession.

The band crashes into a march, and the parade starts across Battery Park. The roar of the crowd tracks into the echoing canyon of Broadway, and the thump of bass drums and blare of trumpets are suddenly muffled as the buildings hide them in their course to City Hall. The crowd has drifted away, and in the deserted park the only sound is the mewing of sea gulls and the monotonous creak of the *Chantier*'s hull against the pilings. I take out my pocket diary, and make a single bleak entry:

"*20 June. Arr. N.Y., 1200.*"

Early next morning, while I am pouring a mug of coffee in the galley and reading all about the parade in the Sunday papers, a car honks on the pier, and the lone driver steps out and climbs the gangplank. At first I do not recognize Grover Whalen in business clothes; but then I spot the telltale white

carnation in his buttonhole and inquire politely if there is
someone he is looking for. Whalen grins.

"I'm looking for you. Floyd Bennett said you'd never seen
New York. Thought you might like to take a little tour of the
city with me."

So at last I have my own parade up Broadway, with the city's
official greeter as my personal escort. The financial district is
deserted on Sunday morning, and only a few street cleaners are
sweeping the last of yesterday's confetti and ticker tape into the
gutters. At City Hall they have already removed the bunting
from the bare wooden stands. We drive through the narrow
streets lined with silent skyscrapers, and I tilt my head and look
up between the converging walls of concrete and glass at the
tiny wedge of blue sky. Once when I was skiing in Norway as
a boy a snow bridge gave way under me, and I was pinned for
several hours at the bottom of a deep crevasse, and I have the
same trapped feeling now. Whalen recites proudly the sta-
tistics of this greatest of all cities, how many hundred miles of
trolley tracks and how many million tons of shipping and how
many dozen elevators in the Woolworth Tower alone; but, as
always, my mind is on airplanes and flying. What will happen
when the big multi-engine transport planes try to land beside
these man-made peaks? New York will have to build enormous
new airports many miles out in the open country, I think; and
I say, "Some day they will have landing places right on top of
these high buildings maybe."

Grover Whalen laughs. "That's way off in the future, Bernt.
You'll never live to see the day."

I think of the seething throngs that will fill these streets
tomorrow, the snarling taxicabs, the traffic stalled at every in-
tersection, and I itch to be out of the city and in the free sky
lanes at the controls of an airplane again. I wonder when I shall
be starting on the new expedition that Commander Byrd has
promised.

Whalen halts the car and points to an enormous department store, covering two city blocks. It is called Wanamaker's, he tells me, and he was once the general manager. "Here's where they're planning to put the *Josephine Ford* on exhibit," he says casually. "Harry Bruno has arranged it with Rodman Wanamaker, and the Byrd expedition will get $30,000 to help defray expenses." He adds: "Harry tells me you'll be right here with the plane."

I cannot believe my ears. "But I'm a pilot."

"That's right. They want somebody on hand at the exhibit to answer questions."

Of all the things I wanted least in the world, this is it. The *Josephine Ford* is caged inside a red velvet rope, on a flag-draped platform in the middle of Wanamaker's store, and day after day from morning to night I must stand like an exhibit myself, while customers hold up their children to see the pretty airplane. They all want to know how I crank it up to start, for instance, or what makes such a big thing stay in the air. One elderly lady examines the landing wheels thoughtfully. "Tell me, young man, how many miles do you get to these tires?"

Still worse are the teen-age girls, who seem even more interested in me than the plane. They giggle and nudge one another and point at me, like a prize bull at a county fair. One girl exclaims in a shrill voice that carries all over the store, "Ee-ee, lookit his big boycep muscles!" and I hear another one snapping gum behind me and whispering to her friend: "Ain't he cute, Moitle! Like Francis X. Bushman almost." Now I have a fair Scandinavian complexion and blush very easily, and when my cheeks flame pink and I stammer something in Norwegian they all jump up and down and squeal with delight. I think if Captain Amundsen were to come into Wanamaker's I should fall right through the floor.

From New York the *Josephine Ford* is taken to Philadelphia,

to be shown at the Sesquicentennial Air Races. I am about
ready to quit the whole job and go home when Harry Bruno
drops by the exhibit and asks me to come to a dinner with him
and meet some people he knows. I have met enough people
already, I tell him, but Harry insists. "This is different, Bernt,
this is your kind of people."

They are members of an organization called the Quiet Bird-
men; and they do not even mention that they belong, but they
cherish the honor deeply. Most of them are survivors of World
War I, and the membership is spread all over the world, even to
pilots they fought once like von Richthofen and Ernst Udet.
One thing they all have in common: they are dedicated to the
future of aeronautics. Here at the dinner are the leaders in
American military aviation, and the future leaders: Hap
Arnold, who has just been promoted to major in the Army
Signal Corps and is being ribbed by his companions about his
exalted new rank, and Captain Carl Spaatz, and Lieutenant Ira
Eaker, and Benny Foulois, and Jimmy Doolittle, and one
slightly older man in civilian clothes, fine-looking and dyna-
mic. I am as awestruck as a small boy when Harry Bruno introduces me to General Billy Mitchell. In Norway last year we
followed the story of his court-martial with astonishment; in
my own country this man is already revered as a prophet of the
new air age, and we could only surmise that petty politics
forced his resignation from the active service of his nation. I
listen, hardly breathing, as he talks about the coming greatness
of air power. In his outspoken way he does not hesitate to
lambaste the Navy and the Army for their shortsighted testi-
mony during his trial. He comes up to me after dinner and asks
if I know Byrd. I reply that I was a member of Amundsen's expedition, and have only talked a few times with Commander
Byrd. "He is very well known," General Mitchell remarks with
a wry smile, "but nobody knows him very well."

I understand that smile a little better when the account is

finally published which Byrd had been writing on the *Chantier*. His book *Skyward* reveals that he personally led the fight against Billy Mitchell's proposal to Congress for a separate United States Air Force, and instead wrote a substitute bill for the creation of a Bureau of Aeronautics within the Navy Department. In his own words Byrd describes how he made daily rounds of Congress, working tirelessly to bring about the defeat of Mitchell's plan, and he concludes: "General Mitchell was finally squashed . . . I believe he was sincere but his sincerity was the ruthless pertinacity of a zealot." I am new to this country, and I cannot know which man is right; but one thing I do know tonight, as I see the fire in his eyes, and that is that Billy Mitchell is not squashed yet.

There is no mistaking a short peppery Hollander in the group, none other than the famous designer of our big trimotored Fokker. He has been staring at me all through dinner, and at last he comes over and asks bluntly in an accent even thicker than my own: "I haf seen you some place before, no?"

"It was in 1923, at the air meet in Göteborg, Sweden, when I was there with the Norwegian Air Force."

Tony Fokker's face lights up. "Sure, now, of course, you were one of those boys stunting the new fighters. What the hell are you over here doing?"

I explain that I am here on exhibition with the plane that he built, and he grunts, pleased, and scribbles an address on the back of his card. "Any time that you show up at the factory in Hasbrouck Heights, there is a job for you waiting."

Harry Bruno has good news for me as he drives me home. The Guggenheim Foundation, which has been set up as sponsor for aeronautical progress in the country and to make the American public more air-minded, has agreed to finance a tour of the *Josephine Ford* around the United States. Floyd Bennett will be the pilot, and I shall be with him as co-pilot.

Now at last I am airborne again. The *Josephine Ford* completes its climbing turn, and behind us Mitchel Field dwindles and merges with the green landscape of Long Island. To our left, across the East River, the giant skyscrapers of Manhattan have shrunk to toy size, herded together in a tight group on the little island. Wanamaker's store is somewhere down there, and I think of the stream of women shoppers moving in and out through the revolving doors, and the millions of people fighting for space in the narrow streets. I pull the dog-eared diary out of the pocket of my flying suit, and make an entry:

"8 Oct., 1926. Lv. N.Y., 0912, J. Ford tour."

Our tour began in Washington, and proceeded to New York, and Harry Guggenheim himself was at Mitchel Field last night for the send-off ceremonies, along with Commander Byrd. There were press interviews and speeches and a Chamber of Commerce banquet, a taste of what we shall experience from now on at every stop. Our two months' junket will cover almost nine thousand miles and touch down at fifty cities from coast to coast. It begins to seem that I shall never be free from facing crowds, inflicting my awkward Norwegian accent on strangers; but between banquets at least I can be here in the cockpit, seeing this new land below me like a map endlessly unrolling.

Floyd Bennett is handling the dual controls, and from the right seat as I navigate I watch his big-knuckled hands moving lightly across the throttles, adjusting the three engines to perfect synchronization. I have familiarized myself with the intricate operation of this aircraft, and now more than ever I can appreciate Bennett's skill as a pilot. His fingertips trail back and forth across the instrument panel like those of an organist, attuned to the plane's rhythm, sensitive to the slightest variation in pitch, drawing out the full symphony of the engines with his master touch. We skirt the northern suburbs of the city, and he asks me: "Are we going to follow the river or the railroad?"

"Why not fly across country direct?" I suggest. "I'll give you a compass course, and after a while I'll check the ground speed and tell you when we'll be there."

We drone across the Westchester hills, over wooded areas and mountains where there are no landmarks or signs. The country is as new to Bennett as to me, and I can see that he is uneasy. "Sure you're on the right course?" he asks once.

"*Ja, ja,* don't worry one thing: we'll be at Albany in just forty minutes."

We land within one minute of our estimated arrival time, and Bennett gives me a sidelong glance as we climb into a waiting limousine. I have a blurred impression of the State Capitol as we drive at top speed directly to the Chamber of Commerce luncheon. After a tasty meal of chicken à la king and peas, Bennett starts the speech that Harry Bruno has prepared for him. He admits modestly that he is only an aviator, not an orator, but that in his belief Byrd's polar flight has proved once for all that flying has come of age, and no horizon in the world is beyond man's reach today. The applause has barely died down before we are back in the limousine again, and I have a blurred impression of Albany from the other direction as we speed to the airport, and take off for our next stop at Syracuse.

Bennett levels off at fifteen hundred feet altitude, to follow the curving New York Central tracks. The air is bumpy, and we have to fight a slight headwind. "Maybe there are more favorable winds upstairs," I urge, "and anyway we'd save twenty minutes on a straight heading to Syracuse."

"I'm not used to that kind of navigating," Bennett admits. "I like to be able to read the names on the railroad stations, and know where I am."

In the Royal Norwegian Air Force we were trained in flying by dead reckoning over a country in which there were few railroads or highways on which to depend for finding one's route by purely visual means. Dead reckoning navigation, in the air as aboard a ship on the high seas, depends upon noting carefully your compass headings, the elapsed time on each heading, and the speed of the plane through the air, which corresponds to the mariner's speed data obtained by reading his taffrail log. It is also necessary to observe any drifting of the plane, which may be thrown off its calculated course by the effect of the wind. These constitute the main elements of this form of navigation. In 1926, however, radio ranges for the guidance of aircraft on cross-country flights are already being experimented with. Of course, it is also possible to rely on the more elaborate method of celestial navigation, using a sextant equipped with an artificial horizon with dampening devices. These slow down the oscillation of the bubble, caused by the rolling and pitching of the plane, sufficiently so that one can obtain more accurate readings of the instrument.

Our tour continues from Syracuse to Rochester, then Niagara Falls, then Buffalo—always the same chicken à la king and peas, always the same prepared speech, over and over. I groan to Bennett while we are flying to Cleveland that I can recite his talk by heart now, and he says grimly: "Okay. If you know it so well, you can give it yourself tonight." Now I have stuck my big foot in my mouth, and the others won't let me back out, so that night at the Cleveland Chamber of Commerce dinner I face the roomful of city dignitaries and begin, as I have heard Bennett start so many times: "I am an aviator only, not an oriay-tor, you bet." Bennett doubles up, and the whole audience rocks with laughter. On the way back to our room at the hotel he insists that my speech is the biggest hit yet. He is still chuckling to himself as he comes out from the shower,

The *America* after ditching on the French coast.

Commander Byrd signing the Golden Register of the City of Paris at the *Hôtel de ville* during the gala reception after the flight of the *America*. Standing beyond the table (*left to right*) are Balchen, Acosta, and Noville.

Test-flying the *Floyd Bennett*, Commander Byrd's trimotor Ford, at Winnipeg for the South Pole flight.

(*Left to right*) Bernt Balchen, Floyd Bennett, and Charles Murphy shortly before the Greenly Island relief expedition.

drying his lanky frame with a towel. "From now you're the oriay-tor, Bernt, I'm only the aviator, you bet."

I am standing at the open window, listening to the dull rumble of traffic in the street below. "We're both only aviators," I insist. "Platform speeches aren't for you or me." I stare at the smoking stacks of the steel mills that smudge the night sky. "How about that flight to the Arctic together that we talked about on the *Chantier?*"

"I've got a better idea." Bennett has wrapped the towel around his middle, and he flops onto the bed. "How would you like to fly the Atlantic?" he murmurs. "Commander Byrd did speak to me about a transatlantic flight, but I haven't heard anything further about it recently. Possibly you and I could do something about it."

We do not sleep that night. Hour after hour we sit on the edge of our beds and talk, exploring the exciting possibilities of the idea. The Raymond Orteig Prize of $25,000, announced seven years ago, is still waiting to be picked up by the first one to fly the ocean. Okay, *ja*, but where would we find an airplane? I ask. Maybe the *Jo Ford*, Bennett says promptly; Harry Bruno could talk to the Guggenheim people. Could it carry sufficient fuel to make the trip? I get out the little pocket slide rule that I always carry, and my calculations show that it would be possible to take off the big Fokker, despite its heavy overload. How about range, though? We resolve to keep the most accurate data during the rest of our trip, noting the *Josephine Ford*'s maximum speed and fuel consumption in our logbooks, to make sure it could fly nonstop to the other side.

We can talk of nothing else as we leave the Midwest and head across the continent to Los Angeles, hopping from banquet to banquet, while Bennett and I spell each other at oriay-ting. With this vision of flying the Atlantic before me, I find I am actually enjoying the tour now. The crowds still laugh at my Norwegian accent; but I have come to know that their laughter is friendly, and realize this is a newcomer's chance of a lifetime to get the big view of America, to appreciate its tremendous promise, and to meet in every city the leaders in modern aviation. What's more, my experience in speech-making is helping me to overcome my difficulties with the language, and I assure Bennett that pretty soon I talk American as good as him, you bet.

From Los Angeles we swing back through Texas, and along the Gulf coast to Mobile and Pensacola, and now at last, several tons of chicken à la king and a couple of million peas later, we are flying north to Washington to end our tour. Tomorrow I will phone Harry Bruno to start negotiations for the *Josephine Ford,* if we can get permission, to fly the Atlantic.

There is a telegram waiting in Washington. Bennett reads it and hands it to me without a word. Commander Byrd orders us to deliver the plane to Detroit. He is presenting it to the Ford Museum for a permanent exhibit.

Bennett and I sit silently in the cockpit as we fly to Detroit where Commander Byrd is waiting. The *Josephine Ford*'s engines hum smoothly, its propellers turn with the same undeviating precision mile after mile. My eye runs over the instrument gauges, and automatically I note down the speed and fuel consumption for the last time. Still figuring, though it looks like an academic question now, I run over the data I have compiled on the tour. "Tell me," I ask Bennett, "what do you get for our average cruising speed?"

Bennett takes his own log out of the leg pocket of his coveralls. "Let's see. About seventy miles an hour."

"So do I." To fly across the Atlantic from New York to, say, Paris—a distance of about 3,600 miles actual flying, or say 3,700 to be on the safe side—would require about 53 hours' flying time. That would mean breaking the world's endurance record for sustained flight.

"If the *Josephine Ford* had those bigger Wright Whirlwind

engines that have just come on the market," I tell Bennett, "I believe we could do it. With those babies we'd get an extra thirty horsepower, or close to it, per engine."

"That's right, *if* she had them," Bennett shrugs. "Well, it doesn't matter now. We won't be flying this bucket across the Atlantic or anywhere else. You'll be working in the Fokker factory, and I'll be looking for a job." He tilts a wing. "What's that wind sock down there say?"

We circle the Detroit air strip, and come around for the final approach. I think back to the first time I saw the big Fokker rafted ashore on lifeboats through the churning ice of Kings Bay. It has come a long way to end its brave life here in a dusty museum. The tires screech, and the *Josephine Ford* settles on the grass and rolls to a stop for the last time.

THREE

RIM OF THE ARCTIC

1927

Uncle Tony, everybody calls him, and he knows the lowliest grease monkey in his factory by his first name. He kneels in a pool of oil beside a mechanic working under an engine mount and argues heatedly: "Damn to hell, Joe, there's too much bend in that gas line—it won't feed right." "But the intake valve's got to go somewhere." "So we put it on the other side, see? Isn't that simple now?" Tony Fokker wipes his greasy hands on the seat of his pants and scurries on to the next operation, while the mechanic nods his head in grudging agreement.

He was born in Holland and started manufacturing planes when aviation was still a wild-eyed dream. Before World War I he offered his designs to both Great Britain and the United States, but neither government was interested. Then he took them to Germany, where they were adopted by the Kaiser's Air Corps, and the famed Richthofen and his Circus all but defeated the Allies over France. When the German army finally surrendered, Fokker managed to work his way here to the States, and organized the Atlantic Aircraft Corporation. He is erratic, wildly impulsive, given to sudden inspirations; there is a story that he held up the first scheduled flight of a new air liner for weeks, while he installed a passenger toilet he had just invented, something unheard of at the time. But Uncle Tony is a perfectionist, and his planes are the last word in design and aerodynamic efficiency.

He is into everything around the plant, pausing beside one of his draftsmen and jabbing his thick forefinger at the blueprint—"Not so much hump there in the wing, Charlie, you cut down the airfoil!"—or running to join a gang on the assembly line and lend a hand with a chain hoist, or personally setting a timing mechanism with the delicate touch of a watchmaker. I see him scoot out of sight at the far end of the assembly floor, and a moment later he has circled the factory and is standing behind me again, peering around for another problem to straighten out. He is short and chunky, with bright pink cheeks that he puffs out when he is harassed, and I think of a shaved Santa Claus, confronted by all the chimneys in the world at the same time.

His Dutch blue eyes pierce me like steel fragments, the first day I report at the plant. "What you like to be doing here, Bernt?"

"First it would suit me fine to go through your shop and get familiar with all your techniques, this steel-tube structure which is new to me yet, and your laminated wings, and see how your aircraft are assembled."

He nods "Okay" and is off on his way to the forge room, grabbing a sledge-hammer as he runs, and I move slowly down the assembly line. I have always been impressed with the simplicity of the Fokker design, the clean lines of the fuselage with almost no guy wires or struts, and the thick leading edges of the wings like the powerful pinions of a gull in flight. There are both single- and tri-motor planes under production, and the factory is working on a revolutionary new single-engine model specially adapted for the Arctic. It is called the Fokker Standard Universal, a sturdy high-wing job, and my fingers itch to handle its controls as I see it rolled out on the line. Bob

Noorduyn, Fokker's assistant, asks me if I have ever flown a type like this, and I say, "No, we have nothing as advanced as this in Europe." Noorduyn sees my eagerness and grins. "Why don't you take it up and see what you can get out of it?"

I can feel its great lifting power as I ease back on the stick, surging upward and banking in a steep climb. I have never felt better stability in the air, it has nice flying characteristics, and its rugged build and large cargo space are destined to make it the pioneer bush plane of Canada. I shoot several more take-offs and landings, and turn in a detailed report on its performance.

Next morning I am on the assembly floor when I get a call to go to the front office at once. Nobody ever knocks, so I walk in. The desk is piled with charts, the floor is littered with samples of aircraft material and working models, and Tony Fokker whirls in his swivel chair red-faced, clutching my report in his fist. I wonder if my job at the factory is already over after ten days. His eyes squint suspiciously: "Just what was that work you did in the Norwegian Air Force?"

"I was assistant to the chief test pilot at the Naval Aircraft Factory."

Uncle Tony's face is like a blast of fire from an overcharged engine. "Why the hell for damn didn't you say so?" he explodes. "What are you doing down there on that assembly floor? You're a test pilot now."

He is always explosive, always making instant decisions. His mind is faster than his tongue sometimes, and when he is too excited to fumble for the English word, he breaks into machine-gun German. I can speak the language, and so more and more he confides his problems to me. He is an intuitive trouble shooter, a self-taught pilot and a very good one. On one occasion we have some vibration in a twin-engine bomber we are testing, and our department has worked in vain for days to locate it. Uncle Tony goes up with us on a test flight, and I see him wandering back through the cabin, fuming to himself. Suddenly he kicks out one of the windows and pokes his head through the hole. "It's a strut in the tail assembly," he grunts, and that is all we need to fix the trouble.

Time never means anything to Tony Fokker, and this is one reason he and I get along so well, because to me too, when I have a problem I want to solve, it doesn't matter whether it is five o'clock in the afternoon or in the morning. Many a night we work in the factory long after everyone else has left, or spread out our work sheets on the living-room table, in his home, or cruise over the week end on his yacht, talking nothing but planes. Sometimes I think he never sleeps. Once I am awakened in my boarding house at two o'clock in the morning by a bombardment of small stones tossed against my bedroom window. The landlady knocks at my door, frightened, and whispers: "There's some maniac outside. Shall I call the police?" Uncle Tony is standing below on the lawn, waving excitedly. "Bernt, Bernt, come now," he yells. "We go to the factory."

We work at the plant for three days without rest. A big gold stampede has started in northern Ontario, and a rush order has come in to deliver some Fokker Universals to Western Canada Airways, to transport miners and equipment. Uncle Tony realizes that the bush pilots have no experience on skis, and he is worried that the landing gear on the Universals is not rugged enough to stand the pummeling. I describe how we sawed strips from lifeboat oars at Kings Bay to reenforce the skis, and we work out alterations in the design that will hold up in the roughest landings. The modified planes are shipped north a week later, to take part in the world's first airborne gold rush.

Now in early March I am down at the Hackensack River, testing the floats that will have to be installed in place of skis after the spring break-up comes to Canada. As I taxi up to the ramp, Uncle Tony's Lancia sport car careens down the hill and squawks to a halt beside the pier. He is hopping mad, I can tell at a glance.

"Whatever you are doing, stop it," he bellows. "You have to catch a train."

"What train?" I gasp as I pile into the car beside him and he stamps on the accelerator.

"The first train, of course."

"Where to?"

"Hudson," he says impatiently, taking a corner on two wheels.

I brace myself as we swerve around an oncoming truck. "Where is Hudson?"

"It's in Ontario where you're going," he replies, glaring back at the truck driver and squeezing the rubber bulb of his horn indignantly. "Where else would it be?"

"But what am I going to Hudson for?"

"Because they've scattered my beautiful planes all over Canada, that's why." He throws both arms in the air, and the Lancia mounts the curb. Uncle Tony grabs the wheel again in the nick of time, and glowers at the curbstone. "All upside down on their backs in the snow," he moans. "All wrecked."

He pumps the bulb of his horn furiously as we go through a stop sign, zigzag down the street, and slam to a stop in front of the factory. "I'm giving you my three best mechanics to take with you." I follow him through the door, and we bolt up the stairs. "There's a train leaving at eight o'clock tonight," he adds over his shoulder. "You have three hours."

He charges into his office, sweeping all the charts off his desk onto the floor as he searches for my railroad ticket. He locates it in his coat pocket, and yanks open his desk drawer. "Here, take these," he says, grabbing a wad of greenbacks and stuffing them into my hand. He hesitates, and snatches another fistful. "Better take these, too; you'll be gone a long while."

Back at my boarding house I dump a bureau drawerful of

clothes onto the bed, cram them into my old rucksack, and arrive at the railroad station just in time to leap aboard the last car. The following morning we cross the Canadian border into Ontario, and head north through the big spruce forests, snow drifted and silent. At one the next morning, the conductor awakes me. "Next stop's Hudson," he says, "God help you."

Our little party climbs down the steps onto the hard-packed snow, and the train pulls away into the darkness. The stars are blinking bright in the night sky, and the train whistle fading in the distance is answered by the howl of Malemutes. We make out the light of a lantern bobbing toward us, and someone yells in a French Canadian accent: "By gar, you de Fokker people from de States? How you like dees cold?"

I fill my lungs with the sharp clean air, and shout back: "I like it fine, you bet."

We follow the lantern down the railroad embankment along a narrow path, and ahead of us I see the pink glow of a Yukon stove, lighting the windows of a snow-covered shack. It is little more than a lean-to, but the lantern's rays reveal an impressive sign over the door: "Western Canada Airways." This is the administration building, ticket office, freight station, and passenger terminal for the whole flying gold rush.

As we push open the door and stamp the snow from our feet, a group of men around the pot-bellied stove peer at us curiously through the murk of spruce-wood smoke and stale tobacco. The warmth is welcome, and my three mechanics make for the stove at once; one of them, a youngster from Jersey City, lifts his coattails and extends his rear end toward the heat, chafing himself gratefully. A short dark-bearded member of the group shuffles toward me in beaded slippers, and holds out his hand.

"I'm Rod Ross, Airways superintendent here. You're Balchen, I take it." We shake hands, and he introduces the others.

"This is Tommy Sears, and Al Cheeseman, our maintenance chief." He jerks a thumb toward a lanky figure seated behind the stove. "And this is Captain Stevenson. One of our pilots."

Stevenson is scrunched so far down in his chair that he is almost sitting on the back of his neck. His legs are propped on a high shelf, a pair of moosehide moccasins comfortably crossed, and a curved pipe is hooked in his mouth, the bend of the stem following the line of his long angular jaw. He waves a hand languidly in greeting.

Rod Ross tells me briefly what has happened. Two of our Fokkers are down—one only ten miles from Hudson, the other almost thirty miles out in the bush. They had hired a couple of new pilots, Ross says, who had no experience in winter flying, and they allowed themselves to be caught in bad weather and tried to make a landing in a snow squall. They misjudged their distance, and the ski tips snagged in the snow and flipped the planes onto their backs. There is one Universal left at Hudson, he tells me, and after a night's sleep I can take it in the morning and fly over the downed planes to inspect the damage.

The young mechanic from Jersey City is fidgeting beside the stove, and his eyes move around the little room in embarrassment. He inquires in a low voice: "Which door is the men's room?" Captain Stevenson unlocks his moccasined feet from the shelf, clambers to his full height, and rips a page from the Eaton mail-order catalogue hanging on the wall. He opens the outside door, and points to the darkness and swirling snow. "There's the whole wide world, sonny boy," he drawls. "If you can't help yourself, you're no man for the north country."

The sun is up before we are, the following morning, and we step out of the bunkhouse and blink in astonishment. Last night's silent wilderness has suddenly become a bustling community of tents and log cabins, and the paths of packed snow between the buildings are swarming with prospectors lured to this fur-trading post by the news of the gold strike near Hudson. They have come from all over Canada and the United States, and even Mexico, Texans in ten-gallon hats and New Yorkers in derbies and raccoon coats, all with just one thought in mind: get in and get rich and get out again. Nobody has made any money yet, but already the usual painted camp followers and card sharks are beginning to move into Hudson, waiting for the first stampeders to return so they can extract the gold nuggets from their pokes. Most of these tenderfeet have no idea of the hardships they will encounter on the trail, and this morning I see a couple of men starting out with suitcases, wearing low rubber overshoes for their hike to the nearest strike, ninety miles away. They are brought back to Hudson a few days later, frostbitten and disillusioned.

After surveying both wrecks from the air, I return to Hudson and hire a couple of dog teams, and load the sleds with spare airplane parts and sleeping bags and a tent. With my Jersey mechanics bundled in Hudson Bay parkas they have borrowed for the trip, we set out for the first wreck. The high-wing monoplane is upside down in the middle of a frozen lake, and we set up camp on shore and go to work. With the temperature thirty to forty below, the freezing wind numbs our gloved hands, and I have to warn my young companions to watch each other's faces for a telltale white spot on a cheek or nose. First we must take the whole plane apart, unbolt the skis and undercarriage, remove the engine, and disconnect the body from the inverted wing, half buried in the snow. We put our shoulders to the stripped fuselage, and roll it over right side up. Now we cut three tall spruce poles in the forest and build a tripod out on the lake, hoist the big wing into the air and swing it over the fuselage and lower it carefully into place.

When we have put the whole plane together again, we straighten out some of the bends in the tail surfaces, and try to realign the motor frame with our crude tools before welding the broken tubes. We do not have the heavy equipment to true it exactly, and when the engine is installed it tilts a little on one side. The result is that when I start flying back to Hudson I cannot hold a straight course, and I approach the lake in a series of wide circles. At the end of the last circle I crab down to a landing. Stevenson is standing at the parking place as I step out, rubbing his chin thoughtfully. "You Scandahoovians always fly sideways?" he asks with a deadpan expression.

By the end of the week we have the second plane in commission again, and the mechanics take the train back to Jersey with ill concealed relief. They are sorry for me, because Uncle Tony has wired me to stay a little longer and instruct Western Canada's new pilots in ski landings and cold-weather operations; but this suits me fine. This is almost like being in Norway again: the same dark pines blanketed with fresh snow, the same ptarmigan shooting and jigging through the ice for pike and whitefish. From my plane, as I fly Stevenson on his check rides, I even look down on the same big herds of *elg*—but over here they call them moose—browsing the willow tips along the creek bottoms, their hot bodies steaming in the sub-zero cold.

Steve has never flown in winter in the Canadian bush before, but I could not have a better pupil. He picks up quickly all the cold-weather tricks: how to run the skis up onto a pile of brush when the plane stops at night so that they will not freeze to the snow, and how to drain the oil immediately from the engine. I teach him to open the pet cock and let the oil run right down into the snow, where it freezes into a solid lump which can be melted in a bucket the next morning. When I start the engine at forty below, I drape a canvas cover over it and put a plumber's blowtorch underneath the makeshift tent to heat it. While the engine is warming I work the propellers back and forth with my hand to tell when the cylinders have thawed out enough to crank. Then the heated oil is poured back into the engine, and I climb into the cockpit and prime it. I have designed these Universals at the Fokker factory to be cranked from the cockpit—a safety factor for ski and float flying, and the Canadian bush pilots like it very much.

Steve and I fly many trips to the gold camps together, and when we sit down at a new spot I teach him the Norwegian trick of reading snow from the air, looking for hidden obstacles and judging the shadows to find a level place. Snow never stays the same, but changes constantly with temperature and pressure and age. Soon Steve is making long trips alone. One day while he is away comes a hurry-up call for a load of drills and dynamite for Squaw Lake, a remote strike in the bush country where no plane has ever landed before.

Three hours later I graze the spruce tops and slap my skis gently on the shore of the lake, and I shoulder into my rucksack and ski to the tar-paper mess hall, which as always is the biggest building in camp. The cook, a strapping Irishman with a black woolen undershirt unbuttoned on his hairy chest and a flour sack tied around his middle, is baking a batch of prune pies, dogged at every step by a half-wit Indian helper. The ripe odor of the boy's greasy dungarees rises above all the other smells in the kitchen, and the cook sniffs at his assistant in disgust.

"Sure an' the only way he could be dirtier," he confides to me, "would be to be bigger."

The boy gawks at me open-mouthed, and drops one of the pies upside down on the floor, and the cook scrapes it back into the pie pan and pats it into shape again.

"It's no use, no use a-tall," he sighs. "He'll niver larn. I even tried givin' him smart pills."

I help myself to a mug of coffee. "What are smart pills?"

" 'Tis me own remedy," the cook explains solemnly. "First I start him off on one pill. After a week he says to me, 'I'm not any smarter yet,' so I tell him to take two pills. Still he's no smarter, so I step up the dose to three. Well, finally one day he

holds up a pill and looks at it closer and says to me: 'Say, these
ain't pills, these are rabbit droppings.' 'Ye see, b'y?' I says to
him. 'Now ye're gittin' smart.' ' "

Supper is pork and beans and fried moose meat, and heavy
bannocks made from a mixture of sourdough, which the cook
keeps all year round in a covered chamber pot on a shelf behind the stove. The men pile them like flapjacks on a plate, and
saturate them with bacon grease, and top off the meal with a
quarter-wedge of pie. "We got all kinds of pie here," one of the
miners grumbles to me, "covered, crossbar, and open, and
there's prunes in every one of 'em."

All this grease I like; but I like a little variety, too. I go out
to my plane and get a couple of lake trout, cut them in chunks
and boil them the way we do in Norway. I put on a kettle of
cold water, heavily salted, and drop the fish in. When the water
comes to a boil and the fish float to the top, I take the pieces
out at exactly that moment. The flesh flakes off the bones, and
they are just right to eat. Captain Amundsen told me once that
he uses sea water and boils seal meat the same way, and caribou
also, but never polar bear. The meat of the polar bear has a
high uric-acid content, and its liver can be deadly poison.

After supper all the men tilt their benches back against the
wall and light their pipes while the cook and his Indian helper
clear the dishes away. Someone mentions that a nugget of pure
silver, weighing seventy-five pounds, has just been found at
Echo Bay; but nobody seems very interested. Silver means nothing in a gold camp. There are only two things here they talk
about. A prospector refills his coffee cup from the bubbling pot
on the stove, and sips it contentedly. "That's how I like it, hot
and strong," he nods. "Just like my women."

"Dark, too," a miner at the table adds suggestively.

The first speaker lowers his eyes, sets down his cup on the
sink, and slinks out the door. The others gaze after him in si-

lence, and shake their heads. "Damn tepee creeper," one of
them mutters. "I hate a tepee creeper."

A big Canuck knocks out his pipe on a boot heel, bangs his
chair forward, and starts toward the door. "By gar, a man he got
to do someteeng, dees goddam cold nights," he says defiantly.
"We don't got enough blankets."

A couple of messages are waiting for me when I get back to
Hudson. One is a letter from Floyd Bennett, and I almost jump
out of my chair as I start reading. Commander Byrd is planning
to fly the Atlantic in a specially designed three-engine plane, to
be called the *America*, which is being built at the Fokker factory
for his overseas hop.

I read on hopefully. Then my heart sinks. Byrd has chosen
Bennett as his pilot and Noville as radio operator, but my name
is not included. Bennett writes that he cannot explain the rea-
sons at this time, but there is nothing he can do about it.

My hopes of being on the first plane to fly the Atlantic are
ended, and I crumple the letter in my hand and open the other
message. It is a wire from Uncle Tony:

"Western requests you remain additional month important
job. Stop. Agreeable me if okay you.

"Fokker"

Rod Ross watches as I read the wire, and grins. "Guess you
can blame me for that, Bernt. I asked for you. We've con-
tracted with the Canadian government to supply the planes for
a harbor survey project at Fort Churchill, nine hundred miles'
flying distance from here on Hudson Bay. It'll open up the
Arctic Barren Lands to air travel for the first time. You and
Steve will be doing the flying. What do you say?"

There is only one thing to say when there is a job to be done.
"Ve do it."

Our base of operations is to be at Cache Lake, the end of

the railroad steel in upper Ontario. Here the survey party is
waiting for us to fly them the rest of the way to Churchill,
about two hundred miles farther north. We must bring two
planes from Hudson to air-lift the fourteen tons of equipment,
survey instruments, and drills and dynamite, which they will
use in their harbor project. The government is investigating
the possibility of extending the present rail line from the great
wheat fields of central Canada all the way to the shore of Hudson Bay, and the party is to take soundings at Churchill, and
determine whether a deep-water port can be created here for
the ocean shipping which would come across the Atlantic and
through Hudson Straits to pick up the grain at the railhead.

We set out at dawn on our seven-hundred-mile flight to
Cache Lake. Steve leads the way in the first Fokker, and I follow in the other with Al Cheeseman, who is coming along to
handle our maintenance and repairs. Ahead of me Steve's plane
glistens like a gold nugget in the morning sunlight, and I smile
to myself as I picture him at this moment, the way he always
looks when he is flying: slouched carelessly behind the stick,
eyes half shut and his empty pipe dangling from his jaw, seem-
ing indifferent and even bored but ready to react like a cat to
any emergency. He is aloof and closemouthed, and his sardonic
manner repels any talk of himself; but bit by bit in the long
hours we have spent together I have dug out something of his
past. He was a World War I pilot, and was shot down in
France; his leg was injured in the crash, and he still walks with
a slight limp. It was not from Steve but from Rod Ross that
I learned he was one of Canada's greatest aces, holder of the
Victoria Cross.

Again the question flits across my mind that I have asked
myself so many times: What makes a man choose this life? Why
did this famous wartime flier come here to lose himself in the
anonymity of the Canadian wilderness? There is no public ac-
claim for the bush pilot, no headlines, no parades or ticker tape

or Chamber of Commerce banquets. He flies alone in an open cockpit at sixty or seventy below zero, and his bed at night is a sleeping bag on the floor of the unheated fuselage, or a lean-to in the shelter of a snowbank. He must dig out his cached oil drums from under the drifts, when it is so cold that his feet are like stumps, and fuel his plane by hand. His tachometer locks tight in the icy wind, his oil-pressure gauge goes out, his air-speed indicator freezes up, his turn-and-bank indicator quits, and he flies by feel and instinct alone. There is no more cruel existence, and there are no finer pilots than these quiet heroes who fly the northern bush.

What prompts a man like Steve to take this daily life-and-death gamble, I wonder. He protests that he hates this country, that he wants to go south to Miami where it is warm; but still he stays on, and will not leave. Does the love of adventure hold him here? Is it the challenge which the white unknown offers? Or is it that his cynical pose conceals a deep pessimism, and he is secretly courting the death which he defies every day?

On the afternoon of the second day I see his plane dip below the tree tops, and I come across over the ridge behind him, bank to the right over Kettle Rapids, and follow the winding Nelson River to Cache Lake. Steve has already landed on the lake, and I park my plane beside his. Al Cheeseman and I swing our duffel bags to our shoulders and hike a quarter-mile to the little camp at the railroad terminus. Our sleeping quarters are in a freight car shunted onto a siding. The survey party welcomes us, and we make plans to start for Churchill tomorrow with our first load.

The terrain changes rapidly as we fly over the flat rolling country, crisscrossed with sharp gravel ridges and interlaced with rivers. We cross the divide, and now suddenly all the rivers are flowing north into the Arctic watershed. The black pine forests around the lakes begin to disappear, and the trees are more wind-blown and scraggy, until at last, ninety miles

south of Churchill, the timber peters out entirely and we are in
the permafrost of the tundra. We follow the Churchill River
to the Royal Canadian Mounted Police station and trading post
at its mouth, and the scattered tent camps of the Eskimos. In
the distance are the ruins of Fort Prince of Wales, a medieval
castle in stone, and stretching away into nothingness is the vast
white expanse of the Hudson Bay ice.

Day after day Steve and I shuttle back and forth across this
route, passing each other in flight, as we air-lift the supplies
from Cache Lake to the harbor site. Once on my way back I
make a side trip to deliver some mail from Churchill to the
Royal Canadian Mounted Police outpost at Eskimo Point, and
I run into a violent blizzard and have to sit down on the ice. I
drain the oil from the engine, light my brass primus stove to
melt snow for tea, and crawl into my sleeping bag to ride out
the storm. Early the next morning I am awakened by something
bumping the tail surface of the plane. I open the cabin door
cautiously and stare at a huge polar bear, casually rubbing his
rump against the rear stabilizer. He returns my gaze, shrugs a
white shoulder, and goes on scratching. I wonder what Uncle
Tony will say when I tell him a polar bear has used his airplane
for a back-scratcher.

The storm abates by midmorning, and the fresh-fallen snow
is dazzling in the high noon sun as I head back to Fort Churchill. I fly over a large frozen lake, and the white surface is dotted
with brown specks. The ice was completely bare when I flew
over it last, and I wonder if I am getting snow-blind. I rub my
eyes and look again, and the specks seem to be moving now.
I push the stick forward and buzz the lake, and on all sides, and
as far ahead as I can see, thousands of caribou are trotting
across the ice. As my diving plane spooks them, they scatter
and break into a gallop, with their noses high in the air and
their racks laid back on their shoulders. This is one of the great
sights of the Arctic. Each spring, since time immemorial, these

animals move in massed herds across the Barren Lands, in search of gray reindeer moss. Between Churchill and Cache Lake at this moment are over two million caribou in migration, their brown backs covering the slopes until the hills themselves seem to be crawling. A week later they will have gone without a trace, and the slopes will be bare and silent again.

Al Cheeseman is pacing up and down the shore as I land at Cache Lake in the moonlight, after stopping to gas up at Churchill. He is vastly relieved to see me; they feared that I was lost when I failed to return, he says, and now Steve's plane is long overdue. Next morning, I set out in search.

I take Al Cheeseman with me. He has held the stick a few times, and he knows enough to handle the rudder pedals in an emergency. I check my maps and work out a search pattern of all the little lakes and river beds where Steve may have gone down. After about an hour we sight his plane in a narrow opening in the forest. There is barely enough clearance between the trees for my wing tips as I side-slip into the clearing and halt beside it.

The plane is deserted, and a line of footprints cross the snow and disappear in the deep woods. Oil is spattered over the windshield, we see, and Al Cheeseman recognizes at a glance that Steve's scavenger line has broken. This line carries the used oil from the front of the crankcase down to the main sump, and on the J4B, the first Wright air-cooled engine, the copper tubing is exposed to the full blast of the wind. In the 60-below temperature, the oil had frozen and burst the line, and Steve had made an emergency landing before his engine conked. Al Cheeseman has brought his repair-kit with him, and I leave him to fix the broken line while I continue the search. He has a sleeping bag, and can spend the night here if I do not locate Steve and return before dark.

I can find no trace of Steve from the air, and at last, when my fuel tanks are beginning to show "Empty," I land back at camp, to resume the search in the morning. I have just finished supper when I hear the barking of sled dogs, and above it Steve's voice in a measured denunciation of cold and snow and the whole ruddy country. His lean face in fringed with icicles hanging from his parka hood. He tramped three ruddy hours through the snow, he complains, until he ran into this Indian fox trapper, who has brought him back ninety ruddy miles. His mood is not improved by the discovery that he forgot his ruddy pipe when he left the plane.

We are heating our oil the following morning to take off for the downed plane, when we hear the drone of a motor in the distance. There is no other airplane within a thousand miles, and we stare at the sky incredulously as the second Fokker staggers into view. It is seesawing and wobbling like a wing-shot goose, lurching and yawing as it drops toward the lake, and thumps onto the ice. Al Cheeseman crawls out and reels like a wooden man into the mess hall. After thawing himself out with a cup of steaming coffee he tells us what happened. As the temperature dropped lower and lower last night, the cold of the floor permeated his sleeping bag, and he tried to sleep on his knees and elbows. A pack of wolves surrounded the plane, and all night their bloodcurdling serenade just outside made him shiver still more. At first daylight he decided he'd had enough, and he managed to start the engine and somehow squeezed the plane between the trees and got it into the air. Steve has retrieved his pipe from the cockpit, and he exhales a contented cloud of smoke as Al finishes his story.

"Glad you got back safe, old chap," he remarks blandly. "I wouldn't have had anything happen to this pipe for worlds."

By the end of the month we have moved the last of the supplies to Churchill and are ready to leave Cache Lake and return to Hudson. There is no time to lose: spring is coming almost overnight to the north country; already the loons and whistling swans are winging past us to their breeding grounds in Baffin Land, and we can feel the increasing mildness in the air. The surface of the lakes is honeycombed, and we fear that nine hundred miles south there will be no ice left on which to land with skis. We debate whether to wait another month for the break-up and then substitute floats; but we elect to take a chance. Cache Lake is already covered with a foot of water, and we roar across the ice like a seaplane in a cloud of spray, and our skis fly dripping into the air.

Rain squalls hug our course all the way south, and low clouds force us to fly almost on the deck, feeling our way over the ridges and along the creek bottoms. As we finish our last leg and skirt Lake Winnipeg, we can see the blue water glittering, and Lake Seul, the only landing near Hudson, is wide open. We find a little inlet, in the shadow of the tall trees, where a last frozen patch still clings. We touch skis on the crumbling ice, keeping our planes at full speed, and run them ashore and up onto the brushy bank.

The telegraph operator at Hudson meets me with an urgent wire as I land. The *America*, the three-engine Fokker that is almost ready for Byrd's transatlantic attempt, has just crashed in a test flight at Teterboro Airport in New Jersey. Byrd and Noville and Bennett and Fokker himself were in the plane at the time, and Bennett has been seriously injured in the accident and cannot fly again for many months. I am ordered to return to the factory at once.

I pack my rucksack, and on my way to the train I stop at the Airways lean-to and say a reluctant goodbye. This Canadian bush country is part of me already, and it will always call me back. I shake hands with Rod Ross and Al Cheeseman and the others. Steve is slouched behind the stove; his long legs have climbed the wall, and his moosehide moccasins are crossed on the shelf. I try to persuade him to go to the States with me, as he has always insisted he wanted to, but he explains mockingly that he hates this snow so much he wants to stick around a little longer and see the last of the ruddy stuff melt. The trickle of smoke from his curved pipe masks his sardonic face, and he waves a languid hand as I leave.

Later I read the citation which is given by the Canadian government to Western Canada Airways: "Despite the distance from any prepared base, and severe winter conditions, the Fort Churchill operation was an unqualified success. The selection of this site as the ocean terminus of the Hudson Bay Railway was made possible by these flights. There has been no more brilliant operation in the history of commercial aviation." Western Canada Airways receives the McKee Trophy for the most notable event in British aviation that year, and Captain Stevenson is awarded the Harmon International Trophy as the world's outstanding aviator of 1927. The award is given posthumously: in the interval, a few months after my leaving Hudson, Steve has been killed in a crash at Le Pas. Later the field at Winnipeg is named the F. J. Stevenson Airport, in honor of Canada's greatest bush pilot.

THE GREAT NEW YORK
TO PARIS AIR DERBY

1927

As soon as I am back in New Jersey, I hurry out to the Hackensack Hospital to see Floyd Bennett. His right thigh was fractured in the accident to the *America,* and a propeller fragment entered his back and punctured a lung. The leg is in a plaster cast, stretched toward the ceiling with weights, and the top half of his mechanical bed is cranked up to support his bandaged shoulders. His eyes look heavy with sedatives, but he manages a grin and points to the pulleys and cables that surround him. "Ever fly in a cockpit like this?" he asks me.

Floyd grasps the trapeze bar above his head and hoists himself to reach for the water glass on the table. His hand still shakes, a week after the crash, and I can see that it hurts him to talk; but he tries to tell me how it happened. Tony Fokker had been planning to fly the first test hop of the *America* alone, he says, but Byrd wanted to check personally on its performance before accepting it for his backers, and asked Noville and Bennett to go along with him. All four crowded into the cockpit, and as they came in to land after the flight, Bennett realized that the plane was nose-heavy. There was no ballast at the rear of the ship to compensate for the extra weight forward,

87

and the lack of a passageway made it impossible for any of the party to crawl back into the tail. Floyd had a flier's hunch that they were in for trouble. Fokker made one pass at the runway; but the plane nosed forward dangerously, and he gave it full throttle and climbed again in the nick of time. The gas was running low, and finally they had to take a chance. Bennett motioned to Byrd and Noville behind him to brace themselves. As the wheels hit, he felt the whole fuselage rise into the air, and he remembers flipping the switch. Later I find out that he himself had designed a master switch to cut all three engines at once in an emergency, and this is probably what saved them from fire. The next thing he knew, he was hanging upside down in the wreckage, the blood from his lacerated back streaming down into his eyes, and Byrd and the others were tugging to get him free.

He winces a little. It is more than physical pain: he knows it will be a long time before he can fly at all, and he may never be strong enough to endure the rigors of another major expedition. Things will be difficult for Byrd now with Floyd out of the picture—there just aren't many top-level, all-around pilots and mechanics of his caliber. I do not like to bring up the Atlantic trip, but Floyd does not evade the subject.

"Byrd's getting another pilot," he says bluntly.

"Who will it be?"

He shrugs. "I hear it's Bert Acosta. He's a fine aviator with a big name—he's the logical one, I guess." I am no good at hiding my feelings from Floyd, and he sees the question in my face.

"Probably you wonder why your name isn't on the list. Rodman Wanamaker is putting up the money for the flight. He named the ship the *America,* and he wants an all-American crew. You're not a citizen." He breathes heavily. "So that's how the wind sock blows."

His eyelids are starting to droop, and I move toward the

door, but he opens his eyes again and calls after me: "You've seen the ship at the factory. How long will it take to get it in the air again?"

"A month maybe."

Bennett nods, and his head falls back wearily on the pillow, and I close the door.

I know his feelings, and Commander Byrd's, too. The *America* was scheduled to take off early in May, with the full moon, and at that time there were no other contenders ready. Now the newspapers are full of rival entries in the race for the Orteig Prize: Clarence Chamberlin, who with Acosta set the world's endurance record in a Bellança on April 14th, Captain Nungesser and Major Coli of the French Air Force; Commander Noel Davis of the United States Navy, and a young mail pilot from the Middle West named Charles Lindbergh. And now when their planes are being groomed for the flight the *America* is scattered all over the factory floor, to be redesigned and completely rebuilt. I think back to how the Amundsen camp felt a year ago when the *Chantier* dropped anchor in Kings Bay.

The *America* is a three-engine plane, similar to the *Josephine Ford* but with engines of bigger horsepower, and capable of lifting an enormous load. Its planned weight at take-off will be 15,000 pounds, even to this day the highest horsepower loading ever flown off the ground. The wingspread, increased from sixty-three to seventy-one feet, permits the ship to be airborne with at least three thousand pounds more than the *Ford,* including ample fuel for the Atlantic crossing as well as eight hundred pounds of extra equipment. It will carry a special radio set, waterproof installations in case of an emergency ocean landing, a putty substance to repair leaks in the gas tank, spare sextants and hand compass, and a wind-drift indicator which can be lowered through a trapdoor in the bottom of the navigator's compartment. Thermometers have been installed to give warning if an icing condition makes it necessary for the plane to descend quickly to a warmer altitude. There is every kind of emergency lifesaving equipment: two rubber rafts built into the wings, Very pistols for signaling, and even a kite to keep the wireless antennae in the air and also act as a sail. In addition the ship carries carbide drift flares to light on the water in case of a night ditching. Parachutes, however, we don't carry. They would be of no use over the ocean.

In the center of the plane is the 800-gallon main fuel tank, oval in cross-section, with a dump-valve as a safety factor, to spill all the fuel in a few seconds. The empty tank will give added flotation if the plane is down in the water; and, should one of the engines cut out during the flight, the crew can spill surplus gasoline to reduce the weight so they can continue on two engines.

To overcome the nose-heavy condition, we decide to relocate the navigator's compartment behind the main fuel tank, where it will distribute the weight better. The crash has shown the need for some way to get from the cockpit past this tank to the navigator's compartment. Now we construct a catwalk, leading aft from the cockpit under one side of the oval main tank, so that a man can slide back and forth on his belly. Steel cables are stretched from the fuselage to the outboard engines, at the request of Commander Byrd, so that if necessary a crewman can crawl out in mid-flight and balance himself in the slip stream to work on a dead engine.

Now we are very busy at the Fokker plant, working around the clock to complete the modifications and the rebuilding of the *America*. Uncle Tony himself is like a whole swarm of bees, yelling orders until he is purple in the face and then doing everything anyway, and I think I do not see my boarding house bedroom more than a couple of nights all the time we are working. I have a cot in the hangar and grab meals at odd times at a quick-lunch counter near the field. There, one day, I run into a young pilot with the Gates Flying Circus, whose head-quarters are at Teterboro. He is named Clyde Pangborn, and he is the picture of the early barnstormers in his leather jacket and polished boots and helmet and goggles, and we sit on our stools side by side and talk flying.

Day and night the work goes on, and at last, in a little under three weeks, we have the wrecked plane flyable again. On May 13 I roll it out of the factory hangar and, after a couple of take-offs and landings and minor adjustments, I ferry the *America* over to Roosevelt Field on Long Island, the largest private air-field near New York, which has been leased by Rodman Wana-maker for the Byrd flight.

On my way I fly over Curtiss Field, right next to Roosevelt. Clarence Chamberlin's Bellanca is already there, I see, parked before a hangar, and I notice that another ship has just landed. It is a single-engine high-wing monoplane, and a crowd has gathered about it. I circle Roosevelt Field, set the *America* down on the grass, and taxi to the main hangar, marked above the door in big white letters, "The America Trans-Oceanic Co., Inc.," with the Stars and Stripes flying overhead.

The flight crew is waiting to receive the plane. Commander Byrd is as young-looking and as courteous as ever. He is slim and handsome in his flying clothes, high-laced boots and regula-tion breeches, and his dark curly hair is unruffled by the wind. George Noville, who is to be the radio operator on the flight, wears similar high-laced boots and aviator's pants. His face, round and square-jawed behind horn-rimmed glasses, is a strange contrast to Byrd's, and the straight line of his mouth is expres-sionless. He and Byrd are talking with some newsmen, and while they are busy I introduce myself to the *America*'s new pilot, who is casually dressed in a gray tweed suit and tweed cap.

Bert Acosta is a fabulous figure in aviation, one of the top pilots in America if not in the whole world. He was a noted

Army flight instructor during the First World War. After 1918 his sensational aerial stunts were the talk of us all in Norway. Acosta is one of the finest acrobatic pilots ever seen. A flier with a marvelous sense of coordination, he is an expert at such stunts as upside-down flying at low altitude, picking a handkerchief off the ground with one wing tip, and other hair-raising feats that leave his audiences at fairs and air meets breathless. It is the romantic rather than the scientific kind of flying that he stands for. He is what they call in the movies a "sheik," olive-skinned, with a close-cropped black mustache and sleek hair parted in the middle, and a low, musical voice. I can see the Mexican-Indian in his sharp profile.

The newspaper photographers have posed Byrd and Noville in front of the plane, with "America" showing on the fuselage, and Byrd calls to Acosta to join them. While the pictures are being taken, I ask one of the reporters about the little silver monoplane I noticed at Curtiss Field as I flew over.

"Belongs to that mail pilot," he says. "It's called *The Spirit of St. Louis.*"

Already the race for the Orteig Prize has fired the country's imagination. Titles such as "The Great 1927 New York to Paris Air Derby" are being invented by newspapermen, and daily headlines report the position of the various contestants who are seesawing for first place: "LINDBERGH HERE FOR SEA HOP!"—"BYRD JOINS RIVALS IN OCEAN JUMP!"— "WILL CHAMBERLIN LEAVE TOMORROW?" An air of secrecy surrounds the contenders, while constant reports from overseas of new entries add to the suspense. Drouhin, holder of the French endurance record, has been conducting clandestine tests with a Farman biplane. Tarascon is trying out a new Bernard-Marie-Hubert. Coste plans to fly the ocean in a Bréguet with a Hispano-Suiza engine. Nungesser and Coli are poised in Paris to speed westward at any moment.

Disasters whet the macabre appetite of the public. Captain

René Fonck washes out in his big Sikorsky, cartwheeling in flames off the end of the runway at Roosevelt Field and killing two of his crew. Sensational extras announce that Commander Davis has been killed in his Keystone Pathfinder biplane: "'AMERICAN LEGION' IS WRECKED ON TAKE-OFF AT HAMPTON, VA." On May 8 word is flashed that Nungesser and Coli have left Le Bourget Airdrome at Paris in their heavily loaded Levasseur, the *White Bird,* bound for New York. All that day the papers scream the latest rumors: A destroyer reports sighting their plane near Land's End. The *White Bird* has been heard off Nova Scotia. Nungesser and Coli have passed over Boston. Then the rumors die out, and the next day's papers carry a huge black headline: "NUNGESSER AND COLI LOST." They have vanished like spume in the wake of a wave, and search parties comb the silent Atlantic in vain.

Now the public interest reaches fever pitch. The New York to Paris race is the story of the year. With four men already killed, two missing, and three planes lost to date, preachers denounce from the pulpit the needless waste of lives and equipment; and this only adds to the excitement of the thrill seekers. Their cars jam the roads to Curtiss and Roosevelt fields as they flock to gape with morbid curiosity at the last three surviving planes entered in the Air Derby. Rodman Wanamaker offers his two rivals the use of Roosevelt's longer runway, and editorials applaud his generous gesture. Wagers are made, and the odds shift back and forth like just before starting-time at a horse-race. Each new delay brings insulting boos from the angry fans; Byrd ruefully displays an anonymous letter calling him a coward. "You never had any idea of flying the Atlantic," the note accuses. I wonder how much money the writer has on the *America* to win, place, or show.

All the competitors' private troubles are front-paged. Every subway reader knows that Charles Levine, Chamberlin's backer, is still looking for a co-pilot for the *Columbia.* This single-

engine plane, with a Wright J-5 engine and an exceptionally
efficient wing design and great range, is to become one of the
most successful and famous types in American aviation history.
Chamberlin tried first to hire Acosta as copilot, but lost him to
Byrd. Then he offered the job to Lloyd Bertaud, a mail pilot;
but they disagreed on terms, and Bertaud is bringing an injunc-
tion against him. Levine gives out a statement that he has decided not to pick a pilot until just before take-off: "I want all
the candidates to have their hearts in the race, and if one is
chosen now the others would probably be sore." Chamberlin
himself comes to me on the quiet, and asks if I will go with him
as copilot and navigator of the Bellanca and split the Orteig
Prize; but I cannot fly the plane of a rival manufacturer while
I am still chief test pilot for Fokker, and I also feel an obliga-
tion to the Byrd expedition because of Bennett.

The only contender nobody knows much about is Lindbergh.
I have run into him here and there, but he keeps to himself,
always preoccupied and quiet. The reporters have dubbed him
"The Flyin' Kid," and it is generally assumed that he is out
of his class and could never make it across the ocean alone in
his tiny monoplane. The newsmen take pity on this unknown
youngster, and try to talk him out of his long-shot try. "He
won't listen to reason," a reporter complains to me; "he's just
a stubborn squarehead." He realizes my own nationality and
corrects himself in embarrassment. "Swede, I mean."

On Fokker's orders, I have remained at Roosevelt to run fuel
consumption tests and speed trials with Acosta. Uncle Tony
comes over from Hasbrouck Heights frequently to see how we
are getting on. As far as we at the factory are concerned, the
America is ready for its transatlantic flight on the 17th of May.
Every test flight has come off according to our computations,
and Fokker grows more impatient with Byrd's continual defer-
ring of the take-off. "If he don't get going soon," he sputters,
"I myself will buy the plane back and fly it over the ocean, by

Gott!" Always he gets the same explanation: the weather isn't right yet. Several forecasts that seem decidedly promising are passed up because there is a slight overcast. "Look at that sky," Uncle Tony fumes. "Just a little mist only. Any fool could fly it blindfold with both eyes shut."

That afternoon Acosta and I are flying another test hop, to recheck our rate of climb against the computations made at the factory, and Tony Fokker comes along on the flight. The weather is soupier as we get to altitude, but I pay little attention to this. I have logged much instrument time, and on the recent round-the-States tour with Bennett I have practiced blind flying every time I had a chance. I have also spent much time with Howard Stark of Colonial Airlines, who wrote the first book on instrument procedure, and we have worked out many theories together.

Acosta is at the controls, and as we are flying through a solid cloud bank I suddenly feel myself getting very heavy in the seat, and see that the turn-indicator needle is all the way over on one side. I quickly reach for the wheel, and Acosta lets his hands drop from the controls in relief.

"This is one thing I don't know anything about," he confesses. "I'm strictly a fair-weather boy. If there's any thick stuff, I stay on the ground."

After the flight, Uncle Tony is very quiet as we climb out of the plane, and I know his unusual silence is the calm before the storm. He drags me into a corner of the hangar, and there he explodes in rapid-fire German. Now he sees the reason why the flight has been held up. There is only one thing to do. He keeps stabbing my chest with his forefinger. "You, Bernt, must go along in the crew to handle instrument flying and bad weather, or all summer the *America* will still be waiting here, and I am the laughing stock of the whole United States!"

I point out that Rodman Wanamaker will stand for nothing but an all-American crew, and I am a Norwegian citizen.

"Poof! That is nothing," Uncle Tony dismisses the objection contemptuously. "Go take out your first papers."

Often it has seemed in my life that the biggest changes happen very casually, as this one does. The idea of becoming a citizen of the United States has never before crossed my mind. I am a member of the Norwegian armed forces, and have taken it for granted that I will go back to my native land when my job here is over. But all night I lie awake on my cot in the hangar, and the conviction comes to me that it is possible to love each of two countries. I have not realized until this moment that America has become so strong in my heart. Still, I am undecided as I take the train to New York the next morning. Am I being unfaithful to my own homeland, I ask, if I become a citizen of the United States? The two countries have so much in common, I tell myself; they both believe in the freedom of people and want to live in peace with each other and all the world, and if there is trouble they will always fight side by side. Maybe some day as a Norwegian-American I can justify my belonging to them both. I hesitate before the desk in the Bureau of Naturalization, and the girl smiles as she notices my Norwegian accent.

"My mother comes from Oslo," she says. "You want to be a citizen of this country, too?"

I pick up the Declaration of Intention form. "You bet."

When I get back from New York that Thursday evening, Roosevelt Field is bustling with preparations for the christening of the *America*. Rodman Wanamaker has planned a big party for Saturday afternoon, May 21st, and the main hangar is being decorated with festoons of red, white, and blue bunting. Two thousand guests, including the French ambassador and his staff, have been invited to the field for the ceremonies, and large French and American flags are crossed over the speakers' platform which has been erected at one end of the huge hangar.

Fitting skis on the *Floyd Bennett* at Le Pas, Manitoba, before the departure for Antarctica. Bernt Balchen straddling the ski; Floyd Bennett, beyond propeller tip.

The first survey party setting out from the *City of New York* to locate a site for Little America. The ship is moored at the edge of the ice shelf in the Bay of Whales. Bernt Balchen on skis in the right foreground.

Camp at Ver-sur-Mer Inlet, housing men setting up Little America.

Grover Whalen is arranging the festivities, as usual, and there will be tributes from the dignitaries and a speech of dedication by Commander Byrd.

Yesterday's bad weather still hangs on; the sky is overcast, and there is a slight drizzle. The field at Roosevelt is shiny with rain, and the fog settles lower as night falls. I pick up by chance a late weather forecast by Doc Kimball, meteorologist in charge of the New York office of the United States Weather Bureau, who has been supplying regular bulletins for all three contenders: there has been a sudden change, and the weather over the ocean is clearing, with indications of increasing visibility over Paris. I look around expectantly, but cannot see any unusual signs of activity on the field. The *America* is here in the hangar, heavily draped with flags, and obviously Byrd has no intention of leaving until after the christening ceremony on Saturday. Levine is still wrapped in legal tangles, and there is no indication that he plans a daybreak start for the Bellanca. What of Lindbergh? I ask one of the mechanics. Oh, nothing doing over there at Curtiss Field, he says. Lindbergh and some friends have driven into New York tonight to go to the theater.

I stretch out on my cot in the silent hangar, and listen to the drip of rain pattering down from the tin gutters. For some reason I feel the same restlessness as on that midnight when the *Josephine Ford* was about to take off from Spitzbergen for the Pole. Once I waken out of a half-sleep and hear the sticky sound of tires on the wet concrete. An airplane is being towed by truck across the strip, but in the rain I cannot make out what it is. Hours later, it seems, an automobile drives rapidly past the hangar, and I strike a match and look at my watch. It is a little after five. I roll over and try to sleep.

The hangar door bangs open, and Uncle Tony rushes in.

"Get me quick some fire extinguishers. That young fool he is going to take off. Maybe there comes trouble."

His Lancia spurts down the field toward the end of the strip, and I follow on the run. In the grayness of early dawn the dismal light rain is still falling from an overcast sky, but there is no wind at all. Ahead of me, the *Spirit of St. Louis* has been hauled tail first to the starting line, with a canvas wrapped around the engine to keep out the rain. Ground crews pull off the tarpaulin cover, and a murmur goes up from the small group of reporters and policemen standing behind the wing as a lanky figure in leather flying clothes, carrying a bag of sandwiches and a vacuum bottle of coffee, strides through the crowd and approaches the plane. He seems unconscious of the curious glances of the spectators, and looks calm and assured as he climbs into the cockpit.

In a moment the engine starts with a dull roar, muffled by the rain. As I walk down the field for a better view of the take-off, the drifting smoke of the plane's exhaust looks blue in the early morning light. From halfway down the runway, I see the little plane start moving, accelerating very slowly with its tremendous overload of gasoline. I hold my breath. As he passes me, Lindbergh still has not gotten his tailskid off the ground. The plane staggers faster and faster; the end of the runway is only five hundred feet away. Suddenly the wheels lift clear, and the plane lurches into the air. It disappears from sight, into a little depression at the western end of the field, as it dips to gain speed. To the uninitiated it may have looked as though Lindbergh were in trouble. But at the last second the *Spirit of St. Louis* appears again, just clearing the treetops, and is lost almost at once in the solid murk. A masterly take-off! I let out my breath and say: "Lykke paa reisen!" (Luck on the voyage!)

All day long we can think of nothing else. Carpenters and mechanics stand in groups around the hangar, where we are readying the *America* for Saturday's dedication, the radio turned on to catch the special bulletins that interrupt the programs: "Lindbergh is over Cape Cod." "Lindbergh passes Nova Scotia." "Lindbergh crosses the north tip of Cape Breton

Island." All over the whole nation similar groups are standing and wondering and hoping against hope. Office work is halted, crowds gather in front of the newspaper bulletin boards, and in Washington the Senate interrupts its business to hear a special announcement: "Lindbergh is over the Atlantic." Now there is no more word. Housewives hang by their radios, forgetting supper. Services are held in churches. In Madison Square Garden the crowd rises just before the main bout as Joe Humphreys' bull voice calls for a moment of silent prayer. All that night and the next day there is only one topic of conversation: Will he make it?

Rodman Wanamaker has decided to go ahead with his plans for the christening of the *America* as scheduled, and the guests gather at Roosevelt Field late Saturday afternoon for the ceremonies. The opening speeches are heard politely, but it is clear that everyone's thoughts are far away over the Atlantic, following a little plane and its lone pilot. It is almost five o'clock, and Commander Byrd mounts the flag-decked rostrum for the final address. He holds a sheaf of notes and lays them before him on the lectern. Harry Bruno rushes up and hands him a piece of paper. He reads it, and slips his speech-notes into his pocket. He lifts his hand for silence.

"Ladies and gentlemen," he says, "Charles Lindbergh has landed at Le Bourget at 10:22 Paris time."

Chamberlin is the next to get off, and in the copilot's seat is none other than Charlie Levine. With the Paris race won, they have announced no destination (later they admit that their secret goal was Berlin), but will keep flying until their fuel is exhausted. Levine spends his first trip over the ocean emptying five-gallon tins of gas into the main tank. They have to detour around bad weather over the Atlantic, and they put down after forty-two hours at the town of Eisleben, southeast of the German capital. Their flight, made entirely by dead reckoning, has covered 3,911 miles, 300 miles farther than Lindbergh's.

Now only the *America* remains at Roosevelt Field. A whole month has gone by, and we are still waiting for better weather. Three times we have good forecasts for the trip, and three times the plane is hauled to the top of a fifteen-foot incline, with wooden wheel tracks and greased tail-skid slides. This has been specially designed by Tony Fokker to increase acceleration and in effect add another five to seven hundred feet to the runway. With each weather break, word is rushed to the Garden City Hotel, where Byrd and Noville and Acosta are staying; but no one shows up. From his hotel room, Byrd issues statements to the press that it does not seem right to fly to Paris while the receptions for Lindbergh are still in progress, and that furthermore, his flight is not a race but a serious effort to pioneer the transatlantic airways of the future.

The *America* is being towed back to the hangar for the third time, and Tony Fokker has been up all night, waiting vainly for the take-off. When Commander Byrd strolls into the hangar later that morning, Uncle Tony flies into a Dutch rage. His round pink cheeks blow in and out, like the rubber bulb-horn of his Lancia, as he honks with fury. He is sick and tired of all this damn stalling. Byrd can fly the *America* nonstop to hell, for all of him—he is through right now, by Gott. He roars off in his sport car in a cloud of mud and flying grass, and goes for a long cruise in his yacht to cool off.

The next day, the 28th of June, Floyd Bennett shows up at Roosevelt Field. His face is thin and gray, and he shows the effects of his long ordeal as he sways on his crutches. I do not know whether Uncle Tony has spoken to him about Acosta's reluctance to fly instruments, but I see that he is upset. He and Byrd and Grover Whalen talk for a long time in a corner of the hangar. Presently Bennett comes over and puts his big-knuckled hand on my shoulder. His grip is weak, but he is smiling.

"It's all set, Bernt. You'll be on the crew as relief pilot and mechanic." Later, Byrd gives me the news officially.

The spell of good weather over the Atlantic has already passed its peak, and the forecasts are becoming more discouraging every day. Late that night of June 28th, Doc Kimball phones Byrd at the Garden City Hotel that although conditions are not perfect, they are about as good as we can expect for some time to come. There is a cold front building up over the eastern Atlantic, but we should have good visibility until we hit it, and after that we should be able to fly under the clouds. After the phone talk Byrd decides abruptly not to wait any longer, because, as he explains to the reporters: "The transatlantic plane of the future must be able to cope with other than ideal conditions, and perhaps we could gain more scientific and practical knowledge if we meet adverse weather."

We have very short notice. Returning to the field at midnight from supper with my friend Porter Adams of the National Aeronautic Association, I see a big hustle around the hangar. Acosta tells me to get my personal gear together, and gives me the gist of Doc Kimball's report. After the long wait for ideally favorable weather conditions over the whole distance, the sudden decision that, after all, the scientific value of the flight will only be enhanced by bucking a little rough weather comes as a surprise to me. It looks to me as though we may run into considerable turbulence over the eastern Atlantic and I won't be too surprised if there is plenty of opportunity for blind flying. I am not concerned about this, as I stretch out on my cot in the hangar fully dressed, to catch a bit of rest while waiting. I am too keyed up to sleep, but lie there thinking back over all our elaborate tests and calculations. I know we have put the *America* through an exacting test program, and I am confident she will get us to Paris under almost any conditions.

About half past one Byrd and Noville appear. I get up and wander outside for a look at the weather. It is dismal and rain-

ing slightly, but a large crowd has gathered in glistening
slickers around the incline at the east end of the field. By 3:30
A.M. the *America* is gassed up and ready to go. We get a final
briefing on the weather maps; then we take our places in the
plane. Acosta is in the left-hand seat in the cockpit, and Noville
in the copilot's seat where he can keep his hand on the dump
valve in case of an emergency—a safety measure which won't
do us much good until after we're airborne. Commander Byrd
and I climb down through the after hatch into the navigator's
compartment aft of the main fuel tank. Byrd and Noville are
in their high boots and leather jackets, but I am wearing old
blue trousers and a plaid woolen shirt from Canada, because I
know it will be a long flight and I always like to be comfortable.

As I look out through the narrow window to port I realize
that the *America* is in the same spot and facing in the same
direction as Fonck was when he crashed in flames on his Atlantic
take-off. Ours is the first trimotored plane to make the attempt
since then, and no other plane has ever carried such a load. To
get faster acceleration after applying full power, a rope has
been made fast between the tailskid and the top of the incline.
When the engines have been run up to maximum r.p.m., Acosta
will give a signal to the ground crew to cut the rope with an
ax, and the *America* will hurtle on its course.

I glance at my watch. Just 5:20. Outside, the gray light is
growing rapidly stronger, though the cloud ceiling is not more
than 1,500 feet. Beside me Byrd braces himself against the fuel
tank with feet wide apart, his hands gripping the struts. The
engines are being revved up, and I can imagine Acosta up forward in the cockpit, watching the gauge needles climb bit by
bit. Suddenly the rope snaps under the pull of the big props,
and we are prematurely rolling down the ramp. Acosta must
make an instant decision whether to cut the switches, or gamble
on gaining enough speed by the time he has reached the end of
the strip. Through the window my eyes are fixed on the big tire

bumping over the field. Acosta shoves the throttles forward, the plane lumbers past the halfway point, and I know it is too late to stop now. The end of the runway is rushing toward us, and I can picture Noville's hand groping for the dump-valve. Then, at the last split second, Acosta eases the wheel back a little, and there is a little lurch, almost a bump. The tires have left the ground.

Back in the navigator's compartment we relax, and I enter the take-off time in my diary. Below us Roosevelt Field is swallowed in the drizzle as we complete our climbing turn at four hundred feet and head northeast over Long Island, still gradually climbing. I notice two small planes keeping us company, and press photographers snapping us from their cockpits. Then they veer away and vanish astern. My application for citizenship is only a few weeks old, it occurs to me, and already I am leaving my new country behind.

"29 June, 0610. Setting course up coast line, compass 83½°, wind S.W. Clearing."

The ceiling lifts as we cross the eastern tip of Long Island and head over the open water of Block Island Sound toward Cape Cod, our three engines humming smoothly. With our load condition, the air speed is little better than eighty miles an hour, but favorable winds are pushing us up to ninety-five ground miles. We are holding our altitude about 2,000 feet, for it is important to conserve fuel and our optimum range altitude is between 2,000 and 3,000 feet.

The sandy crescent of Cape Cod is under the plane at 7:30 in the morning. Leaving Byrd in the navigator's compartment, I crawl on my stomach through the catwalk, which is almost blocked with five-gallon tins, to the cockpit in order to spell Acosta at the wheel. Noville yields his right-hand seat to me, and goes back to his set in the radio operator's compartment, immediately behind the cockpit. In addition to his sending key, we have an automatic transmitter which keeps sounding the call letters of the *America* when he is not on the air, to enable radio stations to take bearings on the plane and know that we are still airborne.

By now we have a high ceiling, with the sun breaking through the clouds from the southeast in some places. Along the Maine coast the wind, which is blowing offshore, grows stronger, and we alter course five degrees left to compensate for right drift. Noville hangs up his headset and begins transferring gasoline from the five-gallon tins into the large center tank to replace the fuel which we have been consuming at the rate of twenty gallons per hour. He drops the empty cans through the trapdoor in the floor of the radio compartment, and I watch them flashing in the sun, tumbling and sailing away behind us toward the water as we cross the outer Bay of Fundy and approach the rocky shore of Nova Scotia.

The sun is bright overhead when we roar over a fishing village with schooners lying at anchor, but as we leave the thinly populated coastal belt and cut straight across the lonely, lake-dotted barrens of southern Nova Scotia, woolly, white clouds begin to appear unexpectedly, low over the land. The visibility below us becomes steadily more obscured, but I hold the course for Halifax, aided by occasional holes in the thickening white blanket, which was definitely not in the weather program.

"*29 June, 1350. Passing Halifax, N.S.: holding course. Air bumpy. Thickening cumulus.*"

By the time we pass Halifax and head northeastward, a few miles from the coast, the cumulus clouds are like a great flock of giant sheep, cropping the dark forests below us. They huddle together in increasing herds that hide the ridges and sparkling lakes, and the shadow of our plane races us across the pearl-gray top of the undercast. Cape Breton Island is obscured completely, and it is only by my dead reckoning that we can estimate when we have crossed Cabot Strait and reached the coast of Newfoundland. Now the solid fog bank shrouds the earth as far as we can see. There will be no chance to get a visual fix on St. John's, from which we had planned to take our point of departure across the open water. It will be up to Commander Byrd to get star fixes during the night, in order to determine our exact position.

We are still over Newfoundland when Noville appears in the doorway of the radio compartment and hands us a slip of paper with an alarming report. Our gas consumption is far greater than we anticipated. I stare at his figures and rack my brain for an explanation: his results are completely at odds with all our computations based on our flight tests at the Fokker plant. We should have enough gas, I know, to go all the way to Rome if necessary. Nevertheless, his depressing report sows the seeds of doubt even in my own mind, giving me an uneasy feeling in spite of myself, and Byrd gives us the order to reduce r.p.m. as low as possible. Soon, however, as the clouds continue to build up, we must start climbing again in the hope of getting above them. Once more we have to run the engines at high r.p.m. We ascend to 5,000 feet, considerably higher than our optimum altitude for greatest engine efficiency, trying in vain to get above the stuff. Now even our wing tips are barely visible in the milky whiteness that enshrouds us in every direction, and the plane is drenched with moisture.

We ask Noville to recheck the gauges, and once again he insists that the fuel is being consumed much faster than expected. At that rate, we shall never make the other side of the Atlantic if we encounter any head winds at all. Byrd has come up into the front compartment, and he and Noville are standing behind Acosta and me in the pilots' seats. Byrd asks us how we feel about turning back. I look into the blind grayness pressing against the windshield, and again mentally review our situation. The decision to head back must be made now or never. We cannot put down at St. John's or on the crude gravel runway at Harbour Grace, because both are hidden by fog, and there is no other landing place between Newfoundland and the United States. But again I tell myself that Noville must be mistaken. If we were to turn back now I would never forgive myself. I say something to that effect, and apparently the others' feelings are similar to mine. We elect to keep on going.

So we pass our point of no return, and now ahead of us is nothing but two thousand miles of ocean, hidden by the pall of inscrutable vapor that stretches around us, in every direction, for undeterminable distances.

"29 June, 2010, Lv. Newfoundland, heading east 108° magnetic, Alt. 6500; climbing."

Still we are struggling to lift our heavily loaded plane above the clouds, but there is no sign of a top. I have been at the wheel for the past hour and a half while Acosta dozes in the left-hand seat. We have left the coast of Newfoundland, and somewhere below us, hidden in the undercast, are the Grand Banks. Small schooners and trawlers are setting their long lines for cod and dragging the bottom for ground fish, and I can picture the Bluenose fishermen in their oilskins cupping their ears and peering aloft as we drone overhead, and muttering to each other and shaking their heads dubiously. But I would not change places with them. For all the fog and the danger of icing at this altitude, I'd rather be up here in the cockpit, enclosed in milky darkness, my eyes fixed endlessly on the hypnotically glowing dials of the instrument panel, than bouncing around in a dory down there in the heavy ocean swells.

I have never liked the sea. My grandfater had a fleet of sailing ships in Kristiansand, and he would often take me down to see the square-riggers in port, ready to sail for Australia with a cargo of pine logs and trade them for wheat. He was a big man with a white beard and long black frock coat, and he would pound his gold-headed ebony cane and insist that some day I should ship before the mast. But even as a boy I preferred the snow and mountains and fresh-water streams, and the casting for salmon below the falls of the Topdal, or fishing for brown trout in the little alpine lakes.

Blind flying in fog or darkness on a long flight soon becomes a monotonous business, a mechanical operation in which your eyes shift ceaselessly from indicator to indicator as you gently maintain the plane's equilibrium.

It is hard to keep my mind on the luminous dials, hour after hour, and repeatedly I find my thoughts straying back to when I was a boy. I remember my first shotgun, a brand-new single-barrel .410; I was so excited over it that I was ready to burst. I remember a day when I started alone up the mountain side at dawn, through the yellow birch and ash trees red with fall berries, and I saw far above me the metallic glint of a cock capercailzie feeding on lingonberries. Crawling into a gully, I squirmed uphill on my stomach toward the bird, and as I reared up with gun cocked I was looking into the eyes of the big cock, only fifteen yards away. I pulled the trigger as it thundered into the air, and it tumbled to the ground. Throwing down my gun, I dashed forward, fell upon it and wrestled it until it was quiet. Then I slung the bird upside down over my shoulder and carried it home, its beak nearly dragging at my heels. My father saw the blood on my clothes and thought I had shot myself for sure. Later the capercailzie was roasted and brought to the dinner table on a big platter, and I had the first juicy slice off the breast.

This memory reminds me that I am hungry, and I think of the bundle of chicken sandwiches I have stowed under my seat.

I turn to Acosta at my left. "Take the plane for a minute, will you, Bert?" I ask. He nods and obligingly grips the wheel. Taking my eyes off the instrument panel with a feeling of relief, I bend down and grope under the seat for my sandwiches.

I am still in this awkward position when suddenly I feel an invisible weight pulling my whole body down with relentless force. What in—? I strain to rise again, immediately realizing that the *America* is in a dangerous, diving spiral. When I manage to get my eyes back on the instrument panel, it has gone crazy. The rate-of-climb indicator shows that we are plunging downward in a steep dive, and the turn-and-bank needle is over in the corner of the dial. We are out of control and spiraling toward the ocean at dizzy speed. The air speed is fast passing the 140 miles per hour mark, and I know that loaded as heavily as we are, when that needle reaches 160 miles per hour at the outside, the wing will simply let go and the careers of the *America* and her crew will end then and there.

I have to act—fast. I get my hands on the wheel and signal to Acosta, who relinquishes the controls. We have lost a thousand feet already, and our air speed is building up rapidly, so that I have to work very gently to avoid putting too much stress on the whirling ship, already strained to the utmost, and instantly ripping the wing off her. The altimeter drops another five hundred feet as I delicately ease back on the wheel in order to raise her nose slightly and reduce our air speed. Lightly, I apply opposite rudder to roll her gradually out of the bank. Slowly the turn-and-bank indicator edges back toward the level position, and slowly we straighten out of our spiral. At last I manage to level off at 5,000, and I mop the sweat from my face. Then I make a 180-degree turn to get back on course. Byrd comes crawling up through the catwalk, his jacket ripping in his haste.

"What happened?" he demands.

"Oh, nothing much," I answer. "At least, everything is okay again."

Acosta slumps in the left-hand seat, his arms folded. "This instrument flying is one thing I've never bothered with," he says. "You'd better handle it from now on, as long as we're fogged in."

I feel sorry for Bert, especially as he is disarmingly honest about his lack of experience in blind flying. I know he is gifted with exceptional physical coordination and rapid reactions— shown in his masterfully executed take-off at Roosevelt Field. But the whole art of instrument flying is still in its infancy. Many pilots of the old school insist that they can "sense" when they are flying level, and refuse to make the sheer effort of will power necessary to force themselves to rely on their instrument readings when their supposed "instinct" tells them a different story. Now this dependence on a supposed sixth sense has brought us to the brink of disaster, but I am thankful that Bert Acosta has the sound judgment to realize the limitations of the old methods.

Already I have started the slow climb back to regain the altitude we have lost. Steadily I watch the gauges on the instrument panel, my eyes moving methodically from the air-speed dial to the turn-and-bank indicator to the rate-of-climb needle, and back again. I also study the long glass tubes, each mounted before a graduated scale, that show the level of the gasoline in each of our tanks. Noville must be wrong. I suspect the tail of the plane is down a little with the weight, and the gauges may not be registering accurately. True, the fog is forcing us to fly a lot higher than the pre-flight weather forecasts led us to expect. But even so, with the throttle and mixture control settings I've been using, our gas just can't be flowing as freely as champagne on New Year's Eve. Constantly I have to assure myself of this, for if I'm wrong it will be our last celebration.

"30 June, 0100. Climbing out of fog at 8,000 feet."

I have been at the wheel for seven hours, and, though the excitement of the spiral dive and the importance of avoiding a repetition keep my senses alert, I am beginning to be conscious of the fact that I have not slept for forty-one hours. At last, about one o'clock in the morning, we break out on top at 8,000 feet. One moment we are still wrapped in our white cocoon of fog; the next moment we have emerged, like a hatching moth, into a brightness almost like that of noon. The moon shines on a solid stratus layer covering the Atlantic for endless miles, and the dark blue sky above us is pricked with brilliant stars. We level off about 500 feet above the cloud base, and now Acosta relieves me at the wheel.

I stand up and stretch my legs and flex my cramped hands. Noville is on his jump-seat before the radio, trying in vain to make contact, and I tinker with the frequency dials to see if we can raise any station. But no signals break the silence. We have done a litle work with plane radios in the Norwegian Air Force, but radio in aviation is still in the experimental stage. This is my first long-range flight with radio on board, and none of the other planes in the Transatlantic Air Derby was equipped with it. Any signals from the ground—so far, we have heard nothing—must come to us in Morse. We are not, of course, depending on our set for navigation, for there are no regular ground-to-air radio stations anywhere in the world. For navigational purposes we are relying on Commander Byrd and his optical instruments.

Our hope is, however, that at least some ship and ground stations may pick up the call sign which is constantly emitted by our automatic sender, and will thus discover that we are still in the air. Possibly, if such a station happens to have a radio direction finder, it will even take a bearing on us and determine our position. Should we be forced down at sea, we have an emergency radio transmitter in the life raft, and under favorable conditions—that is, if ships or ground stations are within our range—it would be a real asset.

Tearing his earphones off, Noville gives up the radio and bends over the problem of the fuel consumption again. I crawl back to the navigator's compartment, where Byrd is poring over a chart. I sit on the floor to stretch my numbed legs some more.

After a while Byrd gets a message, written on a slip of paper, on the trolley cable that runs aft to us from the cockpit. He hands it to me. It is from Noville and it reads: "Made mistake in first estimate. Have enough gas to fly all the way."

I wish we had known sooner. I might have enjoyed the trip more.

Acosta and I spell each other at the wheel through the night, but along toward dawn we meet a cold front, and towering cumulus clouds loom through the undercast ahead. There is no way to dodge them, and once again we move into solid murk, flying blind. Acosta turns over the wheel to me, and crawls through the catwalk to the navigator's compartment to get a little sleep. Noville, too, has already crept back to the rear compartment to stretch out, and I am alone in the cockpit.

I watch the instrument dials glowing in the blackness, and hold the plane on course through the turbulent clouds. Now and then, as we emerge from the darkness of a cloud mass, I get a glimpse upward between towering peaks, and see their sides turning gold with the first dawn, with blue sky above. I remember once watching the dawn come up near Topdal, after driving all night in a broad sleigh, called a *sluffe* in Norway, pulled by a small *Nordfjord* pony. My companions in the sleigh were asleep, snuggled under heavy wolfskin robes, and I was all by myself in the driver's seat, guiding the horse along a narrow trail and seeing the shadows under the trees grow sharper on either side, and the snow turn from violet to pink and then bright gold in the new day.

Hour after hour the engines drone on, smoothly and faithfully, and I wish Uncle Tony Fokker could hear them. The plane follows a deep valley in the clouds, between white cliffs. Sometimes the white wool comes so close that the wing shears through it; now and again it washes over the whole plane and leaves me in a pink haze until we suddenly cut out into the clear again.

Now the morning sun, flooding the endless ocean of clouds below us, makes the white so brilliant it almost hurts the eyes; but it is good, for a change, to have something outside the cockpit to focus on. Acosta comes creeping up front, and for a while we sit in silence and enjoy the plane and the sky together before I crawl aft for a nap.

"30 June, 1200. Alt. 15,000 feet. Moderate icing."

About an hour later the clouds close in around us again, and I return to the cockpit. Since then I have been climbing through the clouds.

We are following our precomputed compass course of 108° magnetic, along the same route that Lindbergh and Chamberlin flew; but we cannot see the water below us and there is no way of telling how much the wind has drifted us off course during the long hours that we have been on instruments. We hope that at the altitudes at which we have been flying, we may have been getting the benefit of winds from the west to increase our speed through the clouds. At noon a penciled message from Byrd is brought up to the cockpit: "It is impossible to navigate."

Now we are at 15,000 feet, which is the maximum ceiling of the ship. The controls feel mushy at this altitude, and some ice is forming at the leading edges of the wings and on the props, breaking off and rattling against the fuselage.

Noville has been trying in vain all day to pick up a signal on his radio. At last, at three o'clock, while we are ducking in and out of the cumulus, there is a faint stutter on the set. It is a message from a steamer three miles below us, reporting a broken ceiling around 2000 feet, with northwesterly winds. I throttle back immediately, and start descending through the clouds as fast as possible to get out of the icing condition and try to see something to tell us where we are.

According to my dead reckoning, if the prevailing northerly winds have not driven us too far off course, we should be approaching close to the coast of Ireland.

The ceiling proves to be at not much more than a thousand feet, but now, as we let down through the cloud layer, we can suddenly see the endless expanse of tossing, dark blue water. Ridged with whitecaps, it stretches away in every direction to the dim horizon. There is no sign of land, no plume of smoke to mark the presence of any coastal shipping. Plainly we are nowhere near Ireland, and I assume the wind has drifted us far to the southward of our heading. There is nothing to do but continue on an easterly course. That way, I figure, we are at least bound to hit Europe somewhere between Spain and Norway.

"30 June. Sight coast, 1700. Weather fair, slight haze."

I am in the cockpit when at last, at five in the afternoon, almost twenty-four hours after leaving Newfoundland, we make out a faint smudge of land on the horizon. Along its base runs a thin line, darker than the sea. Soon more of the coast lifts above the horizon, and, from its configuration, we can tell that we are looking at the westernmost tip of France, on the approaches to the port of Brest. As I have suspected, we are about 250 miles south of the course for Ireland.

Now, we think, the dangers are all behind, and a sense of release fills the entire ship. It is a beautiful afternoon, with only a light haze in the far distance, and Paris is only a couple of hours away.

As we come in toward the land, Noville is bent over the radio receiver. He hastily scribbles down a message. It is a weather transmission from a French government station, sent blind for our special benefit, and predicts low ceilings and rain squalls for the evening. This forecast fails to dampen our spirits, for we should be at Paris before night. We cross a line of white breakers, and suddenly green meadows are below us, and farmhouses with red-tiled roofs and smoking chimney pots. We are approaching the city of Brest, easy to identify on the north side of the bay, and Commander Byrd comes forward to the cockpit with a message for Noville to send back to Rodman Wanamaker: "It has been a great trip. We all send our best wishes." He takes the wheel in order to pilot the *America* on its last leg.

The message is never sent. Just as we are over Brest, Noville picks up a signal direct from Le Bourget, reporting heavy drizzle and lowering ceilings, closing by nightfall. This is what we all have feared most: to see the goal almost within our grasp, and then have it snatched from us by the elements. The rest of the continent is still giving open weather, and we have enough gas to skirt the stormy low-pressure area and go on to Rome or Berlin; but Byrd has pledged that Paris will be our destination. He announces his decision: "We'll make a pass at Le Bourget."

He makes another decision, which I have never been able to explain since. We could set a course direct for Paris from Brest— there even is a railroad track we could follow right into the heart of Paris and get there before dark. Instead, turning the controls over to Acosta, Byrd shouts to him:

"Fly along the coast. Follow the coast line to Le Havre, and then try to follow the Seine into Paris."

I am familiar with northern France through having flown there before. It is only two years since my last flight into and out of Le Bourget.

"Commander," I suggest, "if we do that it'll take us two or two and a half hours longer than if we set a course direct from here to Paris. By following the Brest-Paris railroad line, we can hit Le Bourget just before dark."

Commander Byrd turns around to Acosta. "Fly as I've told you," he says.

Every moment is critical if we are to reach Le Bourget before it is closed completely by darkness and rain. We will do our best.

We fly along the coast in the failing light. It is starting to get dark as we pass over Cherbourg, and Acosta relinquishes the controls to me, and crawls aft. Rain begins to fall from the high overcast: we are reaching the edge of the low-pressure area. Byrd is in the copilot's seat beside me, peering through the rain-streaked windshield. Now and then we can see the winking lights of little villages along the coast to our right, but the visibility is dwindling fast, and soon the ceiling is down to the hilltops.

We feel by now that our radio set has certainly earned its passage, but unfortunately its usefulness is short-lived. Noville, in shifting his position in the cramped radio compartment, accidentally puts his foot on some wires leading into the outfit, ripping away one or more of them. This knocks the set out of commission for good.

"*30 June, 2030. Over Le Havre, 2,000 ft. Rain: visibility poor.*"

We circle over Le Havre and set a course up the Seine River. Byrd gets up from his seat and goes aft, and I am left alone in the cockpit. Below us I can see the river reflecting the last gray light of the sky, and the black shapes of barges on its quiet water. Picturesque—but I should have much preferred following the prosaic railroad line from Brest, which would have put us safely down on the runway at Le Bourget airport just about now, in this last, swiftly fading daylight.

In a little more than an hour after leaving Le Havre, we are over the outskirts of Rouen. I have been driven down to about 200 feet and can see the wet, cobblestoned streets, but the clouds are right down on the deck now. I have no choice but to pull up to 4,000 feet and set a course for Paris from my estimated point of departure.

"30 June, 2200. Letting down over Paris. Zero zero."

We have been flying at 4,000 feet for about forty-five minutes, and now I start easing down through the solidly pelting rain, hoping to find some hole in the clouds. It is now almost ten o'clock at night. The only light is the dull gleam of dials on the instrument panel, and the blue flames from the exhaust stacks of the motors, still running evenly after forty hours, never missing a beat.

I maneuver for fifteen or twenty minutes, turning and banking to peer down through the inky blackness, then dropping a little lower and circling again. At last I decide the only thing to do is to set course back to the coast, where I hope there is still a fairly high ceiling.

After an hour and a half, flying at 4,000 feet, I let down by instruments and to my relief, break out at least 1,500 feet over the water. To the east, on the horizon, I pick up the lights of the shore, and get hold of Le Havre again. I take a new point of departure and once more set course for Paris. Studying the dwindling columns of liquid in the fuel gauges, I know this will be our last try.

"1 July 0050. Over Paris again. Letting down."

It is almost one in the morning, and by my estimate we are over Paris once more. I descend to 3,000 feet. I do not dare grope my way lower, because the Eiffel Tower is somewhere in the area, a thousand feet high. We circle in the dark, through the driving rain, and once I think I see a flash underneath the wing. I watch anxiously, but there is only blackness. Later we learn that a large crowd has been waiting all night at Le Bourget to welcome us, and they claim that about one o'clock they heard our engines directly above. The weather at the field at that time was heavy rain, 75 feet ceiling, visibility nil.

Our fuel gauges are beginning to register almost empty. Now I know that we shall not get into Paris this trip. We have been fumbling about in this black rainstorm long enough—too long, perhaps. Now it is a question of saving the ship. There is only one chance: to find our way back to the coast a second time, and hope we shall be lucky enough to have a little ceiling left for a landing there. Again I set the *America*'s nose on course for Le Havre, and we drone through the night, my ears anxiously cocked for the first warning cough from a motor burning its last drops of gas. It is after two in the morning when I figure that we are over the coast again, and let down through the clouds. At this time of the year it is already growing the faintest shade lighter. Faintly below me, through the rain-filled air, I can now see the line of the shore. When scattered lights twinkle below, to port, I head for a brighter group and as we sweep over it I see that it is an electric sign on the roof of a big building. It reads DEAUVILLE.

Byrd crawls up through the catwalk and asks our position. I tell him what I have just seen. Through the deafening uproar of the motors, I shout to him that we'll have to sit down—and soon.

His voice, muffled by the roar of the engines, seems to come from far away as he asks me whether a crash is imminent. I tell him, with more confidence than I feel, that I hope the fuel will hold out till we sight a landing spot.

We are flying southwest along the coast. Ahead of us I spot a low, sandy beach, and swoop down to buzz over it hopefully. No use—a whole fleet of fishing boats hauled up on the sand, leaving not the slightest place to set down. I pull the plane's nose up again and level off, both of us straining our eyes ahead along the winding coast.

"1 July, 0400. Gas tanks empty. Preparing to ditch."

Ahead of us the beam of a lighthouse cuts through the graying murk, swinging in a slow circle. I come down over the stone tower and bank steeply, following the beam around and studying the ground below. The meadows are cut up into little fields by stone fences, and there is no hope of landing there. There is a small, sloping beach, and it is littered with small boats. Only the water offshore looks clear. Shouting back and forth to each other, Commander Byrd and I agree that our only chance is to ditch.

As we complete a left turn and make a first pass over the water, our right engine coughs alarmingly. We have only a few seconds in which to ditch. Crawling back to the navigator's compartment, Commander Byrd quickly has three carbide drift-flares in readiness. Through the trapdoor he tosses them into the sea below, about a hundred yards apart. As I come around again, I see them ignite on the surface. I decide to set her down on the middle light, making my flare-out over the first one and judging my height above the water by the third, up ahead.

I take the plane down, all the way down to the wavetops. A hundred feet; fifty feet. The others have gone to their emer-

gency stations, Acosta hunched in the radio operator's seat behind me, Byrd and Noville braced in the rear compartment.
Now we are only three or four feet above the water, and I cut
all three engines and stall the ship in.

A large bow wave engulfs the *America*'s nose as we hit, and
cold salt water is pouring in from everywhere. We come to a
stop and the weight of the engines, all forward of the wing,
draws the nose of the plane gently under the water. I follow it
beneath the surface, and can feel it settle to the bottom.

Unhitching my safety belt, I squirm around in my seat and
kick upward toward the door of the radio compartment, just
behind and above me. The ocean feels wonderfully cool and
refreshing as at last I pull myself up through the hatch over
the radio compartment and fill my lungs with the fresh air.

Looking about in the graying light of dawn, I see that
Byrd and Noville have emerged through the hatch in the roof
of the navigator's compartment and crawled up on the tilted
wing. The plane is floating on its empty main tank. I try to
wriggle up on the wing beside them, but somehow my hands
cannot get a grip on anything and I slide off again backward,
like a greased seal. I cannot understand why everything is so
slippery; then I realize that the oil tank for the center engine
was under my seat, and I am coated with slimy motor oil.

Byrd gives me a hand up and calls out, "Where is Acosta?"
His voice sounds high-pitched and shrill, hard to understand,
and then I realize that my ears are completely out of whack
after two days and nights of roaring engines. The upended
plane is filling rapidly, the leading edge of the wing slowly
settling toward the water. We crawl forward, ready to dive
down and grope for Acosta's body in the fuselage, and at that
moment he appears out of nowhere in the darkness behind us,
thrashing in the water and shouting in the same strange,
squeaky voice.

We pull him onto the wing beside us. Gradually my hearing is getting back to normal, and now I am aware of the uncanny silence, broken only by the *lap lap lap* of the tide running out past the *America*. The plane is floating lower in the water, its heavy nose resting on the bottom at a depth of ten or fifteen feet, the wing barely awash. Later we find that the landing-gear was sheared off by the first impact; but there isn't a tear in the canvas. The shore, some two hundred yards away, seems completely deserted.

Noville has opened the emergency rip panel in the center of the wing, and we haul out a rubber life raft and inflate it with a foot pump, and launch it from the wing. We fish from the plane our most precious items of cargo, a strongbox containing a piece of a historic American flag, which we are to present to the people of France, and a sack containing part of the approximately 150 pounds of mail on board. The flight was sworn in by the Post Office Department as the first official transatlantic mail carrier. Loading these valuables into the raft, we climb in ourselves and push off for shore. We are all exhausted, and it is slow work paddling against the ebbing tide, but at last the rubber raft grates against the sand and we flounder out and haul it up on shore. At least, we have delivered the first transocean airmail from the United States to Europe.

By now it is around four-thirty in the morning, local time. It is a dismal day with rain pelting down, but we cannot get any wetter as we straggle up the hill to a village a mile from the beach. Its houses, surrounded by high fences with locked gates, are dark and quiet. The only sign of life is a French boy on a bicycle, and he takes one look at these strange-looking, disheveled creatures that have come dripping out of the sea, and pedals away in terror. We climb the hill to the lighthouse and hammer on its massive door until the keeper pokes his white nightcap out of an upper window. Noville speaks a little French, and when he explains who we are, the window bangs down and the lighthouse keeper and his wife rush to unbolt the front door and let us in. We ask him where we are.

"Near Caen, department of Calvados," he says in rapid French. "Called Ver-sur-Mer." (Later this place is to be known to millions of American soldiers during World War II as Omaha Beach.)

"1 July, 0800. Tide out. Salvage wreck of America."

Noville and Acosta, exhausted, have been put to bed in the lighthouse, and Commander Byrd and I change to dry pants and sweaters lent us by the lighthouse keeper and trudge back downhill to the crashed *America.* The tide has gone out, and the plane sits forlornly on the sand, half out of water, its stilled propellers stark against the gray sky. We can see the wheels lying a hundred yards down the beach, where they were sheared as we struck the water.

Soon I am soaked to the skin again as I wade around to the offshore side of the plane, to get the rest of the mail and start the task of taking the *America* apart and salvaging what we can. By this time a crowd of excited villagers has gathered, and most of them pitch in to help. Someone brings tools from a local machine shop, and we unbolt the motors and carry them gingerly ashore. Later we remove the wing. The local people are eager to assist in any way, and we labor side by side in the pouring rain, disassembling the plane and carrying it a section at a time to a safe place above the high tide line.

So intense is the excitement in the village that it is impossible to keep the souvenir hunters from making off with little trophies of this historic event. Once I detect five or six residents struggling up the beach, lugging away one of the outboard motors. When we protest, they shrug in surprise and surrender it politely.

But one whole section of the plane disappears completely. It is an eight-by-forty-foot strip of the fabric side, on which is painted in big white letters: AMERICA.

FIVE

THE LAST VIKING
1927–1928

In Paris, as soon as we are brought here by train from Ver-sur-Mer, Bert Acosta and I must go buy some clothes at once. Commander Byrd and Lieutenant Noville have their starched white Navy uniforms, sent ahead from the States and waiting at the hotel, but I cannot appear at a formal banquet wearing my checkered lumberjack shirt and oil-soaked blue pants. Acosta and I are taken to the Paris branch of Rodman Wanamaker's store, which is handling all our expenses; but these French people seem to be smaller than I am, and the suits I try on look as if I'd outgrown them already. So a Parisian tailor works all night to build me a coat and pants in the latest French style, with overstuffed shoulders and peg-top trousers that hang loose and balloon around my seat. All the shoes I can find are pointed, and the clerk wants to sell me a derby even; but I draw the line at that. When I see my own reflection in the mirror of the hotel lobby, I almost shake hands with myself before I know who I am.

Never have I seen anything like the wild hysteria of Paris. Around the railroad station when we arrived the streets were blocked with crowds, and they swarmed over the car and broke the windows and almost tipped it over. We dared not run the

123

motor, and the mob pushed us down the avenue and all the
way to the Continental Hotel, shouting *"Vivent les Américains,
vive Byrd!"* Women jumped on the running board and threw
their arms around us and kissed us until our faces were daubed
with red lipstick. At least they could not see me blush any more.
Gendarmes flung up their arms in despair at controlling the
traffic, and elbowed through the crowds to the car and begged
for autographs themselves.

Morning, noon, and night, the banquets and handshaking
and welcome ceremonies go on, everybody jabbering in French
and squeaking like the swarms of sea birds around the nesting
cliffs at Kings Bay. The Stars and Stripes and the Tricolor of
France are draped side by side in the store windows, and people
line the balconies along the Champs Elysées and the Rue de la
Paix, waving and cheering as we tour the city in open cars to
visit the Arc de Triomphe and Notre Dame Cathedral and the
Eiffel Tower. I remember circling in the dark rain-filled sky
over Paris, trying to avoid the Eiffel Tower; but now after a
week of receptions I almost wish I were up there in the cockpit
again, away from these thronged streets and taxi horns and endless celebrations.

Our daily round usually begins with a formal ten o'clock reception with champagne, and this is hard to face after a night in
gay Paree. Among those many receptions, certain ones will forever stand out in my memory. A particularly moving occasion
comes when we are invited to visit the Invalides, the great military hospital which is also the site of Napoleon's tomb. Here
we are taken into the wards and have an opportunity to see the
men personally. This experience brings home to me the great
number of French veterans who have been left disabled not only
by the 1914–1918 war, but also by campaigns in various parts of
the French colonial empire. I am impressed by this close-up evidence of the tremendous sacrifices the youth of France have
been called upon to make almost continuously in defense of

their country, and the strain thus imposed on the nation.

Another outstanding event is the reception given for us by the Fédération Aéronautique Internationale, at which Clifford B. Harmon presents us with honorary membership. At this affair there is a regular oratorical contest among the dignitaries, each outdistancing the other in eloquence, but as the speeches are in French, I can unfortunately understand very little of them. On this occasion we have the pleasure of meeting the famous Louis Blériot, whose first flight across the English Channel in 1909 opened a new epoch in the conquest of the air, and other pioneers of European aviation in the early days. We are also honored by being presented to Marshal Foch.

One morning I breakfast alone with Byrd, and we have a long talk together over a cup of coffee. An idea has been forming in his mind for some time, he tells me. When he brought me back from Spitsbergen to the States, he was planning another cold-weather expedition. Now at last he reveals what it is. He will attempt the impossible, he says. He has been the first man to cross the North Pole, and now also he will be the first to look down on the South Pole, never flown over before in all history. Bennett and I are to be members of the expedition.

My excitement grows every minute as we discuss the big new adventure. What would be the airplane to use in exploring this unknown continent, ten times as far from civilization as the North Pole mass? Both of us agree that the best plane in the world at this time is the Fokker, and I offer to go to the Fokker plant in Holland, while the Paris receptions are still going on, and discuss with Uncle Tony's European experts the modifications for a specially equipped airplane to go to the Antarctic. I am only too glad to get away from all the banquets and "oriayting," and that same afternoon I fly to Amsterdam.

With the Fokker engineers I go into lengthy technical conferences on the design and specifications for extreme cold-weather flying. We would have to operate on skis, of course, and we would need greater lifting capacity and load-carrying ability at altitude for extra fuel and survival gear. The big-wing F-7 could be modified for the Antarctic expedition, I believe. My cold-weather knowledge, and experience with ski flying, are incorporated in their planning, and when I leave Amsterdam there is already a preliminary design on the drawing boards.

The Paris receptions have finally ended when I get back, and next morning we start by car for Cherbourg, to board the *Leviathan* for our triumphant return to the States. Our motorcade halts for the night at Le Touquet, and after another reception in Byrd's honor we are taken over to the famous Casino at Deauville. The Prince of Wales and some friends are at a large center table. Acosta and I are introduced to his Royal Highness, and he invites us to join his party. With the Prince is a cool and statuesque brunette—a well-known actress, somebody whispers—and I can see Acosta eyeing her with Latin interest as we are seated.

I am beside a distinguished-looking British general, with a drooping mustache and a monocle hanging on a black ribbon, and I try in vain to start a conversation about airplanes. I notice that Acosta's wineglass is being refilled frequently, and he is a hard man to keep up with, even for a Norwegian. While the couples are waltzing, suddenly Acosta pushes back his chair and slaps the Prince of Wales on the shoulder. "How about me dancing with your gal, old chap?" The general beside me stiffens and puts his monocle into his eye, measuring Acosta up and down like some loathsome object, and Acosta takes a five-franc piece from his pocket and squeezes it into one eye and returns the glare. There is a moment of dead silence, and then the Prince of Wales laughs, "Go right ahead, old chap!" and everyone relaxes.

On my way up to the game rooms, my eye is caught by a wall

decoration, stretching forty feet from one side of the balcony to the other. It is the missing piece of fabric from the wrecked plane, which has been sold to the Casino as a souvenir. In big white letters is the name, "America."

Still the celebration goes on aboard the *Leviathan* on our way home. Now it is a double celebration, because Chamberlin and Levine are here, returning to the States after the *Columbia*'s record-breaking flight to Germany, and the joint parties continue day and night, in the main salon and the cocktail lounge and on the dance floor. I am sharing a cabin with Acosta, but I barely see him the whole trip. Byrd does not mingle with the merrymakers, and during the voyage I spend much time with him in his stateroom, discussing the Antarctic trip. I report the results of my visit to the Fokker plant and the new plane they propose to build, with special arrangements for fuel tanks and an advanced type of control valves and the very maximum in wing-loading capacity, designed to operate in temperatures down to 70° below. We discuss the logistics of the polar flight, how to transport the planes to the Antarctic, and how to get them up onto the icecap. I go back to Amundsen's own experience, described in his book *The South Pole*, as we plan how to set up a base for the expedition on the permanent glacier.

Noville and Acosta will not be going to the Antarctic, and more and more Byrd comes to confide in me. During our long conferences in his stateroom and pacing the decks, I come to appreciate the magnitude of the manifold problems of planning such an expedition. Aside from the question of the aviation operations, the logistic problems of transporting a large number of scientists and other expedition members to the Antarctic, and of housing and supplying them there for an extended period, are extremely complex. Byrd plunges into them, often shutting himself in his cabin when I leave and having his meals brought to him there, while he studies his plans and adds up figures of tonnage and costs.

Always our talks on the Antarctic come back to one thing: What would Roald Amundsen say? Amundsen conquered the South Pole by dog sled, his expedition lived for months on the great ice fields, he knows the answers to the problems of food and clothing and existence better than any other man on earth. Byrd remembers Amundsen's unselfish assistance on the North Pole flight, and he tells me, as soon as the New York reception is over, that I must go back to Norway and see Captain Amundsen and get his advice.

The celebration in New York is as wild as the one in Paris, but with ticker tape. The traditional parade up Broadway, the bands and cheers and whoopdedoo, go on all day long, and by nightfall my feet ache from pounding the pavements and my fingers are numb from handshaking. From New York we are taken to Washington to be presented to the President of the United States. I am prepared for another burst of oratory, but Calvin Coolidge extends his limp hand and says in a dry twangy voice: "See you made it." Now we go back to New York again for the climax of the ceremonies, a great banquet at the Commodore Hotel given by the City of New York for the *America's* crew and for Charles Levine and Clarence D. Chamberlin for their flight to Germany in the *Columbia*.

Mayor Jimmy Walker is the toastmaster, and after the usual speeches and tributes he introduces the Secretary of the Navy, Curtis D. Wilbur. My mind is wandering a little, and I am thinking of the coming Antarctic expedition, when Bert Acosta beside me suddenly nudges my elbow. Secretary Wilbur is presenting the Navy Distinguished Flying Crosses to Commander Byrd and Lieutenant Noville.

A puzzled murmur arises in the banquet hall as the audience realizes that Chamberlin, Acosta and I have been overlooked in the conferral of awards. Questions are asked as to why the pilots on the expeditions have not received an award intended specifically for flying proficiency. Secretary Wilbur points out in his remarks that the Navy has no power to confer medals on other

The beginning of the blow at the Rockefeller Mountains. We tried to weight the Fokker down with snow blocks.

The situation at our camp at the Rockefeller Mountains after the blizzard. Our clothes are hung out for drying. Here we waited for a relief plane from Little America.

than Navy men. This explanation does not seem very logical, as the *America's* flight was a private venture, and the law prescribes that the DFC shall be awarded for flights made on duty with the armed forces, and it arouses some verbal and press criticism.

On August 10 I pack my old rucksack and sail on the steamship *Stavangerfjord* for Norway. It is the same rucksack I had on my back when I left for Kings Bay, a little more than a year ago now. I have not told even my mother I am coming, and I am planning to surprise her when I get to Oslo. I wonder if any of my squadron mates in the Naval Air Force are still in Horten. It would be good to see someone I know because so much has been crowded into this past year that I feel almost like a stranger coming to my own homeland again.

Our first port of call is Bergen. As we enter the harbor I see that the waterfront buildings are hung with flags, and a crowd is gathered on the dock. I try to remember what national holiday this can be. Then I hear the sound of airplane engines overhead, and a formation of Hansa-Brandenburgs zooms down over the harbor, buzzing the ship in salute. Suddenly I recognize the wing numbers of my old squadron, and I have to look away for a moment and swallow hard. I would not exchange this greeting for all the parades up the Champs Elysées or Broadway, because the crowd on the pier is shouting my name, and these are my own people saying with their hearts; "*Velkommen hjem, Bernt!*"

There is a luncheon for me here in Bergen. As the ship continues on its way to Oslo it makes a stop of several hours at Kristiansand, and I meet my relatives and old schoolmates there. At Oslo I make out one face among all the hundreds of faces lining the wharf, and my mother rushes up the gangplank and puts her arms around me, excited and happy to hear all I have been doing. I had been worried about finding a hotel room in Oslo, but there is a whole suite at the Grand Hotel waiting for me, and a car and driver standing by; and I am humbled by the speeches in my honor at a luncheon given by the Aero Club of Norway, and without words to reply.

Oskar Omdal flies to Oslo from the Horten Air Base, and I am glad to slip away from all these formal tributes, and go back with him for a reunion with my squadron mates that night at the Officers Club. Admiral von der Lippe, chief of the Naval Air Force, is on hand at the dinner, and here also are Riiser-Larsen and Captain Höver and my cousin Leif Dietrichson, all in the uniform that I no longer wear, because I am on leave status. There is much politeness and clicking of heels in the Norwegian military style, and nothing like the ribald greetings and good-natured horesplay of an American officers club; but behind the stiff protocol is the same fellowship, and it is good to be with my old friends again.

Over highballs after dinner I mention the fine buzz job the squadron did at Bergen harbor, and someone reminds me of a buzz job of my own, five years ago, when I was a second lieutenant at Kristiansand. I was flying a fast Sopwith fighter with an English Clerget rotary engine souped up to do over a hundred miles an hour, they laugh as they recall, and with this thundering speed in my young hands I could not resist swooping down over my uncle's field artillery battery on the drill grounds. The horses and caissons stampeded in every direction when I roared out of the skies at them, and over on the parade field the band threw their instruments away and scrambled for the ditches as I pulled up again in a tight chandelle. I stayed aloft until I was out of gas, and then I had to land and face the music. My squadron mates want to hear about the Atlantic flight, but they are more interested in what happened in France later.

"How did you find the girls in Paris, Bernt?"

"That's easy," I say. "They were there waiting."

There are also special honors waiting for me in Oslo. One is the Gold Medal of the Aero Club. But best of all, on my second day in Oslo, a messenger in the uniform of the Royal Guards appears at the Grand Hotel, salutes, and announces: "Lieutenant Balchen, King Haakon bids you welcome back to Norway, and requests you to appear at the Royal Palace tomorrow."

The next afternoon I stand at attention in the doorway of the King's study, and he rises from behind his desk. He is straight as a candle, lean and tall, with a clipped gray moustache and a stern military bearing, but at the same time gentle and courteous. "Come in, Lieutenant Balchen," he greets me, "you have carried the flag of our country far." He motions me to be seated, and for an hour and a half he questions me with shrewd insight about flying and the future of aviation, what it will mean some day to Norway. I realize the perception and world vision which have made King Haakon a great leader. He is particularly interested to hear of Byrd's proposed Antarctic flight, and as I rise to leave he holds me a moment more. "We are proud that the American expedition is coming to Roald Amundsen for counsel. To honor him is to honor all Norway."

Oskar Omdal, who was with Captain Amundsen on his first attempts to reach the North Pole from Alaska and then Spitsbergen, and later also on the *Norge,* comes with me to visit the old man at Bundefjorden, on an arm of the Oslo Fjord about ten miles out of the city. We cross the fjord by ferryboat, toward a pleasant rolling shoreline dotted with white houses; and Omdal points to one house that is different from all the rest, painted a light grayish blue, the color of the water-sky. This is Amundsen's home, "Svartskog," a two-story villa in the 1890 style, with steep roofs and a high gable surrounded by a small balcony, from which the retired explorer can still look across the sea. It stands well back amid maples and birches and chokecherries, which are turning bright with the first autumn colors.

At the foot of the sloping lawn, a small pier extends a hundred feet out into the fjord; and, from the ferry, I see a lone figure standing on the dock to welcome us.

We walk slowly up the lawn to Captain Amundsen's house. He is still erect and vigorous. His living room is starkly furnished, with dark flowered paper and heavy drapes, and the walls are bare of pictures except one large oil painting of King Haakon and Queen Maud. There are no trophies from his expeditions, for Amundsen does not believe in intruding his personal affairs on his guests. All his pictures and mementoes are upstairs in the private study where he works. This room is his own life, and the door is locked against all others. No one is ever allowed inside except himself.

He sits in his favorite leather chair, beside a smoking stand made in the shape of a lighthouse, and tamps tobacco into the bowl of a long-shanked pipe. He listens with only half-interest to my story of the Atlantic Air Derby, but his eyes brighten as I describe winter flying in the Canadian bush. "You did the right thing going there, Balchen," he nods. "This was your right move. Only in Alaska and northern Canada can one get the experience that the Antarctic requires."

Now he begins to talk about the Antarctic, the bitter cold and violent storms there, how to survive on the ice barrier, how an air base might be established. From his own vast experience, and from all the books he has read, he judges that the best average weather in the Antarctic is at Framheim, his winter quarters, and he recommends that we launch our attack on the South Pole from there. Later, Little America will be built not far from the old site of Framheim.

Now comes the question of a ship to carry the expedition through the pack ice. Amundsen recalls that in 1893, when he sailed for the first time in the Arctic before the mast, it was aboard the *Viking,* an old sealer built in Scotland, and that the ship, now named *Samson,* is in Tromsö at this very moment.

He considers that, of all the vessels available in Europe, the *Samson* is the best designed and best equipped for this type of operation. He offers to get in touch with the owners and secure the specifications and also the price for me to take back to Commander Byrd.

He draws on his thirty years of polar experience to describe the proper clothing for Arctic survival, and gives me a sample of a tight-woven gabardine material that is light and yet windproof. He makes a sketch of the Amundsen parka he has perfected from an old Eskimo design, with an apron pocket in front and a hood sewed to the parka, with a drawstring to pull it tight around the face (the pattern of the U.S. Army parkas in use in Operation Deep Freeze in 1957). Most important of all, he promises to arrange for the sixty-eight-year-old sailmaker and tailor, Martin Ronne, who had been with him on his discovery of the South Pole in 1911, to get leave from the Naval base at Horten and accompany our expedition. More than one member of Byrd's party owe their lives today to the garments and tents turned out by this veteran Norwegian craftsman.

That evening, after supper, Captain Amundsen has his own special nightcap, a brandy toddy in a tall glass, mahogany-colored and consumed boiling-hot. I have never seen Amundsen's like for hot food and drink: his coffee is always scalding, and he swallows it at one gulp without batting an eye. When Oskar Omdal mentions that he has decided to go with me to the States, in the hope of signing on with Byrd as a spare pilot on the expedition, Amundsen nods his head slowly, almost sadly. "You are young, both young," he says, sipping his toddy, "and aviation today is for young people. Old men stay home and write their memoirs." He is just finishing his autobiography, *My Life As an Explorer,* he tells us; but I can see as he talks that he is not in love with words, is ill content with retirement, and would like to be going with us. There is a caged restlessness in his deep-set eyes, a touch of bitterness that he must end his days in an easy-chair by the fireplace. He would like to fight the Arctic ice once more, to die with his straw-filled mukluks on, in the north and the great white silence.

We leave after breakfast the next morning, and he stands on the pier as the ferry pulls away. His lone figure dwindles and disappears from sight, but I can still see the shaggy white eyebrows and great hawk-nose, the face carved in granite as timeless as time itself, the last Viking.

Floyd Bennett has disturbing news on my return to New York the 1st of October: The specially designed F-7 Fokker, ordered by Commander Byrd and under construction in Holland, will not be used on the South Pole flight after all. Byrd has decided instead on a metal tri-motor plane being made by the Ford Motor Company in Detroit—its cold-weather capabilities unknown.

Bennett tells me this when I call to see him at his home in Brooklyn, where he is still convalescing after his accident. He is in charge of organizing the aviation unit for the Antarctic expedition, but he can work only a few hours each day. He hauls himself off the living-room couch, dragging his right foot a little as he slowly crosses the room to greet me. Mrs. Bennett smiles to see me enter. "It does Floyd good to talk to a fellow pilot—he is more like himself," she says. He has lost weight, is coughing a little, and since I saw him last he has developed a habit of licking his lips, as though under some kind of nervous tension.

The reason Byrd has chosen the Ford is simple: Henry and Edsel Ford have made a generous contribution to help finance the expedition, and they are donating the plane. This expedition is no exception to the general rule that such enterprises require abundant funds to defray their expenses. And airplanes certainly add a great extra financial burden.

In the circumstances Bennett and I will have to go out to Detroit and take up one of the models at the factory for a test hop and work out with the engineers the necessary modifications in the design. Byrd has decided on the Ford plane, so it's up to us to see that it can do the job. That's how the windsock blows.

There are many points in favor of the all-metal plane, we find when we arrive at the Detroit factory. It is sturdy in construction; and its wing comes in three sections and can be taken down and crated so that it is easier than the Fokker to transport to the Antarctic. But the most important question, of course, is what we can get out of it in the air; and the next morning, with Ford's chief test pilot, Brooks, we make several flights in one of the factory models. Our preliminary findings are not satisfactory, and when we land we have a conference with the Ford engineers, and give them the bad news. The chief engineer is disturbed, and he picks up his phone and calls Edsel Ford himself.

Ford is easy-mannered and affable, like all great executives when you break through the palace guard surrounding them; and he is determined that the plane which bears his name shall be capable of fulfilling its historic role. He listens intently as we describe the problem. This model carries standard commercial engines, three J-5 Wright Whirlwinds of 220 horsepower each, and we do not feel that the ship has the ceiling or load-carrying capacity required for the Antarctic flight. From Amundsen's winter quarters at Framheim, in the Ross Sea area, the round-trip distance to the Pole is 1,600 miles. About 400 miles from our point of departure, moreover, we shall have to climb to 11,000 feet in order to clear the Queen Maud Range, and maintain this altitude all the way to the Pole and back again. The power of the engines will decrease as we get higher; between sea level and 11,000 feet the reduction in performance will be about 10 per cent.* Even worse, the tests we have just run were conducted with wheels, and we must make a further deduction for the added drag of skis. The fuel load for this distance, plus the safety margin for headwinds and the pay load, gives us a criterion of the gross weight. Based on this, and on the data we have gained from flying the trimotor Fokker, we question whether the all-metal Ford could make the polar flight with its present Whirlwind engines.

Edsel Ford and his staff discuss with us other needed modifications, including winterization of the engines and a new fuel system for the extra tankage the plane will have to carry; and I lay out the design for a special ski gear to carry such a heavy ship. It is agreed that as soon as the plane can be made ready, around the beginning of March, Bennett and I will fly it to Canada and test it on skis under actual arctic conditions.

Oskar Omdal has been signed as one of the pilots with the expedition to the Antarctic, where his experience in cold-weather operations will be invaluable, and meantime I ask Tony Fokker to give him a job at the plant in Teterboro. Uncle Tony is fuming at Byrd because his F-7 Fokker has been rejected, although his feelings are somewhat mollified when it is agreed to purchase one of his new single-motor Super-Universals as a reconnaissance plane over the ice barrier. Somehow Omdal does not fit in at the Fokker plant; he is restless and ready for the first wild adventure that comes along. A Mrs. Grayson, a well-to-do real estate dealer who has no knowledge of long-range flying, proposes to cross the Atlantic in a Sikorsky S-38 amphibian called the *Dawn*, and Omdal leaps at the chance to be her pilot.

It is a useless stunt flight, in my opinion, with this equipment and at this time of year, but I cannot talk him out of it. On December 23rd, despite unfavorable weather reports, the *Dawn*

---

* In 1927, propellers of variable pitch, to make more efficient use of thinner air, were only in the experimental stage.

takes off from Curtiss Field, with Omdal and Brice Goldsborough, the expert who has installed the navigational equipment for almost all the transatlantic flights. Heavy icing is reported off Boston, and after leaving the coast they are never
heard from again. The Byrd expedition has lost an experienced
Arctic pilot, and I have lost an old and valued friend.

In March the trimotor Ford is ready for its winter tests. We
load our cold-weather equipment and specially designed skis
aboard, and fly it from Detroit to Winnipeg, and then north
to Le Pas. Here it is still the dead of winter, and it is possible
to change from wheels to skis. The spectacular strike at Flin
Flon has turned Le Pas into a booming frontier town, with
dog teams and tractors in the crowded streets, and bearded
prospectors and fancy ladies staggering along the boardwalks
arm in arm from one saloon to the next. From Le Pas we move
farther north to Reindeer Lake, deep in the heart of the
Canadian bush that I love. Ours is the first trimotor plane ever
taken into northern Canada, and Bennett has his first taste of
actual sub-zero field operations. Our winterization and heating
equipment prove satisfactory, but the skis reduce the plane's
performance so much that our worst fears are realized. With
these engines we could never make the South Pole.

When we return to the Ford aircraft factory, we present our
test results to the engineers, and it is obvious that there is only
one solution: more horsepower. Plans are worked out to leave
the two 220 horsepower engines as outboards, but to replace
the center engine with a newly developed Wright Cyclone, just
off the test stands at the factory, which could develop 525 horsepower and give us sufficient increase in performance to lift the
load to the altitude we require. To support this heavier center
engine and take the increased thrust, the nose of the plane
must be expanded and reenforced clear back into the fuselage.
While the necessary changes in design are being made, Bennett
and I head back to New York. He has picked up a severe cold

while flying in Canada. We fly our plane back, the quickest way of getting to New York.

I glance at a newspaper in New York. There is a black scare head:

"BREMEN FLIERS DOWN IN LABRADOR."

The *Bremen*, a low-wing Junkers monoplane with a single liquid-cooled 300 horsepower engine, had taken off from Ireland on April 12th, in the race to be the first to fly from Europe to America. Eight previous attempts to cross the ocean from east to west had failed. Nungesser and Coli had tried it last summer in the *White Bird;* Princess Löwenstein-Wertheim, with Captain Leslie Hamilton and Colonel Friedrich Minchan, started from Upavon, England, in an equally ill-fated bid; in March of this year the Honorable Elsie Mackay and her pilot, Walter Hinchcliffe, had left Croydon Airport in the *Endeavor.* All of them had vanished without a trace.

On March 26th Baron Guenther von Huenefeld, backer of the *Bremen* expedition, with Captain Herman Köhl of the Deutsche Lufthansa as pilot, flew from Berlin to Baldonnel aerodrome near Dublin. There Colonel James Fitzmaurice of the Irish Free State Air Force joined them as copilot; and after waiting over two weeks for favorable winds, the *Bremen* set out on the 12th on its east-west Atlantic hop. They ran into bad weather as they reached the coast of North America, and two days passed without any word from the fliers. Then on the 14th a message was flashed to the crowd still lingering at Curtiss Field: the *Bremen* was down on Greenly Island, at the south of Labrador and some fifteen hundred miles north of New York. The plane was damaged, but the crew were safe: the first fliers to complete the crossing from the old world to the new.

Day after day the latest editions carry headlines of the rescue efforts. Duke Schiller, well-known Canadian bush pilot and war ace, takes off from Murray Bay in Quebec in a ski-equipped Fairchild, with Dr. Louis Cuisnier of the Grenfell Mission. Dr. Cuisnier remains at Greenly Island with the rest of the *Bremen* crew, and Schiller flies Colonel Fitzmaurice to Murray Bay. Meantime pilot Fred Melchior speeds north from New York in a Junkers F-13, a sister ship of the *Bremen*, bringing with him Erhardt and Herta Junkers, son and daughter of the famous German designer. At Murray Bay they discuss with Schiller and Fitzmaurice the problem of salvaging the *Bremen*, and it is agreed that they must have a new landing gear and propeller, and also special benzol fuel, since the *Bremen* cannot use regular 87-octane gasoline.

Now the New York *World* gets in on the act. Herbert Bayard Swope, the enterprising managing editor, has assigned his star reporter, Charles J. V. Murphy, to fly to Greenly Island and scoop the rest of the country by wiring a firsthand interview with the stranded German fliers. To give the story even greater drama, Swope asks Commander Byrd to let him use the trimotor Ford, now being readied for the South Pole flight, and hire as its pilot none other than Floyd Bennett. He persuaded Byrd that the publicity may stimulate further contributions to his own Antarctic expedition, and Byrd consents. Bennett has been put to bed with a case of influenza, but he insists he is able to make the rescue flight and carry the replacement gear and fuel to the *Bremen*. He asks me to come along as copilot.

He is pale and shaky, and I seem to have picked up a touch of his flu myself and am as limp as a flounder. We take off on April 18th in a Bellanca, bound for Detroit to pick up the big Ford, and with us are Charles Murphy and Thomas Mulroy, the old chief engineer of the *Chantier*, who will be fuel engineer on the Antarctic trip. By the time we reach Detroit both Bennett and I are running a high fever. Edsel Ford meets us at the airport, takes a look, and orders us to the Ford hospital at once.

I am up and around again the next morning, though weak and nauseated, but Bennett's resistance is lower because of his accident, and he is in no shape to fly. While he remains at the hospital, I oversee the loading of our ski gear aboard the Ford, and transfer the cans of benzol and spare Junkers parts which have arrived from New York. Two days later, on the 20th of April, Bennett drags himself out of bed and climbs into the plane, slumping in the right-hand seat. At dawn we start the nine-hour flight to Murray Bay.

The weather is cold and drizzling, and I am on instruments right from take-off and have to ascend to 10,000 feet before breaking out in the clear. Now, as we leave the Detroit area, I can go down to about 4,000 feet, which somewhat relieves our respiratory systems. Even so, I am much worried about this long flight that Bennett faces in such weather. The heater in the cabin is not working right, but he complains that he is burning up. His forehead is hot with fever, and I ask him if we hadn't better turn around and go back to Detroit, but he shakes his head.

"You handle it a little longer," he mumbles. "I'll spell you later on." He is coughing deep in his chest, and he sinks lower in the copilot's seat beside me and closes his eyes.

I am so weak myself I can barely hold the wheel steady, as we are buffeted by a little turbulence. Bennett rouses himself, and manages a grin. "We're a fine pair to be rescuing somebody else." I grin back at him: "At least, we're flying to the Arctic together. Remember on the *Chantier* how we planned this once?"

He nods and licks his lips, rests against the side of the cockpit and dozes again. During most of the rest of the flight he remains slumped over in his seat corner, and I am glad to see that he can sleep, at least fitfully. He is wearing my leather flying suit, which helps to keep him warm. The weather is clear now,

but the temperature still low, and there is a northwest wind of
about thirty-five miles per hour, which prolongs our flying
time. I am greatly relieved when finally Lake St. Agnes, about
a mile from Murray Bay, comes into view and we can glide in
for a landing there on the ice. Here we will have to change to
skis and get information about weather conditions at Greenly
Island.

There is quite a crowd to meet us. Never before or since,
probably, has the little seaplane base at Lake St. Agnes had the
attention of the world so focused on it. First to greet us are
Colonel Fitzmaurice and Duke Schiller.

We have to help Bennett from the plane, and I hold him up
to steady him. He seems to have passed into a semicoma, and
is carried to a bed in a nearby farmhouse and a rush call is sent
for a doctor. Charlie Murphy sees to these arrangements, while
I, forcing myself to keep going, discuss the rescue operation at
Greenly Island with Fitzmaurice and Schiller, and get started
with the shifting of the landing gear. Also on hand is a Junkers
mechanic, Köppen, an expert on equipment and a quiet efficient
type, and he helps me change the Ford gear from wheels to skis.
The following morning it is good weather, and we are ready
to start north. Murphy has been with Bennett at the farmhouse
all night, and he comes down to the plane while we are loading.
"You'd better figure on Fitzmaurice or somebody to be copilot.
The doctor says it's pneumonia."

I climb the hill to the farmhouse. Floyd Bennett is lying in
an old-fashioned double bed, the springs sagging in the middle.
His face is the color of the pillow, but there are blazing-red
spots on his cheeks. He does not open his eyes, but he runs his
tongue over his dry lips and murmurs: "Have a good trip."

"I'll see you when I get back, Floyd."

There is a trace of a wry grin at the corners of his mouth.
"That depends how the sock blows." His eyelids lift a little.

"One thing I want you to promise me, Bernt. No matter what happens, you fly to the South Pole with Byrd."

One year later I keep that promise.

Colonel Fitzmaurice sits in Bennett's place on my right as we fly from Murray Bay three hours northeast to Seven Islands at the mouth of the St. Laurence River. The main ice has already gone out, and we make a mushy landing on a narrow strip along the shore, and refuel with gas brought from Seven Islands by dog team. We take off again the following dawn, after the soft ice has crusted over during the cold of the night, and fly five more hours along the coast of Quebec and Labrador, to Greenly Island in the Straits of Belle Isle.

On our flight Fitzmaurice fills me in on what happened to the *Bremen*. Strong winds threw them far off course to the north, and when they broke out of the clouds, expecting to see the green spring landscape of the United States, they looked down instead on a winter terrain covered with snow. They had no idea where they were, and kept on flying over primitive forests and patches of ocean, looking for some landmark to guide them. They had been in the air for two days, and their fuel was getting critically low. Captain Köhl spotted what he took to be the mast of a schooner, but when they came down through the clouds they discovered that it was a lighthouse on a small wind-swept island, sticking out of the frozen sea.

They were afraid to sit down on the shore ice, for they had no way of knowing that in the Straits of Belle Isle it is four or five feet thick and would have held them easily. Their tanks were almost empty now, and there was no time to look further. They decided to land on a tiny lake at the very top of the island, and Captain Köhl pointed his plane into the teeth of a howling gale, stalled it in, and dropped the *Bremen* evenly onto the ice.

His safe landing seems even more miraculous when we circle

Greenly Island and bank over the lake. It is less than seventy feet long, only a catchbasin in the hollow of the mountain, with a rocky ridge at one end. The *Bremen* straddles this wall, its landing gear on one side and its tailskid on the other. The wheels are crumpled, and the propeller blades are curled like a pair of steer horns, but there is no other damage. Only the masterly piloting of Captain Köhl, plus a little help from the Almighty, had ever saved the ship.

I land in the lee of the island, on a smooth strip of bay ice, and we are greeted by Baron von Huenefeld and Captain Köhl and also Dr. Cuisnier. I stake out the Ford securely with special steel spikes I have brought for this purpose, and we unload the spare landing gear and hitch it to dog teams, and start up the hill to the stranded *Bremen*. For once I cannot make good time climbing; my legs tremble from the effects of the flu, and for five days now I have not been able to keep any food on my stomach. I am exhausted when I reach the top, and while Köppen and the others remove the broken wheels I take a tarpaulin and wrap up in it and lie in a sheltered niche in the cliff. It is about ten in the morning, and the sun is warm. I wake again about three in the afternoon, and like magic my sickness has left me, and I am able to join the others fitting on the new landing gear.

All that night a heavy blizzard rages, with blasts of wind that seem to shake the lighthouse where we are sleeping. In the morning, we find that the steel spikes anchoring the big Ford have been bent almost double by the bucking plane, but they are still holding. When the storm abates, we go back to the *Bremen*, hitch the sled dogs to the tailskid, and haul it up out of the basin. Then with ropes and tackle we ease it down the hill to the flat ice of the shore. We replace the propeller, and fill the tanks with benzol from the cans I have brought; but we have no luck starting it. Somehow we must get the plane ashore before the ice breaks up. We borrow some extra dogs from the

Indians, hitch the huskies with long lines to the *Bremen's* tail, and start pulling it across the frozen bay to the mainland. There it will be stored in the village, and flown down to the States later in the summer.

That afternoon a dog team arrives from the Point Amour radio station, bringing a message from Tom Mulroy, who has remained in Murray Bay. After we left, Bennett was moved to a small hospital, and as he grew worse Charles Lindbergh flew from New York through a heavy snowstorm to deliver some serum. He arrived too late. The message says briefly: "Floyd Bennett died yesterday."

Now the preparations for the South Pole expedition are in full swing. The target date for our departure has been set for August, and headquarters are established in the Biltmore Hotel in New York. The trimotor Ford, christened *Floyd Bennett*, is being modified in Detroit to accommodate the larger center engine; the Super-Universal Fokker, powered with a Pratt & Whitney 425 horsepower Wasp engine and christened *Virginia*, is ready at the Teterboro plant; and a Fairchild photographic aircraft with the same horsepower, christened *Stars and Stripes*, has been donated to swell our growing invasion fleet. Before we know it, we have a fourth airplane to go with us to the Antarctic, a smaller lighter ship presented by General Aviation. Now we can assault the Pole in mass formation.

I have been placed in charge of the aviation unit, taking Bennett's place, and I am rushing from one factory to another, seeing about special installations and different types of skis, and arranging for all the parts to be catalogued and crated for shipment to the Antarctic. Harold June, a U.S. Navy chief petty officer, joins the expedition in May; he is a first-class pilot and an excellent radio operator and skilled mechanic as well, even-tempered and pleasant in any situation, an invaluable addition to the unit. Also with us now are Dean Smith, a veteran

mail pilot from the New York to Cleveland run, and Captain
Alton Parker, an ex-marine flier, and Captain Ashley McKinley,
a World War I kite-balloonist, to act as aeronautical photographer.

Our expedition is not the only one that is attempting to make
history, or at least headlines, this busy summer of 1928. The
development of long-range aviation has suddenly opened up
new spaces to conquer, and a sort of aerial gold rush is on.
Prospectors of the skies are stampeding in every direction in
hopes of striking it rich over the horizon and bringing home a
pokeful of advertising contracts and publishing rights. Kingsford-Smith in the *Southern Cross* flies 7,300 miles from Oak-
land to Australia. Wiley Post and Harold Gatty come to Teterboro while I am there, and we discuss their proposed flight
around the world. Hubert Wilkins and Carl Ben Eielson, Alaska's leading bush pilot, hedge-hop all the way around the rim of
the Arctic from Point Barrow to Spitsbergen, with a single-
engine Lockheed Vega, exploding once for all Captain Cook's
claims that there was land to the north. Two Italians, Captain
Arturo Ferrarin and Major C. P. del Prete, increase the world's
nonstop distance record to 4,466 miles by flying from Rome to
Brazil. This same summer Bert Hassell and Shorty Cramer set
out from Rockford, Illinois, for Stockholm, Sweden, but wind
up on the Greenland Icecap.*

On June 17th, Amelia Earhart becomes the first woman to
fly across the Atlantic. Byrd has sold her the F-7 trimotor
Fokker which Uncle Tony built for the Antarctic flight, and
she had fitted it with pontoons and named it *Friendship*. With
Wilbur Stultz as her pilot and Louis Gordon as navigator,
she takes off from Trepassey Bay in Newfoundland—and lands
at Burrey Port in Wales the next day. She is a friendly and un-
assuming girl, popular with fliers everywhere, and her slim

---

* Near the very flats where I set up the then northernmost United States Air
Force base at Bluie West 8 in 1941.

build and tousled short blond hair win her the newspaper nick-name of "Lady Lindbergh."

Now also comes word at the beginning of the summer that Umberto Nobile is in Spitsbergen again with another dirigible, the *Italia*. He plans to fly the North Pole alone, evidently for the sole purpose of proving that he can do it without Captain Amundsen. Nobile's nose has been out of joint since he felt he was ignored on the flight of the *Norge,* and he has attacked Amundsen with open spite. Amundsen himself writes, in *My Life As an Explorer,* of the "gross misrepresentations and im-pudent assumptions of Commander Nobile." This is one of the few times I have ever known the gentle old man to speak so forthrightly, but his own integrity forces him to refute Nobile's allegations.

I can imagine the old Viking's sardonic amusement as No-bile sets out on his vainglorious flight. It proves, indeed, to be more vain than glorious. The *Italia* crashes into the polar ice pack north of Spitsbergen, and a world-wide alarm is sounded. Seven nations and twenty-four airplanes join in the hunt for Nobile and his crew. I receive a call from Herbert Bayard Swope of the New York *World,* always alert to cash in on any new headlines, asking me to take the first steamer across the ocean to Sweden, where a tri-motor Junkers is now waiting for me to fly over the ice fields. I point out that it would take me a couple of weeks to get there, and they would save time by finding a pilot already on the spot.

Roald Amundsen is attending a banquet in Oslo, in honor of his good friends Hubert Wilkins and Ben Eielson, when a message is read aloud. The Norwegian government requests him to lead a rescue expedition to find the missing Italians. Despite the slurring attacks that Nobile has made on him, Amundsen is ready. On June 18th, he and my cousin Leif Dietrichson depart from Tromsö in a Latham seaplane to search for Nobile.

A month later Nobile is located by a pilot of the Swedish Air Force, safe on a drifting ice pan north of Spitsbergen. Amundsen does not return. His life has ended, as he wanted it to end, somewhere in the north and the great white silence.

SIX

ANTARCTICA

1928–1930

"10 December 1928. Approaching pack ice, Long. 179° W., Lat. 67° S. Sighted first iceberg, 0815.

Today is gray and gusty, but the sun breaks through the snow squalls sometimes, and glistens on the floating bergs that litter the sea around us. We met the first icy sentinel about eight o'clock this morning. More and still more fragments have been appearing over the horizon since then, brilliant green and turquoise and deep violet as the occasional shafts of sunlight play across them. Now they are marching past us in endless procession, some of them as much as fifty miles long, calved by the great Ross Shelf and borne north by the ocean currents to melt and disappear in the warmer waters we have left behind.

We are nine days out of New Zealand, and our ancient vessel creaks and rolls with the long swells of the South Pacific. Amundsen's old sealer, built in Dundee almost half a century ago and called the *Viking*, now has the imposing name *City of New York* painted on her bow in white letters. She is an old-fashioned three-master, bark-rigged, with square yards on the fore and main masts and one fore-and-aft sail on the mizzenmast. Her stout hull is planked with thirty-four-inch timbers and sheathed with iron-bark to withstand the pressure and steady sawing of the jagged ice cakes.

We are making all possible speed, and our lookouts peer into the swirling snow to warn us if the white periscope of a sunken berg knifes toward us through the waves. We have been losing time, and there is no time to lose. The big Norwegian whaler *C. A. Larsen* is lying off the edge of the pack-ice belt, and we will follow in its wake as it shoves through the frozen barricade to the inner Ross Sea. Beyond this rampart, locked in its own world of eternal glaciers, is the South Pole.

It was this same *C. A. Larsen* which brought us all the way from the United States to New Zealand. She is what the whalers call a "factory ship," a huge ocean-going rendering plant over an eighth of a mile in length, and belongs to a distant cousin of mine named Magnus Konow. The *Larsen* was in the States on her way to the Antarctic whaling grounds, and Magnus offered Commander Byrd free cargo space as far as New Zealand. The lumbering old *City of New York* set out ahead of us, early in August, and we followed on the faster *Larsen* a month later. We put in at San Diego to pick up Commander Byrd, and then Captain Oscar Nilsen set course across the Equator to our southernmost staging point at Dunedin.

There was no sign of the *City of New York* when we arrived at Dunedin on November 5th, so we piled our crated airplanes and sled dogs and supplies on the dock, like a stranded traveler sitting on his suitcases and waiting for the "local train." The factory ship, relieved of its incongruous cargo, steamed south at once to the whaling grounds, accompanied by a small flock of killer ships armed with harpoon guns. In December the blues and finbacks from all the oceans of the world congregate in the Antarctic for the breeding season, more than three million whales. The ships hunt outside the pack ice until it thaws and softens, and then they force their way through the barrier and race each other to the richer plunder that lies on the other side.

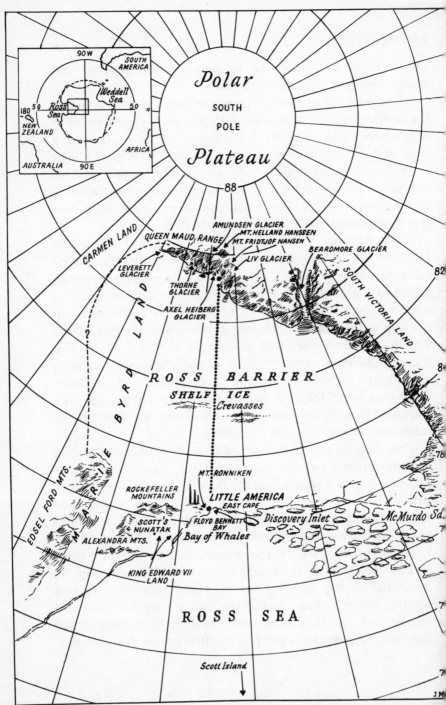

ANTARCTICA, FROM LITTLE AMERICA TO THE SOUTH POLE

This mysterious ring of pack ice, welded together into a solid sinister blockade up to five hundred miles in width, has puzzled oceanographers since it was first discovered in the seventeenth century. Only at this season of the year, in the Antarctic summer, do a few chinks appear in its timeless armor, opening up for a short time only and then sealing tight again. The *Larsen* would have to take advantage of the first break, and she could not afford to delay for us. The success of our whole expedition could depend on our promptly keeping our rendezvous.

Days lengthened into weeks, however, as we waited impatiently on the dock at Dunedin for the *City of New York* to wallow into sight. There was no telling when the pack ice would yield and let the *Larsen* through. The expedition's auxiliary ship, the all-metal *Eleanor Bolling*, showed up on November 18th, but it was not until the 26th that the old *City* came limping into port at last, her crew blistered by the blazing tropical sun and complaining that this was a hell of a way to start a polar expedition. They were expecting a few days of shore leave after three months at sea; but the dock was mountain-high with boxes and crates, and everything had to be stowed aboard the *City* in the shortest possible time.

Now everyone became a stevedore. Fliers and geologists and scientists all pitched in together, their soft hands sprouting blisters and their backs kinked with unaccustomed stooping and heaving. Even Dr. Laurence Gould, second in command of the expedition,* stripped off his shirt and joined the line passing crates from dock to deck. The puffing of steam winches and shriek of pulleys, the rattle of hand trucks up the gangplank, the thump of loads dumped by the swinging cranes into the hold, dinned in our ears all day. By night we were soaked with perspiration and black as the miners at Kings Bay with coaldust.

* In 1958, a college president and chairman of the International Geophysical Year Antarctic Committee.

When the hold was crammed full, we battened down the hatches and started loading the *City*'s decks with canned foods, scientific instruments, clothing, medicines, photographic equipment, dog food, barrels of gasoline, drums of oil, and even several prefabricated houses. All our supplies had to be sorted and repacked to save space, and at least half of them were left behind. Two hundred kegs of chutney sauce, which some bright genius had purchased for the expedition, may be in the warehouse in Dunedin to this day. Our trouble was too much abundance. Every manufacturer in the United States, it seemed, had donated his pet brand of cigarettes or breakfast food in exchange for the coveted slogan "Used on the Byrd Antarctic Expedition," and even Commander Byrd's skill as an organizer could not cope with the problem of fulfilling all his commitments and still staying afloat.

We had another problem: the *City of New York* had to be an expedition within an expedition, a self-sustaining unit able to survive alone in case the thin plates of the *Bolling* should be sprung in the pack ice. In addition to the key personnel and all our supplies, we had to carry the eighty-six sled dogs, each boxed in a separate kennel, ranged in rows on the poop deck and on top of Commander Byrd's cabin. We could not possibly transport all our airplanes on this little 500-ton ship, and after much debate we stowed the Fairchild, the photographic and mapping plane, in two crates between the foremast and mainmast. The Ford and Fokker would be picked up later by the *Bolling*. The fourth gift plane never left Dunedin at all. Every last inch of remaining deck space was taken up with seventy-five tons of spare coal in sacks, and by the time we were ready to depart the overloaded *City of New York* had settled so low that water showed above the Plimsoll line. A trip from bow to stern over the heaped decks was like a mountain-climbing expedition.

Even under full sail, and with our coal-burning steam engine hammering its hardest, the old *City* cannot do more than six or eight knots. Time is essential, so we pick up a line from the faster *Bolling* and she takes us in tow. Our stubby bow smashes hard into the waves, shipping green water with every plunge, and the deck cargo shifts and groans ominously. The lower yard of the mainmast is so close to the top of the crates that we must take a reef in the sail to keep it from sweeping everything overboard. Once a gust of wind bellies out the mainsail and boosts us ahead, and the straining towline slacks and dips into the sea. We swarm over the freight like a bunch of monkeys to haul the canvas up just in time to avoid a rear-end collision with the *Bolling*.

We have been keeping a sharp eye all afternoon for any sign of Scott Island. Somewhere on our course lies this elusive outcropping of rock, called by Captain Robert F. Scott "the loneliest of islands," whose very existence has been doubted by veteran whaling skippers. At five o'clock Sverre Stroem, a giant Norwegian ice pilot who has come from the old country with the vessel, climbs the rigging to the crow's-nest and shades his eyes to scan the horizon. Suddenly we hear his bellow: "Land ho! *Styrbord!*"

A few snowy petrels rise from the water and circle the ship. Now in the distance we can see a weird silhouette, like an elephant's head, rearing out of the sea. Scott Island is the last lone peak of a submerged mountain chain, drowned during prehistoric times, which once connected the Antarctic continent with New Zealand. The bare knob of basaltic rock rises almost perpendicularly, two hundred feet above the ocean. Beyond it is a smaller hump of rock a quarter-mile long, like the back of the elephant, washed with waves. The top of this fantastic monument is snowcapped, and its gray sides swarm with thousands of petrels and sooty shearwaters nesting in the crannies. As we come closer, we can make out patches of brownish green moss around its summit.

We take a long look as we sail on south. This is the last
vegetation we shall see for almost two years.

*"10 December, 0415. Cross Int. Date Line, Long. 180°, Lat.
68° 50' S. Yesterday is today again."*

At dawn we cross the 180th Meridian, so that today is still
the 10th of December; but this December 10th is not like the
other one. The wind has increased in violence, whistling through
the rigging, and the driving snow blots out the sea and the sky.
We pound and pitch on our way between titanic ice chunks,
some of them weighing hundreds of thousands of tons. They are
moving against the wind, only about a fifth exposed, their great
submerged bulks propelled by powerful currents.

Once in a smothering snow flurry the *Bolling* stops short to
avoid a head-on impact with a mountain of ice. Her whistle
fails to warn us, and we race our engine full speed astern to
avoid ramming her. At the same moment our towship starts
forward again, and the steel cable comes hissing out of the
wave tops and parts with an eerie wail. The frayed end lashes
across the *Bolling*'s stern, and the men hurl themselves to the
deck to keep from being beheaded. Two sailors jump over the
side and hang from the rail by their hands, ducking the writh-
ing steel coils. The broken cable runs wildly off the drum and
slips overboard, and now the little *City* is on her own.

Late in the afternoon there is a faint glow in the blue-black
water sky, the shimmer of reflected ice fields, and a call comes
from the crow's-nest: "Pack ice ahead!" Already I can feel the
first cold breath of the frozen world. The blood of my Norwegian ancestors stirs inside me, and I fill my lungs with the keen
freshness. The Malemutes scent it, too, and start howling. Now
we can see from the deck an unbroken white prairie of ice
before us, undulating with the roll of the long swells. Here and
there are small patches of open water, the crushed ice like

streaks of foam, and as the upended slabs grind together the
green sea is forced up between them and sluices down again
over their sides. Deeper inside the pack all motion ceases, and
as far south as we can see it stretches to the horizon in a solid
and silent mass, challenging our advance.

We turn east and grope our way along the outer edge of the
pack, looking for the *Larsen*. The gray sky is thick with snow,
which turns to slush on our slippery decks and quickly freezes.
The *Bolling* has long since been lost to view in the gathering
gloom, and the Magnetic South Pole, six or seven hundred
miles to the west, makes our compass vacillate as much as a
hundred degrees. At last our radio picks up a faint wireless
wave from the whaler, and we set a course in the direction of
the signal. Stroem is perched in the lookout's barrel on the
masthead, and just at evening we hear his booming cry: *"Larsen
dead ahead!"* We round a white slab and glide into an ice-
locked bight just inside the floe. Here the *Bolling* is hove to,
and beyond is the big factory ship.

We have made our rendezvous in time.

*"11 December. Drifting with pack ice. Bolling departs Dunedin,
1100."*

During the past twenty-four hours the ice mass has carried
us back and forth across the International Date Line so many
times that we cannot tell if today is yesterday or tomorrow. I
am not sure without a sextant whether to date this entry in my
diary the 11th or 12th or even 10th again. At least, I know it was
the day before today that we tied up alongside the *Bolling* and
started to transfer coal. All night the bags have been coming
aboard the *City* in slingloads, then to be passed across the
heaped cargo from hand to hand, and dumped below into our
bunkers. The dirty job is finally completed, and at eleven

o'clock this morning the *Bolling* casts off and heads back to Dunedin to pick up the crated Ford and Fokker.

We have caught up with the *Larsen* none too soon. Already the pack ice is softening and spreading, and the other whalers in the area have their steam up, poised to slip through the barricade. Sometimes we can make out the smudges of their funnels on the horizon, vessels from Norway and England and even Japan, all congregated here to hunt in the shadow of the South Pole. Every winter Norway alone sends more than a score of expeditions to the Antarctic, each mother ship with five to seven killer boats; and their crews earn a year's livelihood in the hundred-day hunting season. Twenty-four thousand whales are harvested annually in these waters, producing over two million barrels of oil, valued at 400,000,000 kroner—about $60,000,000. The pelagic industry is a great factor in Norway's economy, producing meat and bone meal and fertilizer and oil for cooking and oleomargarine and even shaving soaps and cosmetics. Sometimes a killer boat strikes it rich by finding a floating nugget of ambergris, worth its weight in gold.

At noon a chaser from the *Larsen*'s fleet, on its way to the hunting grounds, comes alongside the *City of New York* with a message from Captain Nilsen. He has just had word that a sister ship of the *Larsen* is starting through the pack ice to the Ross Sea, and the *Larsen* herself will be getting under way in a couple of days, as soon as she has cleaned up on a pod of blue whales feeding in the area. The chaser's gunner is Captain Jorgensen, another acquaintance of mine. He yells up to me, "Like to come along for the hunt?" I yell back, "Ja, you bet!" and hurdle the *City*'s rail and jump aboard.

This killer boat is a complete unit in itself, with its own galley and living quarters for the captain and a crew of fifteen men, and able to cross the ocean alone. It is built along the sturdy lines of an old Viking ship, 110 feet long, with heavy steel armor reenforced by tons of concrete. Behind the harpooner's platform in the bow is a 30-foot mast, the fishing rod. The fishing line is a half-mile of 12-inch hawser, with a breaking strain of fifty tons, and the leader is a 250-foot length of hard-twist Manila hemp, a kind specially woven for this use by only two companies in the whole world. I think of the tiny Yellow May fly I like to use on the brown trout of the Topdal River, as I look at the whale-fishing hook. The harpoon weighs a hundred pounds, with 2½-foot flukes which will spread open when the line is tightened. Embedded in its point is an explosive charge to detonate inside the whale.

These Norwegian killer boats are wonderfully seaworthy, but they roll worse than anything I have ever been in, doing everything but turning over completely and coming up on the other side. We are making fifteen knots. Occasionally we pass a red blotch floating just under the surface of the water. This is called *krill;* a form of plankton like shrimp, it is the source of all life in the ocean, and amid these patches of *krill* the whales are feeding and occasionally breaching. We pass a pair of *spekkhuggers,* small killer whales, butting and trying to tip over an ice pan on which some gray seals are basking, surprisingly unconcerned. But we are looking for the great blue whale, the *blaahval,* largest creature that lives or has ever lived on earth.

The whalers post themselves along the rail, scanning the sea intently. Suddenly the lookout in the masthead barrel sights a feather of steam off our port bow. *"Babord!"* His shout is chorused by the others: *"Blaast!* There she blows!"

The monster blue sounds as we race toward it, and a sailor in the crow's-nest directs the killer boat in its wake. Captain Jorgensen is standing behind the cocked harpoon gun, peering through the open sight and following the underwater bulge of the cruising whale. I should like to try a shot myself, but only a *skytter* is permitted to do this. Harpooning is a jealously guarded craft in Norway, handed down from generation to generation. Jorgensen's father and grandfather were *skytters* before him, and his own apprentice son stands behind him now, studying every move.

The hundred-ton *blaahval* surfaces again, and Jorgensen maneuvers his gun on its swivel, and fires at a range of thirty yards. As the harpoon head buries itself in the whale's shoulder just above the fluke, its whole back arches and it plunges in a boil of foam. An instant later there is a muffled explosion under water. Now the great blue takes off in headlong terror, dragging us behind. With our 1,000 horsepower engine full astern, still we are being hauled at seven or eight miles an hour through the slush and jagged ice. The whale dives under a floating pan, and we ride right up on top of the ice, our keel carving it in two as we cross the pan and drop into the sea on the other side. Ahead of us looms another floe as big as the killer boat itself. We slam into it full tilt, the boat careens on its side, and one rail goes completely under water. The line streaks out, the wooden drums smoking, and the spring in the belly of the ship contracts and snubs the whale to a halt.

Once more it sounds, staying down for ten minutes. Our winches reel the line back in as we creep up. At last its scoop-shovel snout appears at the surface, shooting up hot vapor mixed with blood, and Jorgensen takes quick aim and sinks home the second harpoon. The whale shudders in a death spasm, exuding blood and oily foam with a final massive sigh, and the water is redder than even the *krill*. We come alongside, and one of the sailors drives a hollow lance into the monster's belly, pumping it with compressed air to keep it afloat. We loop a rope around the tail flukes, and drag the bloated carcass to the *Larsen*.

As I climb a rope-ladder up the blood-streaked side of the *Larsen*, it is hard to realize this is the same trim and clean-smelling factory ship which brought us down to New Zealand. Lengths of blubber hang over the scuppers, and streams of salt water are flushing the half-frozen gore from the decks. Power saws rasp as they cut through the bones of a whale, and the odor rising from the pressure cookers below envelops the whole ship. Above the steady clamor of steam winches resound the screams of skua gulls and shearwaters and albatross, attracted by the refuse that floats astern.

The gate in the *Larsen's* bow is open, and our whale is dragged up the slip way to the flensing deck, which is the size of a football field. Here the fatty overcoat of the whale is scored into strips, which are peeled off by the winches. The strips are dumped into steam vats flush with the deck, the lids are screwed back on, and the blubber is rendered into oil, which later is pumped below into storage tanks. Then the dark red carcass is dragged to the rear deck, the size of a second football field, where slicing knives on winches cut off the meat and bones, which are later cooked for oil and ground up into meal. In less than an hour our hundred-ton *blaahval* has disappeared below the decks, and another blubbery leviathan is riding up the ramp.

That night at supper on the *Larsen*, I enjoy a delicious fresh whale steak, smothered in onions and with beer and *aquavit*, followed by coffee later in Captain Nilsen's cabin. I know that our polar expedition has been a nuisance to him, and the whole crew looks on our scientists and amateur sailors with silent disdain; but there is only the warmest hospitality aboard, and Nilsen's cabin wall is hung with American and Norwegian flags side by side. When the killer boat brings me back to the *City,* I have good news. Tomorrow at midnight the *Larsen* will run the blockade to the Ross Sea.

"15 December. In tow Larsen, proceeding Ross Sea."

Always I like to be high up somewhere, high over everything else, flying above the clouds in an airplane cockpit, or scaling a mountain peak in the wintertime; but here on the *City of New York* the best I can do is the crow's-nest. I climb the mainmast and sit a long while in the lookout's barrel as we force our way mile after mile through the pack ice. The sun is a little lower at midnight, but now in the Antarctic summer it is above the horizon at all times, and the slanting rays tint the snow and sky with lavender and pink and gold.

I take out the little color box I always carry in the pocket of my jacket, wet the paintbrush with my lips, and try to catch the fleeting colors on my sketch pad. Strangely, nothing is white. The floes reflecting the sky fade from cerulean blue to gray, and my brush wipes in some neutral brown to show the patches of water between them. Now comes a towering berg, shoved through the pack ice with irresistible force by the ocean current, and I select some turquoise blue mixed with green for the cleaved side where the berg split off the Ross Glacier. For the sky itself I wash together soft blues and grays and a light olive-brown; and I tip the edge of a cloud with salmon-gold where the sun touches it for a moment. I work fast, because the colors merge together and change more rapidly than I can paint.

We are moving as slowly as a glacier ourselves across the endless plain. The *Larsen* leads our strange procession, thirty-five times the size of the little *City* she is towing, like a great whale with a seal swimming behind. She cannot ram the ice mass at full speed, for fear of crumpling her bow, and so she inches up to a pan cautiously, nudging it until it gives a little, and then surges forward at full speed and shoulders it aside. Sometimes the pans tilt and slide one on top of another, and then topple off again in front of us as we follow in her wake.

Any moment it seems as if the *City* must be crushed like an eggshell. Our helmsman astern is unable to see where he is going, and a sailor on the fo'c's'le and another hanging in the rigging shout directions aft. The momentum of the *City* still

The *Floyd Bennett* emerging from its snow hangar at Little America
in preparation for the South Pole flight.

My friend Stroem and myself (*right*) building the sledge I designed
to carry the survival gear for use in case of a crash landing between
Little America and the Pole.

The survival equipment we took with us on the South Pole flight, against a possible forced landing. The *Floyd Bennett* is in the background.

We are warmly welcomed at Little America on returning from the flight over the South Pole.

carries her forward whenever the *Larsen* halts, and we reverse our engine and dodge right or left to keep from running
underneath her overhanging stern.

In our own wake are the five killer ships, like a file of baby
seals. The path that the *Larsen* has cleared closes again quickly
to only a zigzag line of inky water, and the little boats race
through the ever narrowing lane, bucking their steel bows
against the broken ice and shunting it aside. Behind them the
breach in the fortress mends, and no one can tell that we have
passed through.

The men of the Byrd expedition stand on the deck in little
groups, watching a family of Adélie penguins belly-whop happily on the ice cakes alongside us. Now and then a snowy petrel
appears suddenly out of nowhere like a ghost, so pure white
that only its black eyes and beak are visible against the floes,
and as suddenly is gone again. There is a sense of increasing
tension, and the men shift restlessly from one side of the ship to
the other. Our course is due south along the International Date
Line, and in crossing the deck they go from today to yesterday
and back again. It does not matter, because yesterday and today
and tomorrow are all one in this eternity of ice.

From the crow's-nest I look down on the foreshortened figures of my shipmates. Dr. Larry Gould is lounging at the rail,
his hands rammed in the pockets of his gabardine windbreaker
and a curved pipe clamped in one corner of his mouth, studying
the ice floe with meditative interest. "Taffy" Davies, our chubby
little physicist, crouches in the bow, peering into his gravitome-
ter through thick-lensed glasses. Russell Owen, the newspaper
correspondent, is making notes with his gloved hands on a
crate directly under me, turning out a dispatch for *The New
York Times*, which has purchased the exclusive rights to the
expedition's story. Up on the poop deck "Cyclone" Haines, our
cautious meteorologist, eyes the weather dubiously, unwilling
to commit himself on what it will be like tomorrow. The whim-

pers of the Malemutes change suddenly to eager howls, and I
see Arthur Walden, the veteran dog musher from the Yukon,
start across the deck toward them. His short wiry figure darts
from kennel to kennel as he dishes out a bucket of feed. Our
old sailmaker, Martin Ronne, does not even lift his eyes to
the crashing ice cakes around the ship; he has seen all this before, on his earlier voyages to and from the Antarctic with Captain Amundsen some seventeen years previously.

As for our leader, Commander Byrd, he is not in sight at this
moment, and I imagine that he is probably fully occupied at his
desk, where he spends much time these days. Working alone for
long hours in his cabin on the poop deck, he is starting his new
reminiscences. And he must have much detailed planning to do
on various aspects of the expedition. I wonder idly sometimes
who will be the lucky pilot to fly him over the South Pole. He
has said nothing about it to me, so I have no idea. Of course,
I would like to know him better, but he is too busy to have
much time to talk. Well, there is an old Norwegian saying that
a sailor has no secrets from his mates, and perhaps I shall become better acquainted with him while we are all living together for a year in the isolation of the polar ice.

After we have fought our way through the pack for eight
days, one morning there is a dark band across the sky, the reflection of open water. Martin Ronne glances up for the first
time, and nods in satisfaction. The floes become more scattered,
the ice around us grows mushy, and just before noon we feel
the first gentle swell. The sheer whiteness disappears, and suddenly in its place is the smooth expanse of the Ross Sea. One
of the killer boats races past us in pursuit of a spouting whale,
a white wave curling at its bow. We cast off the *Larsen*'s towline,
and her winches haul it in with an exhaust of steam like a vast
sigh of relief. The big factory ship moves away, accompanied
by her brood of killers, a few hopeful skua gulls wheeling in her
wake.

Now we make our way alone across the Ross Sea toward the Bay of Whales, where we hope to set up our base camp near Amundsen's old site on the Ross Shelf. The excitement grows every hour as we start on the last leg of our long voyage, and the petty squabbles and touches of cabin fever that have developed during four months at sea are forgotten. On December 25th, Taffy Davies finds some absorbent cotton in the ship's pharmacy, and puts on a flowing beard and a red parka the color of his round apple cheeks. His students at McGill University in Montreal would certainly never recognize their staid professor of physics as he ducks his knees and pats his pillow-padded stomach to play the role of Santa Claus at our Christmas party.

The party is never finished. One of the men glances over his shoulder, leaves the group quietly and climbs to the bow. Another joins him, and then another, all staring mutely ahead. Soon the whole expedition has gathered at the bow rail, looking in awe toward the south.

A majestic white precipice rises a sheer hundred feet above the sea, like a Great Wall of China carved in ice. At the water's edge it is honeycombed with caves of grotesque shapes and convolutions, blazing like the facets of a diamond as the light rays explore them. A massive chunk splits off silently and drifts away, and another mile-long iceberg has been calved. In every direction the white silence extends to the horizon, unreal as a lost world in the midnight sunshine, magnificent beyond the ability of man's mind to comprehend.

I enter in my diary: "*25 December, 2400. Off Ross Shelf.*"

The Ross Shelf is a large mass of floating ice, the size and roughly the shape of Texas, five hundred miles across and stretching inland over four hundred miles to the base of the Queen Maud Mountains. The ice mass is advancing slowly, breaking off at the edge, which extends far out over the ocean.

No one knows the width of this vast cantilever apron, or where the sea beneath it ends and the land begins. This is the gateway to Antarctica, the nearest approach by water to the South Pole.

The Antarctic continent is five and a half million square miles in extent, almost twice the size of Europe, almost half as big as all of North America. The icecap that covers it is a million times greater than the floating ice pack at the North Pole. If the temperature in the Antarctic rose 10° C., the melting ice would lift the levels of the world's oceans two hundred feet, inundating all the great coastal cities. Every building in New York less than twenty stories high would be under water, and the Mississippi valley would be flooded.

Antarctica is the world's only uninhabited continent. Its isolated position has made it impossible for mammals to migrate from other continents, and, apparently, no land life except some minute arachnids exists here. A few fossils have been found in coal seams, indicating that once there was a tropical climate; but today its temperatures register lower than in any other spot on earth. At Little America we never recorded higher than 38°, only 6° above freezing, and our scientists figured that in the interior it might drop to 100° below. The sole living things to be seen in this loneliest and coldest of all continents are the seals and sea birds, the whales and the penguins.

The ever present penguins meet us as we jump ashore at Discovery Inlet—little Adélie penguins the size of waddling ducks, and groups of giant Emperor penguins more than half the height of a man. They stand in single file in their stiff white shirts and black Tuxedos, weaving a little and teetering impatiently from one foot to the other, like slightly inebriated dinner guests waiting their turn at the men's room. They show no sign of fear as we walk among them, and they dismiss us with a casual nod, touching beak to breast, and then shuffle off with a Charlie Chaplin shrug. One of the seamen makes the mistake of trying to pick up a big Emperor. There is a blurred tangle of arms and wings, and the sailor is sent reeling by a left jab with one flipper, followed by a stiff right cross with the other. The rest of the penguins flap their flippers together enthusiastically and call for another round, but the seaman has had enough.

We make a reconnaissance trip on skis at Discovery Inlet, but there is no place for our base site here, so the *City of New York* moves on another seventy-five miles along the edge of the Ross Shelf, to the Bay of Whales. This was the location of Framheim, Roald Amundsen's winter quarters sixteen years ago; but to our disappointment the Bay is frozen over from East Cape clear across, four or five miles, and there is no chance to unload directly onto the Shelf. There is a strange sense of violation as we drift outside the silent Bay, a feeling that we are intruding on a past that belongs to Shackleton and Scott and Amundsen himself, all of them now dead. The men line the rail soberly and stare at the icy slope of the Shelf that will be their home for the next fourteen months.

First we must look for a base site, and we hope at the same time to find the site of Framheim. Commander Byrd orders two dog teams made ready, one driven by Arthur Walden and the other by Norman Vaughan, a football player from Harvard and a good outdoor type. Walden in his fur parka, with big wolfskin mitts slung around his neck, is like a picture out of the Klondike gold rush. The teams are wild as timber wolves after being cooped up on the *City*, but Arthur has been handling sled dogs for thirty years. He harnesses his lead dog Chinook at the head of the line, and the old husky steadies his teammates with a low warning growl until Walden gives the command: "Jeech!"

Carl Petersen, our radio operator, is skiing beside Walden's sled, and Byrd rides with Vaughan, while ahead Chris Braathen and I blaze the trail. It feels very good to be ashore at last at what is to be our new home for almost two years. We pick our way across the jumbled bay ice and work up a natural snow ramp to the top of the hundred-foot shelf. The day is overcast, and the haze and complete absence of shadows distort everything as we travel south along the coast. This is the famous polar "white-out," which is so deceptive and tiring to the eyes that it often causes snow blindness and infection. We are looking for Mt. Ronniken, one of Amundsen's landmarks, and suddenly Braathen yells: "There's the peak ahead!" He starts to ski toward it at top speed, but it is only a hummock of snow directly in front of him, no more than shoulder high, which in the tricky light he has mistaken for the mountain. On the other hand, sharp sastrugi before us turn out to be a high-pressure ridge still a mile off.

There are no shadows to warn us, and at any moment we may pitch blindly down a deep crevasse; so we decide to make camp in a little valley. There we roll up in our reindeer bags for the night, the first members of the Byrd expedition to sleep on the Antarctic Continent. Next morning the haze lifts, and we wake to discover that we have camped in an inlet in the Shelf ice, only a little higher than the Bay itself. We climb a gentle slope to the east and come to a plateau surrounded by low hills. This is the ideal location for our base, Byrd decides, with plenty of space for the camp site, easily reached from the Bay and offering easy approaches for a landing field.

It is December 31st, we remember suddenly, and Pete and I prepare a feast on our primus stove of pork and beans, peanut butter, and canned apple sauce for dessert, and we all drink "Skaal!" to the New Year with a cup of hot tea made from snow water. Pete rigs up a bamboo pole as a mast for his antenna and cranks up his four-watt Burgess transmitter, run on dry-cell batteries; and that night we dispatch the first message ever sent from Antarctica. The message is relayed from our ship to the States, and tomorrow's *New York Times* announces in headlines that Commander Byrd has named his base Little America.

Next morning Byrd and Braathen leave with the dog teams for the *City of New York,* while Pete and I remain at the camp waiting for the supplies to start arriving. Now we can relax and explore our new home at the end of the earth. If you stuck a hatpin in the globe at Spitsbergen, and drove it down through the very center, the point would come out here at the Bay of Whales. We reconnoiter the whole area on skis, looking for any relics of Framheim; but there is no sign of Amundsen's old base. We conclude that the Ross Shelf has moved forward through the years, and the exact site has toppled into the sea with the ever advancing ice.

Now comes the first dog team back from the ship, bringing Larry Gould to supervise the building of the camp. He takes charge with that quiet air of authority we have all come to respect, giving orders in a low pleasant voice. He is a born scientist and a natural leader in the field. We set up a full-scale real estate agency on the glacier, allocating lots to the various undertakings. The largest of our prefabricated houses will be our mess hall and sleeping quarters; and we dig a five-foot-deep excavation in the hard-packed snow and sink the frame to keep it from blowing away. Here in the Antarctic the winds build to gale proportions in a matter of minutes, drifting the snow and burying everything from sight. If you leave anything lying around, you mark it immediately with a pole, or you will never find it again.

Soon a small town is growing up around us. The administration building, where Commander Byrd will have his quarters, is located two hundred yards from the mess hall, so that our whole camp will not be wiped out in case of fire. This is one of the greatest perils of a polar expedition, for a conflagration would be the end of everything, surely. We dig a snow tunnel to get from one building to the other, and line the walls with food boxes to shore them up and at the same time give easy access to our supplies. We also build storage rooms, as annexes to the tunnel; these are made of snow blocks and covered with flat tarpaulins so that the driving snow will not collect more deeply than necessary on top. After the first blizzard the whole camp disappears from sight, and the only things sticking out of the drifts are the smokestacks of the houses and our three radio towers, which will keep our base in constant communication with the outside world.

Our crated Fairchild has been unloaded from the *City,* and we assemble it on the bay ice. Taking it up for a test hop, I have my first look at Antarctica from the air. I can see the Bay of Whales cutting deeply into the frozen expanse of the Ross Ice Barrier. The ice of the Barrier everywhere reveals evidences of constant change and movement. I can see pressure rolls building up, and whole sections of ice forced up over adjacent areas with a vast sliding motion. Definitely, our camp is not in a stationary spot—changes are taking place all the time which will greatly influence the shape of the Bay of Whales.

I shuttle the Fairchild to our new landing field, a natural plateau conveniently located just north of the camp housing. On January 27th, Cyclone Haines, our meteorologist, announces in his guarded manner that he guesses the weather's about as good as we're likely to get, and we make our initial exploratory flight.

I am in the pilot's seat, and Harold June is sitting on a folded sleeping bag in the rear cabin, operating the radio. Commander Byrd is in the middle of the plane with his navigating equipment, sun compass and drift indicator. Even on a short flight we must carry seven hundred pounds of emergency equipment, enough to last for six weeks in case we have to sit down anywhere away from base.

We take off eastward from the Bay of Whales, following the

edge of the Ross Shelf. About a hundred miles east of Little America, we pass over Scott's Nunatak, a dark mass of rock thrusting up some 1,200 feet above the ice. Ahead of us on the horizon are the Alexandra Mountains, which Scott reported in 1902. Beyond them are the gray outlines of King Edward VII Land, looking as though it might be a number of islands joined together by the sea ice.

We run into a snow squall, and as we have no de-icing equipment on our plane, we alter course to the south, dodging the overcast. I call Commander Byrd's attention to a group of high mountains looming on the horizon. A total of fourteen peaks are sticking up through the ice, with here and there a bare ledge exposed, and the bulging snow traces the lines of their buried ridges. No human eye has ever seen this range before. Byrd names it the Rockefeller Mountains, in honor of John D. Rockefeller, Jr., one of the chief contributors to the expedition.

On our way back to Little America, we find a welcome sight. The *Eleanor Bolling* has made its way unaided through the pack ice and is tied up beside the *City of New York*. Aboard her are our two longer-range planes, the Fokker and the tri-motored Ford in which we will attempt the flight across the Pole.

The ice in the Bay of Wales is breaking up fast, and to save time we decide to take a chance and unload the planes directly onto the Shelf. There is a low spot in the overhanging glacier, only four or five miles from camp, and the *Bolling*'s sharp steel prow chips off a hundred and fifty yards of bay ice and carves herself a wharf in the ice foot, only fifty feet from the Barrier itself. Deadmen are sunk into the top of the sloping glacier, and with a block and tackle operated by the ship's winch we haul the sections of the Fokker safely to the top of the Shelf.

We do not know that the edge of the Shelf where we are working is hanging by a delicate thread. At nine o'clock this morning the sections of the Ford have been unloaded onto the ice foot, and as one of the mechanics is starting up the slope, he sees a crack appear suddenly between his feet. He jumps, and as the rest of us scramble for safety at his warning cry, the whole slope slides ponderously into the sea, carrying part of the Shelf with it. Below us, our ice wharf splits apart and sinks before our eyes.

To our consternation, we now see the center section of the Ford's wing lying on a floating ice fragment, entirely surrounded by a slowly widening belt of black water. The floe tilts more and more as it drifts toward the bay, threatening to slide the precious piece of wing into the sea. We bridge the gap between the floes with planks ripped from the airplane crates, crossing by these treacherous gangplanks to the bobbing cake, where we hook a block and tackle to the center section. It is swung back onto the ship in the nick of time.

Now we work without rest to get the Ford ashore before any more of the Shelf collapses. The *Bolling* moves to a new position, so close that its superstructure scrapes off little chunks of the overhanging ice as it rises and falls with the swells. The *City of New York* is tied alongside, lashed by ropes to the *Bolling*'s outer rail, and both crews unite in a desperate race with the glacier. Two sets of blocks and tackles are working at top speed, and at last we hoist the Ford's heavy fuselage to a secure place on the Shelf. Only a few crates of supplies remain to be unloaded.

About seven o'clock that night, just after supper, I am on my way up from the fo'c's'le to the *City*'s deck. There is a deafening roar like a salvo of cannons and before me I see the keel of the *Bolling* roll up out of the sea. At the peak of her heeling, her mast and bridge rest against the Shelf, and only the straining hawsers attached to the *City* keep her from turning turtle.

Hundreds of tons of ice from the disintegrating glacier have cascaded onto the deck of the *Bolling*. They spill into the sea as the big ship cants over, and, relieved of their weight, she slowly rights herself again. All around us the Bay is boiling, and huge chunks of the shattered glacier come shooting up out of the maelstrom. High on the broken edge of the Shelf, one of the meteorologists is clinging to a rope, his feet kicking in the air forty feet above the churning sea. Another member of the crew, one of the mechanics, is floundering in the water, trying to climb onto a slippery ice cake. He cannot swim, and Commander Byrd yanks off his coat and dashes to the taffrail to dive overboard after him. Some of the men try to restrain him, but he tears loose and jumps overboard anyway.

No one can survive more than a few minutes in the ice-filled brine, and a sailor from the *Bolling* vaults the rail into the water, grabs a floating plank, and starts paddling toward Byrd. We have lowered a lifeboat from the *City*, and in the excitement everybody tries to crowd in. One of the party fears the overloaded boat is in danger of capsizing, and he in turn jumps overboard. Now we have four men in the water, and another still dangling in space from the edge of the Shelf.

The meteorologist is hauled up by helping hands, and one by one we fish the new members of the Polar Bear Club out of the water, none the worse for their frigid dunking. They are taken to warm quarters below, stripped and rubbed down with brandy, and what is left in the bottle they drink. We take a hasty count of personnel, and discover that miraculously nobody has been lost. Taffy Davies glances at the shattered glacier's edge and remarks thoughtfully: "This kind of thing could discourage immigration down here."

Late in February the *Bolling* and the *City* finish the unloading and depart with ill concealed delight for the more tranquil waters of New Zealand. The last of the whalers has steamed for home, and the wall of pack ice has sealed tight behind them. Our base camp is the only human habitation within the entire Antarctic Circle.

One thing has been worrying Larry Gould, and that is how

to make a geological survey of the Rockefeller Mountains. Their discovery has presented him with an unexpected new area to explore, and there is no way to fit another trip into next summer's crowded program. He would like to visit the range this fall, before the Antarctic darkness ends all our flying activities. The Ford has already been stored in a snow-block hangar for the winter, but the Fokker is assembled and has been test-hopped. Byrd agrees that if we hit a spell of fair weather Gould may make the flight.

On March 7th when I get back to Little America from a twenty-five-mile ski trip, Gould is waving to me at the end of the strip. Cyclone Haines has figured out that the weather probably won't get much better than it is, so he guesses we might as well start now as any time. I grab a bite, throw my rucksack into the Fokker and climb in after it. Harold June comes along again as radio operator, and Larry Gould sits in the rear of the plane, gripping his theodolite between his knees.

We have a rough take-off from Little America, because a recent blow has left the field like a corduroy road with ribbed sastrugi. I set a course east for the Rockefeller Mountains, about a hundred and forty miles away, and climb to 8,000 feet and ride on top of a solid undercast. It is breaking up as we reach the range, and I come down through a hole in the clouds and find a good 3,000-foot ceiling underneath. There is a patch of blue ice at the southern end of the range, a frozen lake formed in the summer by melting water; and in this blank white world it is good to have any color to judge height and distance. June drops a couple of smoke flares, to give me wind direction, and I turn and come in for a landing on the blue ice patch. I hear a funny ticking on the plane's skis and I look down and find they are grazing the slope of a hill. I flare out and sit down, and taxi to the northern shore of the lake.

Our landing place is about two miles from the Rockefeller

Range. The snow is packed as hard as a bone and littered with fist-size boulders, blown here by the wind. It is a disturbing omen of what these mountain gales can be like. We sink dead-men in the snow, rope the plane securely, and stretch our tent under the left wing tip, fastening some of the guy lines to the skis and landing gear.

After a good night's sleep the three of us climb over gentle ice and snow slopes up to the 1,200- and 1,000-foot summits of the two nearest peaks, and by forward triangulation determine the positions of the rest of the group. I make some quick sketches to support Larry Gould's triangulations. The wind is starting to blow hard, but this afternoon we find a patch of exposed rock, and Larry chips off a fragment. He shakes his head. It is nothing but granite, nothing to give him even a glimpse into the geological history of the Antarctic.

The following morning the wind is blowing too hard for Gould to resume his explorations, and so we stay in our sleeping bags, enjoying a luxury breakfast in bed cooked over our primus stove. The canvas strains and balloons with each gust, and we glance at one another with a sense of foreboding. Shortly before noon there is a sharp report like a .22 rifle. The two guy lines attached to the landing gear have snapped, as the plane heaves with the wind, ripping a hole in the tent. We scramble out and shovel frantically to pile snow on the skis and weight them down so that the plane will not slide any farther. The wind increases, and the Fokker starts moving again. Gould jumps onto one of the skis, and June stands on the other, as I pile on more snow to hold them. As soon as there is a little lull, we cut snow blocks and pile them around the landing gear, and I make another deadman out of one of our skis and secure the plane a little better.

We try to assure ourselves that the worst is over; but about three o'clock the wind starts up harder than ever, and the plane lurches once more. Now the wind is so strong we can barely stand up against it. I fight my way inside the plane, and glance at the air-speed indicator. It is registering a steady 60 miles an hour, with gusts up to 90. One of them lifts the left wing, and the whole plane quivers and seems about to take off.

While June and I hang on for dear life, Gould gets a ball of heavy silk mountaineering line from the grub chest, throws it over the wing tip, and flings himself to the ground, tugging at the line with both hands. June makes a second loop with the line and holds on, while I start shoveling snow once more to strengthen the wall around the ship. It is all I can do to grip the handle, because the wind is blowing the shovel blade around like a kite. Right now I think we could use a log chain for a wind sock.

We battle the wind for three seemingly endless hours. The blowing snow stabs into our faces like needles; the air is so thick with it that I can hardly see as far as my hand. Gould and June, lying flat on the ground and hanging to the lines, are numb with cold. At last I have piled enough snow blocks so that our buried skis will hold the plane; but there is no way of telling whether the wind will increase even more during the night. We agree that the only safe thing is to take everything out of the plane and dig it down in the snow, out of reach of the gale. We remove the radio receiver, but cannot dismantle the transmitter. Now if anything happens we shall be unable to send a message.

Our tent is a shambles when we crawl inside. Snow has been driven through the large rips in the canvas where the guy lines tore loose, and our food and sleeping bags are almost buried. The temperature has risen, along with the wind, and the melting snow has soaked everything. We repair the torn canvas with safety pins, scoop out the slush, and creep inside our bags, soaked with sweat, to wait the storm out.

It is not very comfortable waiting, that is sure. For two days we lie in our clammy sacks, while the barometer climbs hope-

fully and then drops to the bottom of the glass, the lowest
readings I have ever seen. Anywhere else at least a cyclone
would be coming. Once or twice the wind slacks off enough for
us to attempt a take-off, but our radio picks up a message from
Little America that they have snow and zero-zero conditions
there; and by the time their weather lifts, our wind is building
up again. We can see it coming down the mountain side, like
puffs of smoke foreboding another big blow, and the propeller
blades of the anchored Fokker turn slowly around as the air-
speed indicator in the cockpit registers over a hundred miles
an hour. After that, none of us enters the plane any more.

That night the snow is starting to erode around the block
wall. We try to repair it as best we can, but now we cannot
even stand on our feet outside. I notice that the propeller is
whirling so fast that I cannot follow the blades with my eye,
and I calculate that with a cold engine the speed of the gusts at
this time must be in excess of two hundred miles an hour.
There is nothing to do but crawl inside the tent and take it.

Along about midnight there comes a far-off moaning, building to a roar like an approaching express train, down the
mountain and across the snow toward us. It hits with the boom
of an artillery shell landing, and then everything is dead quiet.
I sit up in my sleeping bag and look through a slit in the snow
blocks we have piled around the tent. Where the outline of the
Fokker's wing was above our tent, now there is only empty
space.

"It's gone!" I say to Gould and June, and they both reply
wearily, "Oh, the hell with it!" and we lie back in our reindeer
bags and go to sleep.

The hurricane is still howling next morning as I start for
the wreck, a couple of miles downwind. A sixty-mile blast knocks
me off my feet, and from then on I proceed to the plane at a
rapid clip, on the flat of my back. I manage to brake myself
with my ski pole and sheath knife and stop beside the plane.

Right away I can see that Uncle Tony's handsome bird will
never fly again. The gale lifted it vertically out of the cradle of
snow blocks, and flew it right side up, but backward, all the
way. The landing gear crumpled forward when it struck the
hard snow, and the whirling propellers hit the skis and curled
up in the shape of tulips. Worst of all, the generator-transmitter
in the ship has been ruined, and there is no way to send word
to Little America of our disaster.

Immediately I begin thinking of the serious consequences
this loss can have if by any misadventure our other long-dis-
tance plane, the Ford, should be forced down south of the
Queen Maud Range during our flight to the South Pole. We
have been counting on the Fokker for support of the other
parties in the field or if a rescue attempt from the polar plateau
should be necessary. We no longer have a long-range plane in
reserve to take off the Ford's crew in case of a crash landing
south of the towering ice barriers which would bar the way to
the lighter and shorter-range Fairchild.

Throughout the day we hear our friends at Little America
vainly calling us on the radio. They cannot understand why we
do not answer, and they want to know the reason. During the
afternoon we pick up a more urgent message: "Explain your
silence." In the evening they send another message: "If we do
not hear from you tomorrow, search parties will set out at
once." We shut the radio off, because there is no more use
listening. We have no idea how long it will take the dog teams
to find us. We have enough food to last a month, at least, and
fortunately the gas tanks in the Fokker were not broken, so
there is fuel to keep us warm.

The dismal days drag by at our makeshift camp. Were I
alone, I feel sure that I could make it back to Little America
overland without too much trouble. The distance is about 140
miles, and I am used to making fifty miles a day or more on my

skis. Neither of my companions has had any practice in skiing, however, and naturally I cannot think of leaving them.

A week later Larry Gould is working down at the wreck, retrieving some scientific instruments, and June and I are inside the tent cooking a pemmican stew. The plumber's stove is sputtering so loudly that we fail to hear the drone of the airplane engine overhead. Not until it has landed do we see that clear weather has finally brought the Fairchild, with Dean Smith at the controls and Commander Byrd himself a member of the rescue party. Later Russ Owen tells me that back at Little America, Byrd was beside himself with anxiety when no word came from us. "If they are lost, my work is done," he kept saying, "and the public will never forget it, either." Before take-off, Owen says, he sat swinging his helmet between his knees and staring morosely at the floor. "Is there no end to it?" he exclaimed. "I have had almost more than a man can bear."

They circled the wreck and spotted Larry Gould alone, and at first they thought the rest of us had perished in the crash. Commander Byrd's face is white as he steps out, and we can see how greatly relieved he is that all of us are there, hale and hearty. He takes his sleeping bag out of the plane, walks a little ways off, folds the bag carefully, and places it on the snow. There he kneels in prayer with his back to us. After a few moments he rises again and comes back, and we begin to load the rescue plane.

On April 17th we see the sun for the last time, a thin painted fingernail that scratches the northern horizon for a few minutes and then is gone, not to appear again until the end of August. Now Little America settles down for the long winter wait. The men start growing whiskers according to their own ideas of how an Antarctic explorer should look, the chins of the youngsters sprouting peach fuzz in assorted pastel shades, and the older men cultivating Dundrearys and black spade beards and pointed Vandykes. Gummy, the cook, is the envy of the camp with his flaming red beard that looks like the rear end of a mandrill. A few of the smart ones remain clean-shaven, for a man's breath in sub-zero cold will frost the whiskers and irritate his face.

We are entombed in a glacier at the bottom of the world, in a total silence broken only by the occasional rumble of an ice-quake as the Ross Shelf shifts and settles. Most of the life in camp is under the snow. The men pop corn over the stoves in their barracks, and play endless games of cribbage and poker with different colored beans for chips. They scrounge bits of material, robbing one another like a colony of pack rats, to make pipe stands and bookshelves over their bunks. Old Martin Ronne is busy at his sewing machine day after day, stitching parkas and sleeping-bag covers, and we work out together a new type of barren-land shelter.* One of the scientists brings Ronne a sensational pattern he has just invented for a trail mask, with slits for eyes. Ronne inspects his design, and shrugs: "*Ja,* I make one like that for Captain Amundsen once. He said no good."

We show movies now and then to pass the time, and every Saturday night we have a two-way broadcast with the United States, in which the men can talk directly with their families and friends at home. I have no relatives in the States to say hello, and one night a chorus girl from the Ziegfeld Follies in New York takes pity on me. To my surprise a message comes to me on the loud-speaker, and the State-side radio operator reads in a mocking voice: " 'Hello, big boy, I been noticing you never get no messages from nobody, so here's one from me. If you and I was down there together, baby, we'd melt a hole right through the ice.' " I answer that I hope to see her when I get to New York, but I never get her name.

---

* It came to be called the Balchen-Ronne tent, and was used by the United States Army in Greenland during World War II.

June 21st is midwinter in the Antarctic, and the men celebrate by putting on a musical show. There is a husky chorus
line in ballet skirts, with rolled-up wool socks stuffed inside
their shirts for bosoms, and platinum-blond wigs made of frayed
rope. Sverre Stroem pumps his accordion, and the doctor prescribes liberal doses of medicinal spirits for everybody from his
pharmacy, and later that night we wind up at Blubberheim.
This is Arthur Walden's hut, made from the crate which con-
tained the two outboard engines for the Ford, and heated with
a blubber-burning stove. It is only ten feet square, but now
twenty-two men crowd inside, singing and clinking cups to the
turning point of the winter.

After this party some of us have a little trouble finding our
way back to our barracks, and one of the mechanics never
makes it at all. He is deathly afraid of dogs, but in his present
condition all he worries about is a place to sleep, so he crawls
right into a kennel with Walden's fiercest husky. Next morning
we find the husky curled on the snow outside, and the mechanic
in the kennel on his hands and knees, yelling for help. His
whiskered face appears in the kennel opening for a moment,
and ducks back hurriedly as the dog bristles and growls.

"Somebody get this ferocious sonovabitch away," he pleads,
"or I'll be in here all winter!"

It is too stormy to go outside now, so for exercise Sverre
Stroem and I lace on the big gloves and spar a few rounds each
day in what I think must be the world's coldest gymnasium.
Stroem, an amateur boxer in Norway, is a well-set-up six-footer.
We put on exhibition bouts to entertain the men, and I instruct
some of them in self-defense. Commander Byrd works out every
day alone, keeping in condition with weight lifting and routine
calisthenics. At Annapolis he was on the acrobatic team; and
now, to demonstrate his agility, he challenges Stroem to Indian
wrestling, foot to foot. Stroem flexes his big muscles just once,
and Byrd goes flying head over heels and gashes his forehead

on the stove. Stroem is very upset, apologizing and wriggling like an overgrown boy.

Members of all polar expeditions are inevitably subjected to environmental conditions vastly different from those they have been accustomed to enjoying in civilization. During the winter night, these unnatural conditions—the eternal cold, the darkness, the high winds, and enforced confinement in austere and fairly cramped quarters—naturally exert a certain depressing effect on the men of an expedition, and occasional tensions and unrest tend to arise among them. In such conditions, and with the general lack of privacy, each man's true self will invariably emerge and stand revealed to his companions. There is no doubt that the type of man best fitted for a wintering party in polar regions is the man who is not only physically fit, but also even-tempered, with inner intellectual resources, and not overly sensitive.

Splendidly equipped and manned as it is, our expedition is not exempt from these psychological pressures from the environment, and everything is done to offset their effects as much as possible. For this purpose, it is of the utmost importance, during such a stay, that a work schedule be set up in such a way that every member of the party has a certain amount of work to perform daily. At Little America this system is used to good effect. Larry Gould, the second in command, has the task of delegating many of the camp chores. These go to different men each day, so that no one has an undue amount of the more unpleasant work, such as dishwashing, snow shoveling, and cleaning of latrines. Our day usually starts with Larry, who bunks next to me, and myself, getting up at seven o'clock in the morning and calling the rest of the men in our barracks. Breakfast is at eight and then the camp work day begins, except for those who have been on night duty. A list has been posted the day before assigning the chores for the day. In these assignments, everyone is in-

cluded; even Commander Byrd cheerfully takes his turn at
washing dishes and setting tables. I might add that it is no
small job to wash dishes for, or wait on, forty-odd hungry men,
especially when that is not your regular trade. However, this
system has the effect of helping keep all members of the expedition psychologically and physically occupied. This somewhat
lessens the tensions.

In addition, of course, each of the scientists and technicians
has his own specialized work to do—meteorology, physics, glaciology, radio communications, and so on. In our spare time during the winter darkness, many of us study. I have brought with
me the latest literature on aerodynamics and mathematics,
which I use in available hours to brush up for my eventual return to my work as test pilot in the States.

On August 24th we have a few minutes of daylight, and now
spring comes fast to the Antarctic. The northern horizon grows
redder, and one day, at high noon, a shaft of sunlight comes
streaming across the snow, turning the sastrugi purple-blue and
gilding the lower sides of scattered clouds in the cold turquoise
sky. At last the time has come to make ready for the grand
climax of the expedition.

During the winter I have been working on the performance
computations of the Ford for the polar hop. I have rechecked
them in detail with the previous performance tests, made up my
fuel consumption curves, and determined which revolution and
power settings will be needed for the various stages of the flight.
The total weight of the plane, counting fuel and crew and all
our equipment, should be in the neighborhood of 15,000
pounds—twice the weight for which the commercial model,
with its smaller engine, is certified. No less than 1,400 pounds
of this overload will consist of the essential survival gear and
supplies for use in case we run into bad luck and are forced
down on the ice. In addition to tents, sleeping bags, and extra

clothing, we must load into the plane enough emergency food
supplies to last for forty-five days if necessary. This would be
far from an excessive amount in the event of a forced landing
on the high, glacier-rimmed polar plateau. It represents, however, the maximum weight that four men could expect to haul
by their own efforts if they were forced to hike back. As a means
of transporting the emergency gear and rations in the event of
disaster, the plane will carry a light but rugged hand sled that
I have designed especially for a party of men to drag over the
ice. It is just about the worst method of traveling there is—
man-hauling your own supplies.

Now we start working on the Ford in the snow-hangar. We
change the gasoline system to a central collector type, with
fuel lines leading to all the tanks—five in the wings and one
126-gallon tank in the fuselage—which can be refilled by hand
with 5-gallon cans. With this central system we can pump the
fuel into any wing tank we desire by means of wobble-pumps
located next to the pilot's seat. A glass-tube gauge measures the
exact amount of fuel in each tank at all times. I have completely
reworked this system during the winter, considerably simplify-
ing it from the factory design. The outside temperature is still
thirty or forty below, and every time we touch the frozen metal
it peels the skin from our fingertips. We fire up the big blubber
stove until the hangar is reasonably warm, and use blowtorches
as close as we dare to the engine, so we can work with our bare
hands.

On the fourth of November, Dr. Larry Gould and a six-
man party, traveling with a total of forty-two sled dogs, take
their final departure from Little America for a 450-mile journey of exploration southward to the Queen Maud Mountains.
The main purposes of this overland geological expedition are
four: first, Gould and his men will establish a series of depots
along a line pointing from Little America toward the Axel
Heiberg Glacier, at the foot of the massive Queen Maud Range.

Meanwhile, at the foot of the Glacier, supplies and gasoline will be landed by plane from Little America.

In addition, from their position between Little America and the Pole, the geological party can give the plane crew the weather conditions at the mountain range itself, the most critical point of the whole flight.

A third important assignment for the geological party, after they have set up their line of caches, is to stand ready, during the flight to the Pole and back, to act as an emergency rescue team in the event of a forced landing. The abrupt termination of its radio tone will serve as the signal that the plane has landed on the ice. Should this happen on the polar plateau, the geologists will attempt to take dog sledges up the Axel Heiberg Glacier, as Amundsen did on his push to the Pole. Then, pushing on across the plateau, they will leave another emergency food cache for the fliers at the southern end of Mt. Helland Hanssen, between the Queen Maud Mountains and the Pole.

The first party to reach either this cache or the one at the foot of the Glacier will leave word there as to its further plans. In this way, there is a remote chance that if the worst happens and the *Floyd Bennett* is forced down on the high polar plateau a rescue can be effected by dog sledge, though it will inevitably be a desperate attempt.

Finally, quite apart from their operations in support of the South Pole flight, Gould and his geologists are responsible for an important and extensive program of exploration and surveying. They will work eastward along the Queen Maud Range and into the virtually unknown Carmen Land area adjoining it. They plan to remain in the field, in all, close to three months.

On the same day that we see the Gould party off from Little America, all hands turn to and begin to dig out the Ford from its winter cocoon of snow, in preparation for the polar flight. The wing sections are still on the sleds, just as they were hauled from the Bay of Whales, but buried now under eight-foot snow-drifts. We shovel them free and lift them onto empty gas drums. With blowtorches, working under a tarpaulin, we melt the snow inside the wingtips. Then we bolt the wings to the fuse-lage. To get the plane out of its frozen prison, we dig an incline from the snow revetment in which it lies, and I start up the center engine. The power of the big Cyclone pulls it up the ramp without difficulty, and I taxi it to its parking place beside the take-off strip.

Now, from a design I have made during the winter, based on my experience in the Royal Norwegian Air Force, we build a shelter on runners—a framework of two-by-fours covered with tarpaulins, with a workbench and vise in the rear. This shelter we slide on the runners over the nose of the *Floyd Bennett* and cover the engines: it is high enough for us to turn the propellers inside. The door is closed, and the shelter is heated with blow-torches so that we can work on the engines with our bare hands. In the Norwegian Air Force we have always called this type of shelter a "Noah's Ark"; and soon everybody here uses that name.

Working inside the Ark, in a few days I have all the engines tuned smoothly. Now I take the big trimotor up for its first hop, making load and speed and fuel consumption tests, and find that all my earlier computations are correct. The *Floyd Bennett* is ready for a depot-laying flight to help establish the emergency cache of food and gasoline at the foot of the Queen Maud Range.

Byrd has not yet announced who will fly him to the Pole, but it is generally assumed that the honor will go to Dean Smith. The choice of Smith as the pilot on the depot-laying flight is now anounced. Harold June will be his copilot and I am to remain in camp.

The *Floyd Bennett* takes off on schedule with Byrd, Smith, June and Captain Ashley McKinley on board. Some hours later they report by radio that they have set up the cache and are returning, and at seven o'clock in the evening, that they are passing a crevassed area about a hundred miles from Little America. When they fail to arrive, I warm up the Fairchild and set out in search, keeping in constant radio contact with Little America in case they get any further news of the long overdue Ford. At the very edge of the crevasses, I sight a black patch on the snow, and land beside them. They are unharmed, but their tanks are bone-dry, and it is good that I have brought an extra hundred gallons of gasoline for just such an emergency. After they have refueled I offer to give them a hand to get their engines started; but they insist that they can take care of this themselves, and so I head back to Little America.

Still the Ford does not show up. We wait all day, puzzled, and at night Carl Petersen and I take off again, carrying more gas and also repair tools in case there has been an accident. They are still in the same place, unable to start the engines and so busy trying to get to the bottom of the trouble, that they barely speak to me when I arrive. We put on the heaters, and in less than an hour all three engines are turning smoothly. Commander Byrd and the others pile into the Ford and take off so fast that Pete, who is working inside the tent, doesn't even hear them leave. We pick up the gear left on the snow, jam everything into our little Fairchild, and rejoin them at Little America long after midnight.

Next morning, with the air of someone who has important business on his mind, Byrd takes me for a walk. He is still concerned about last night, I can see, and he demands to know why their fuel consumption was higher than expected. I reply that I cannot give the answer immediately. Since the flight tests before the depot-laying trip bore out the correctness of my computations, perhaps the trouble was that the mixture was not leaned properly. I am still confident of the accuracy of our test results. However, I promise Byrd that to make doubly certain, we will again go over the *Floyd Bennett's* entire fuel system and recheck the engines completely. Obviously, if there is anything wrong it must be eliminated before undertaking the South Pole flight.

"I am going to assure both you and whomever is piloting that plane," I tell Byrd, "that our figures are right, before the *Floyd Bennett* takes off."

Byrd pauses and then raises another big question that is bothering him. Why, he wants to know, were the pilots not able to get the engines started last night? For that I can offer no explanation except the obvious one that the motors have to be heated properly before being cranked up.

Byrd keeps on walking, his lips firm, his expression thoughtful. Then he turns to me, and some of the strain seems to have left his face.

"All right," he says, "get started right away with those fuel and engine checkups—just to make sure." I sense that the conference is over, and we turn back toward the barracks. "Oh, and by the way," he adds, "I'll want you to pilot the plane. You will fly to the South Pole with me."

At last I can keep my promise to Floyd Bennett.

"28 November, 1929. Weather okay, preparing polar take-off."

This is Thanksgiving Day, and it is a special Thanksgiving for sure. Last night we received a radio message from Larry Gould, on the dog trail a hundred miles from the Queen Maud Range, reporting that weather conditions in that general area are ideal. Cyclone Haines weighs Gould's information, watches a couple of weather balloons dwindle to pinpoints in the sky, takes a reading on his barograph, wets his finger in the wind, and give his official verdict at noon. The weather may be better or it may be worse, but he guesses that right now it is about as good as it probably ever will be. So we will either make it or not.

Now the final arrangements get under way. The mechanics check and recheck every inch of the Ford from nose to tail. An exact setting is made on the plane's chronometer, against a time-tick broadcast from the United States. Everyone in camp wants to be in on the take-off, and a volunteer ground crew forms a bucket line, passing 5-gallon cans of fuel to other volunteers on the wing who top off the tanks. Another group of eager helpers feeds a steady stream of equipment into the plane, every item carefully counted and weighed. At the last minute Byrd decides to add two 150-pound sacks of food, as a still further precaution, and now we are carrying more weight than planned.

The three engines have been run up, and the rest of the crew boards the *Floyd Bennett*. Harold June sits beside me on the right as copilot and radio man; Captain Ashley McKinley is in his position as photographer; and Byrd will be navigator and flight leader. Shortly after three o'clock he comes out of his headquarters in a big fur cap and parka and polar bear pants, poses a moment beside the plane as the movie cameras grind, and waves to the crowd. The door slams behind him, and I rev up the engines.

The skis jerk loose, and the heavy plane slides forward over the snow. I taxi in a wide circle and up a little incline at the end of the flying strip to get full advantage of the slope. I look back at Byrd. He nods, and I give it the gun.

"28 November. Take-off, 1529, heading due south, wind ESE."

The plane hesitates a moment, pointing eastward into the eighteen-mile wind, and I flip the rudder to break the skis loose. A few seconds later the tail ski is off the snow. I nose up, quickly gaining altitude. The weather is clear and ideal, and after a few minutes we pick up Gould's dog-trail, a tiny scratch in the snow, and follow along its meridian, at that point 143° 45′ W. We pass his 20-mile food depot, then the 44-mile depot. We have climbed steadily to 1,500 feet, heading for the South Pole.

Hour after hour the ribbed expanse of the great Ross Shelf rolls under us. Byrd has spread Amundsen's old charts on his navigator's table, and we are looking down on the sledge-route he blazed, doing ninety miles an hour where he made twenty-five miles on his best day. I take my pocket slide rule from its worn leather case, and make a quick check. Our dead reckoning figures correctly. Everything is right on the nose.

Three hours and forty-five minutes out of Little America, we sight some dark specks on the Shelf ahead. It is Gould's survey and support party, waving to us as we roar overhead. We drop some chocolate and cigarettes, and a few messages which have come into camp since they left twenty-four days ago. We have flown the first transocean mail, I reflect, and now we are pioneering the airmail service in Antarctica.

"28 November. Sight Queen Maud Range, 2050. Climbing full throttle."

Soon the Queen Maud Mountains loom ahead, ranked in stately file against the horizon; here and there the brilliant blue flash of glacial ice lights dark gaps in the range. It is a land of a million years ago, right out of the ice age. June, with his earphones strapped to his helmet by a long cord, moves fast to empty the last of the 5-gallon cans of gas into the fuselage tank, and drop the empty tins through the trapdoor. A pound of weight less could make the difference over the Hump. McKinley adjusts his big mapping camera, ready to aim it to port or starboard.

The engines have been operating at cruising speed, 1,580 r.p.m. for the center Cyclone and 1,600 for the outboards. I hope the big Cyclone will stand up all right; it is brand-new and I have not had time to break it in fully. So far, it gives no sign of heating. I open up all three engines full throttle, 1,750 for the biggest one and 1,700 for the two smaller, and we rise steadily toward the only two passes in the Queen Maud Range. We are about fifty miles north, holding course on meridian 163° 45′ W. I watch the altimeter needle climb: 3,000, 4,000, 5,000.

Ahead lies the big decision. One approach to the Pole is over the Axel Heiberg Glacier, the pass which Amundsen chose. He reported this pass to be 10,500 feet at its highest point. It is a long and gradual ascent, flanked by towering peaks far higher than the maximum altitude of the Ford, and its summit is hidden in clouds. The other approach is over the Liv Glacier to its right, named by Amundsen for Dr. Nansen's daughter and completely unsurveyed. We can see it bending in a wide curve to the west of south, mounting to the top of the Hump, and disappearing in a white blur that may be the polar plateau. We estimate its elevation to be about 9,500 feet, and the summit is clear. We decide to swing right.

The Liv Glacier is like a great frozen waterfall, halted in the midst of its tumbling cascade and immobilized for all eternity. Sheer cliffs rise above us on either side, and the canyon narrows as we wind our way upward. A cataract of ice looms ahead, and there is no room to turn around now. We are at 8,200 feet, just about the Ford's ceiling with its present loading. I wave frantically to catch the attention of June, who is bent over his radio, and signal him to jettison some of our weight. His hand reaches for the gasoline dump-valve, and I shake my head and point to the emergency food. He kicks one of the 150-pound sacks through the trapdoor, and the plane lifts just enough to clear the barrier.

A final icy wall blocks our way, steeper than all the others. A torrent of air is pouring over its top, the plane bucking violently in the downdraft, and our rate of climb is zero. June jettisons the second sack, and the Ford staggers a little higher, but still not enough. There is only one thing left to try. Per-

haps at the very edge of the downdraft is a reverse current of
air, like a back-eddy along the bank of a rushing river, that will
carry us upstream and over. I inch my way to the side of the
canyon, our right wing almost scraping the cliff, and all at once
we are wrenched upward, shooting out of the maelstrom of
winds, and soar over the summit with a couple of hundred feet
to spare.

On the other side of the Hump lies the polar plateau. The
snow meets the sky in an empty horizon, and somewhere in its
center, about four hundred miles away, is the Pole. We set our
course along the 171st meridian, leading south like all merid-
ians to the axis of the globe.

"29 November, 0100. Approaching South Pole."

Since midnight the mountains have been fading away behind
us, and by one o'clock they are out of sight. During the climb over
the Hump we were on maximum power setting for almost
ninety minutes. The right outboard engine backfires, and
misses a couple of beats, and June reaches for the dump-valve
again. At our altitude of 11,000 feet, two engines could never
keep the Ford airborne. I figure that I may have leaned the
mixture a little too thin, and adjust it just a fraction. The right
outboard picks up and runs smoothly once more.

According to my dead reckoning, we should be at the Pole in
another fourteen minutes. Our position is Lat. 89° 40′ S., about
twenty miles away, so our goal must actually be in sight at this
moment. I send a message back to Byrd on the trolley cable that
connects the cockpit with the navigator's compartment. Fourteen
minutes later, at 1:14 in the morning, Byrd sends a message
forward on the trolley for June to broadcast to the base:

"We have reached the South Pole."

We make a circle in the direction which would be westward,

except that here everything is north. The trapdoor behind me
opens, and Byrd drops an American flag on the spot, weighted
with a stone from Floyd Bennett's grave, and we turn north
again. I am glad to leave. Somehow our very purpose here seems
insignificant, a symbol of man's vanity and intrusion on this eternal white world. The sound of our engines profanes the silence
as we head back to Little America.

From Little America, Byrd's message has gone to the outside
world. Russ Owen tells us later that the signal from the *Floyd
Bennett* was actually picked up at *The New York Times* station,
direct from the South Pole, and transmitted by loud-speaker to
the jammed streets in Times Square. All over the world the
headlines are carrying the news; and when we arrive back at
camp shortly after ten in the morning of the 29th, the members
of the expedition are lined along the strip, cheering as we
taxi to a halt. The whole flight crew is picked up and carried
on swaying shoulders to the mess hall for a celebration.

I have been sitting so long in the pilot's seat that I am
cramped and sore, and so I slip out of the mess hall quietly and
take my skis. With Sverre Stroem and Chris Braathen I head
out for a couple of hours on the white slopes. This I like better
than all the celebrating.

On the 10th of January, 1930, Larry Gould returns from his
eleven weeks' survey trip to the Queen Maud Mountains. He
has made some important finds, but one is more important to
me than all the rest. Beside the trail, he came on a small cairn
of piled stones, containing a can of kerosene and a waterproof
packet of safety matches and a note written in Norwegian, the
penciled words still clear. He hands it to me, and I translate it
for him:

"6th-7th January, 1912. Reached and determined the Pole on the 14th to the 16th of December, 1911. Passed this place on the return, with provisions for 60 days, 2 sledges, 11 dogs. Everybody well."

It is signed "ROALD AMUNDSEN."

This photograph of the Queen Maud Range in Antarctica was taken from the *Floyd Bennett* during the flight to the South Pole.

At the Fokker factory, Teterboro, N. J., in 1930: (*left to right*) Eddie Rickenbacker, Bernt Balchen; the three members of Kingsford Smith's crew, Van Dyke, Stanaghe and Saul; Kingsford Smith and Tony Fokker.

Dr. James H. Kimball, then head of the New York office of the U.S. Weather Burea and friends at the testimonial dinner given for him by transatlantic flyers in 193

Among those present were (*front row, from the left*) Clarence Chamberlin, Amelia Earhart, Dr. Kimball, Ru Elder; (*front row, from the right*) Lowell Thomas, Colonel James Fitzmaurice; (*rear row, second and third from le* Charles A. Lindbergh, Frank Courtney; (*rear row, right*) Bernt Balchen.

SEVEN

NEW HORIZONS

1931–1941

It is the middle of June when the ice-scarred old *City of New York* wallows into her home port for a tumultuous welcome. The day is steaming hot, and I wish I were again in the Bay of Whales with the floating bergs. Admiral Byrd (promoted after the South Pole flight) has disembarked at New Zealand and traveled ahead; but he comes out with the harbor boat to rejoin the expedition. Coming aboard, he goes into his cabin on the poop deck and changes from his white Navy uniform into clothes like those he wore on the South Pole flight, with big fur cap and breeches and new knee-high hunting boots.

Now begins another official whoopdedoo, like the ones after the North Pole flight and the Atlantic crossing. The same clicking of newsreel cameras, the same parade and ticker tape, the same drum major leading the band, even the same reception in front of City Hall. Mayor Jimmy Walker takes a look at me and grins. "You here again, Balchen? Seems all I do is shake hands with you on these steps."

From New York the whole expedition proceeds in a special

train to Washington, for a banquet given by the National Geographic Society. Dr. Gilbert Grosvenor, president of the Society, meets Byrd at the station; and at the formal dinner Vice-President Curtis delivers a speech of congratulation, and President Herbert Hoover presents Byrd with the Society's Gold Medal.

The following day we are all taken to the White House for the next honor. President Hoover's manner is genial, not like the shy reserve of Calvin Coolidge, and his sincere smile makes us all at home. He has been an engineer and traveled to far places, and we have much in common as we chat together while the photographers are lining up their cameras. Then the President congratulates each member of the expedition for having been awarded a Special Congressional Medal.

There are further honors. The Navy Distinguished Flying Cross is awarded to all the pilots of the expedition—Byrd and June and Smith and McKinley and Parker—except me. Even Carl Petersen, my radio man, receives it for flying with me in the rescue of the stranded Ford. Once again it is explained that this medal cannot be given to me because I do not belong to the armed forces of the United States; but I recall that the *Bremen* fliers, two Germans and a Free State Irishman, all aliens, received this identical decoration, and I wonder what has prompted my not receiving it. The only thing given to me is a letter.

It is handed to me as I come out of the White House, just after being received by the President. A stranger stops me outside the gate, and asks if my name is Bernt Balchen. I reply, "*Ja*, sure," and he hands me an envelope and disappears. I tear it open on the spot, puzzled. It is a subpoena from the immigration authorities. I have broken my residence by going to the South Pole; my first citizenship papers are therefore void, and I am to be deported to Norway.

The newspapermen outside the White House look over my shoulder, grab the subpoena, and race for the nearest telephones.

That afternoon the story is on all the front pages. I am reading the papers back in my hotel room, sick at heart. For years I have been thinking of this country as my own; it is a part of me deep inside, and now I wonder why this has happened to me.

The telephone rings beside the bed, and a high-pitched voice fairly blasts my eardrums.

"This is Fiorello La Guardia, Representative from New York. I'm a Quiet Birdman, too." He is so excited that he sputters, and I can only make out a few phrases. ". . . goddam outrage . . . talked to the President . . . introducing a bill tomorrow."

"What bill?" I manage to cut in.

"To make you a citizen, of course. Shipstead of Minnesota and a couple of other good Scandahoovian Congressmen are here with me, and we're bringing it up on the floor of the House first thing in the morning. Just called to tell you not to worry."

Shortly afterward a special bill is passed by Congress and signed by President Hoover, granting me rights to full citizenship. This is bigger to me than any medal.

Life for me is always adventure after adventure, and the ones I remember most do not always end with ticker tape and parades. Now when I look through my diary, going back over the decade that followed my return from the South Pole, a cavalcade of names crosses the pages: Moscow and Berlin and Singapore and Manila, Hitler and Roosevelt, Amelia Earhart, and Ernst Udet and Hap Arnold—a whole lifetime crowded into ten years. Sometimes a date and place in my log seem to leap out at me, and suddenly I am living the scene again in my mind.

"18 October, 1930. Newark, N. J."

I have been at the Fokker factory since I returned from the Byrd expedition, working as chief test pilot, and one afternoon Eddie Rickenbacker, vice-president in charge of sales, phones and asks me to demonstrate one of the new F-12s. A wealthy Texas oil man is interested in purchasing a Fokker, he says, but first the customer would like to see its performance. We are flying over the East River side of Manhattan when the fuel line clogs, and the engine sputters and quits cold. Luckily I have altitude, and I begin a long glide, ducking between a couple of smokestacks and skimming an apartment house roof, and make a dead-stick landing on the Newark Airport, light as a feather. The oil man climbs out, his knees buckling, but I smile nonchalantly.

"Safest plane in the world," I assure him. "Flies without even an engine."

The sale is made, and later Rickenbacker calls me on the phone. "Pretty risky business," he remonstrates, "cutting your engine right over the city."

"Anything to help the sales department," I reply.

"20 May, 1932. Harbor Grace, Newfoundland."

The fog on the Newfoundland banks has rolled away by evening, and the single-engine Lockheed Vega is fueled and preflighted. Back at the old Fokker factory in Teterboro I had installed a large gas tank in the fuselage, and a new fuel system, and also made some changes in the cockpit layout so it would be more convenient for Amelia Earhart on her flight. Yesterday, the 19th of May, I flew her to Newfoundland, and this afternoon we landed at Harbor Grace. While she is resting at the little hotel I get a favorable report on the weather, and set up the throttle curves and make a flight plan. Now I call her at the hotel and tell her it is okay for take-off.

She arrives at the field in jodhpurs and leather flying jacket, her close-cropped blond hair tousled, quiet and unobtrusive as a young Lindbergh. She listens calmly, only biting her lip a little, as I go over with her the course to hold, and tell her what weather she can expect on the way across the ocean. She looks at me with a small lonely smile and says, "Do you think I can make it?" and I grin back: "You bet." She crawls calmly into the cockpit of the big empty airplane, starts the engine, runs it up, checks the mags, and nods her head. We pull the chocks, and she is off.

On May 21st she lands in Ireland, the first woman ever to solo the Atlantic.

"8 January, 1934. Floyd Bennett Bay, Antarctica."

We are anchored to the floe ice in the Ross Sea, in a small bight of the Bay of Whales named Floyd Bennett Bay. Our ship this time is another old Norwegian sealer, the *Fanefjord,* which Lincoln Ellsworth, the financial backer and leader of our new expedition, has rechristened *Wyatt Earp.* Ellsworth is a great admirer of the Kansas frontiersman, and one of Earp's original six-shooters hangs over his bunk. We are carrying on board a long-range Northrop, the *Polar Star,* in which I will attempt to fly Ellsworth across the Antarctic continent to the Weddell Sea. Ellsworth had dreamed up a plan to catapult the plane from the ship's deck; but I talked him out of that if I am going to be the pilot, and instead we will take off on skis from the solid bay ice.

Chris Braathen is along with the Ellsworth expedition as flight mechanic; and this morning, as soon as the *Wyatt Earp* is secure, we strap on our skis and head toward the site of Little America, about twelve miles from our anchorage. No human eye has seen Byrd's old base since we abandoned it four years ago. A heavy overcast lies on the snow like a second white blanket, and the dog trails and red flag markers that used to lead from the bay to the camp site have long since disappeared. Only the radio tower, sticking out of the drifts ahead, guides us to our former home.

Everything is buried like an ancient city under lava, silent and dead—only the smokestacks of the mess hall and administration building are still above the snow. Everywhere the drifts have smoothed and flattened out, and there are not even mounds to indicate the other buildings now. Buried far below me, as I ski along the lee side of the camp, is the packing-box house that was Arthur Walden's Blubberheim. Near the old landing field is the bare framework of Noah's Ark, and we take off our skis and cook our lunch on the workbench, lighting a primus stove and making a pemmican *hooch*. The burner of a plumber's blowtorch sticks up through the snow, and I see the names of a couple of our mechanics, Benny Roth and Pete Demas, scribbled in pencil on one of the wooden uprights.

A group of penguins, the sole residents of Little America now, circles us happily as we emerge, touching beaks to chests and clapping their flippers together in delight at human company again. They follow us like children, waddling and belly-whopping to keep pace, as we make our way across the sastrugi to the former landing field. The big trimotor Ford is just where we left it when we departed for the States, the tail sticking out of the snow. Chris Braathen skis over to investigate the buried Fairchild, and I climb through the escape hatch of the Ford's cockpit, and lower myself into the pilot's seat.

Instinctively my hand closes on the wheel, and I finger the ice-locked controls. Once more, sitting here alone, I seem to be fighting the heavy plane up over the Liv Glacier. The snow-packed windshield is a solid wall of ice looming ahead, and a gust of wind that shakes the exposed tail is the sudden updraft that boosts us the last few feet across the Hump. The wind dies, and the silence around me is the white eternity of the South Pole.

Something catches my eye, lying forgotten on the floor of the cockpit beside my seat. It is the slide rule I used on the flight across the Atlantic, on the round-the-States air tour with Floyd Bennett, and then over the South Pole. Often I have wondered what happened to it. I pick it up and slip it back into my pocket.

"19 February, 1936. The White House, Washington."

Our ship stopped at Montevideo, Uruguay, on our way back to the States after the Ellsworth Expedition ended. We had made two unsuccessful attempts to cross the Antarctic Continent by air: first, when our plane was crushed by the breaking up of the bay ice; second, when we had to turn back twice on account of impossible weather. In Montevideo I found awaiting me a cable from Hjalmar Riiser-Larsen, asking me to come to Norway at once and help in the establishment of a Norwegian air line. At that time, and to this day, Norway's merchant marine is third in all the world's shipping, and the country depends for its livelihood on chartered transportation. The five largest steamship companies had been farsighted enough to realize that transportation in the future must also look to the skies, and they had decided to pool their resources and develop a civil air transport system, so that Norway could compete with other nations in the coming age of aviation.

In the twenties an international air race was on. Big nations like Germany, limited by the Treaty of Versailles to non-military aircraft, were nevertheless producing transport planes which could be converted quickly to other uses, and were building up an industry which would become the basis of a military machine in case of war. In many of the new planes, the requirements of commercial travel were not even considered.

These foreign manufacturers were heavily subsidized by their governments, whereas Norway's aviation leaders depended upon private financing and equipment. Their first need was to convince their own government that additional funds must be provided out of the nation's small and stringent budget, if Norway were to hold its own in the race.

Under the leadership of the brothers Rudolf and Thomas Olsen, heads of the great Fred Olsen Steamship Line, and Thomas Falck of the Bergenske Steamship Line, a national airline had been formed, called the Det Norske Luftfartselskap. Riiser-Larsen was named manager, and I was made second in command, planning the routes and flying the runs. Our only air fields were a couple of military stations, small and inconveniently situated. The plan was first to build up a seaplane service to the most important cities on the coast of southern Norway, and then later extend this service to northern Norway. For the first year, we chartered a trimotor JU-52 from the German air line Deutsche Lufthansa, for the southern operations, and for the northern mail run we bought a single-engine Junkers seaplane.

At the beginning of last June (1935), I had gone to Travemünde in Germany to accept this plane for DNL. Travemünde was officially a commercial seaplane station, but already it was one of the Luftwaffe's main training bases for the Baltic Sea patrol. Knowing the restrictions of the Versailles Treaty, I was interested to see on the field some Heinkel twin-engine bombers, also some Messerschmitt single-engine fighters. The Luftwaffe officers received me very cordially, and made no bones about the fact that this was a military station with a rapid build-up: they told me they expected to have a large fighting force here in a short time. They let me climb into the cockpit of one of the bombers, and I noticed that the leather seats and rudder pedals were much worn, and asked one of the mechanics: "How much flying time does this airplane have?" "Oh, we

NEW HORIZONS   201

have the third set of engines in it now," he shrugged. I was allowed to inspect the engine installation and armament of the
Messerschmitt fighters, and watched their daily machine-gun
practice on the range. Also in Travemünde I saw the Arbeits-
dienst and the Hitlerjugend drilling with their spades, singing
and goose-stepping as they marched, and it was plain to me that
here the German Wehrmacht was coming into being.

Immediately after returning to Oslo, I saw my old friend
Ambassador Tony Biddle at the American Embassy and described to him the signs of booming industry to be seen all over
Germany now, the great activity everywhere, the build-up of an
industrial capability that could handle an all-out Blitzkrieg
some day. As an American citizen, I felt it was my duty to
report this; I gave the same information to the Norwegian government, expressing the opinion that the Germans had broken
the Treaty of Versailles by operating aircraft to which they
were not legally entitled, and it did not bode a peaceful future
for Europe.

As Norway's air transportation gradually expanded, the pros-
pect of long-range ocean flying was more and more in my mind;
and in February, 1936, I went back to Washington to find out
whether an American company would be interested in an agreement with DNL to pioneer a transatlantic route. On February
18th, in the lobby of the Mayflower Hotel, I ran into Postmaster
General James Farley. At luncheon with him and Harllee
Branch, Assistant Postmaster General for aviation, I told them
of the proposed plan. They both pricked up their ears when I
mentioned that DNL was trying to make contact with Pan
American for a Norway-USA air route. Jim Farley sat in silence
for a moment, and then he said: "Bernt, I think the Boss would
like to hear about this. How about coming over to the White
House with me tomorrow?" Now from my diary I quote the
complete entry for that following day:

"This forenoon Jim Farley takes me in to see Franklin D.

Roosevelt. Present at the meeting are: the President, Farley, Branch and Ross McIntyre. When we come in, the President reaches out his hand and smiles: 'Well, Bernt, I haven't heard from you in quite a while. I understand you're over in Norway now. What are you doing there?'

"Farley breaks in to relate our meeting yesterday at the Mayflower, and asks me to outline DNL's plan to the President. I do this. FDR asks a lot of questions, indicating his interest in air transportation, and says: 'I think you are doing an extremely valuable job for us, and you must continue this for our mutual benefit.' Then he orders Farley and McIntyre to arrange a hearing with the State Interdepartmental Committee at once, and wishes me good luck and says he will personally follow the developments."

Later, we concluded a bilateral air agreement between the USA and Norway and, as a consequence, an operational air agreement between Pan American and DNL. The Norwegian company bought a Sikorsky S-43 for the operation, but developments hit an unexpected obstacle. It turned out that British Imperial Airways had already been negotiating with Washington for a transatlantic service, and our plan had to be deferred until they exercised their option. There was no telling when this would take place. Great Britain, like Germany, was concentrating right now on its own military air force for the dark events that were fast taking place in Europe.

"*2 August, 1937. Hotel Continental, Moscow.*"

I am in Moscow as a representative of the Norwegian Government, to extend an official invitation to the Soviet Union. In Bergen, in a couple of years, Norway plans to hold an International Polar Exhibit, and I have been instructed personally to invite Professor Otto Schmidt, the German-born North Pole explorer who is head of all Arctic research in Russia. Permission for my trip has been granted by the Soviet Embassy in Oslo. I have been fully coached in just what to say to Schmidt, and even the number of my room at the Hotel Continental in Moscow was assigned before I left Norway. I landed at Nukowo Airport, a tremendous sand lot with no runways marked, where I saw the hangars stored with Russian military planes, and many other warcraft on the field. Uniformed police from the Cheka took me at once to the Intourist Bureau, and my American passport was promptly confiscated. Back at my hotel room, as further evidence of Red hospitality, I find that all my baggage has been searched in my absence. It is ransacked again and again each time I leave the Continental.

Everywhere I go the secret police trail me; but once I manage to slip my guards and take a stroll alone in the city away from the tourist conducted tours. There is nothing but slums, filth, and abject poverty; many of the houses even have no windows. At the Museum of the Russian Revolution, which an endless file of people is entering and leaving, Mongols and Slavs and ragged peasants from all over the Soviet Union making their required pilgrimage. I join the line, curious to see what is inside, but the police spot my clean street clothes and tell me bluntly that foreigners are not welcome. So I go back to the hotel, take off my coat and tie and belt and muss my hair to look like a Russian, and this time I go right through without any trouble. Inside I stand and gape with the crowd at Lenin's death mask and other sacred relics of the Bolshevik Revolution, including an exhibit of Communist propaganda in every foreign language. I even recognize some items of subversive literature, copies of which had been seized in Norway during the general strike in the early twenties.

Late this afternoon word comes to the hotel that Otto Schmidt will see me at last. I have met him in New York and

know he speaks excellent English; but when I shake hands with
him and say, "How do you do, Professor?" he looks quickly over
his shoulder and then replies in German, "We do not speak
English here." So we switch to German together, and he describes his recent North Pole flight, how the Russians took off
from Franz Josef Land, which he says will henceforth be a
permanent base for their work in the polar regions. He adds
that it is the intent of the Soviet Union to have twice as many
stations in the Arctic as all the rest of the world together. At
this moment the door bursts open, and a husky girl strides in,
followed by a uniformed policeman carrying a sub-machine
gun. She tells me in German that she is the interpreter, and from
now on Otto Schmidt speaks to her in Russian, and she trans-
lates into German for me. During the rest of our conversation
there isn't much of anything said.

The other mission in Moscow for which I have been cleared
is to interest Aeroflot, the Soviet commercial air line, in co-
operating with DNL to open an air route between Moscow
and the United States via Norway; but they reply suspiciously
that if such a route is ever developed they will do it themselves.
In every way their manner reflects deep distrust of foreigners:
they are Mongolians, all of them, in their way of thinking, and
if I say to a Russian "How do you do?" he tries to figure out
what I mean by that, and what I am really up to. It is impressed
on me once more what a dangerous enemy the whole world has
here, working constantly to undermine the liberties of all free
men and pervert their minds. We in Scandinavia have had the
Russians as neighbors for centuries; we have come to abhor
their cruelties, and are only too well aware of their ambition
to reach the Atlantic across our conquered countries. Our whole
military training has been for defense of our eastern frontier,
and here today in Moscow I am convinced that I was right,
back in 1918, when as a youth I fought in Finland against the
Red with the White Army under Field Marshal Mannerheim.

"28 May, 1939. Adlon Hotel, Berlin."

This evening I am standing alone at the bar of the Adlon Hotel, sipping a Martini. I have just returned from a visit to the Junkers factory, where I ordered some spare parts for the JU-52s we are using in DNL, and I observed the recent great expansion at their plant. Twenty thousand workers are at the factory now, and Stuka bombers are rolling out at a fast clip. On the way back to Berlin in the afternoon I saw the field at Oschersleben lined with four hundred Messerschmitt-104 fighters, all ready to fly. On all the roads tanks and heavy artillery are rumbling, the steam-roller *Wehrmacht* limbering up for the blitzkrieg, and on the streets of Berlin are men in uniform everywhere.

I remember, here in Berlin a year ago, standing on a balcony of the Kaiserhof Hotel and hearing Goebbels introduce *Der Führer*. For an hour Hitler harangued the mob of 250,000 Nazis in the square below; and as he finished speaking the swastikas and torches waved, and the roar of *"Sieg Heil!"* from a quarter-million throats was like an ocean tide rising. But back home nobody paid any attention when I told them.

Suddenly the Adlon bartender stiffens and stands at attention, and in the mirror I see a fine-looking officer in the uniform of a Luftwaffe general, with big white lapels and a shining leather-visored cap. As he lifts a cocktail to his lips, his eye catches mine in the mirror, and he turns with a broad smile: "Bernt Balchen! What the hell brings you to Berlin?" It is Ernst Udet, the great German flier of World War I whom I have met at a Quiet Birdmen meeting in Cleveland, where he was attending the air races. Udet has a great liking for the States and he asks about his many friends there, especially the Navy ace Al Williams, for whom he has the highest regard. After a couple of Martinis together, he invites me to his apartment for dinner. It is possible that another old acquaintance of mine will drop in later, he says.

We leave the Adlon in his gigantic black Horch, even bigger than a Cadillac, with two chauffeurs and two footmen, a swastika flag flying from each fender. Soldiers click their heels at attention as we roll down Unter den Linden and halt at his apartment house, guarded by SS police in brown shirts. After an excellent supper we sit in his living room over cigars and brandy and talk of Arctic flying. He mentions that he has flown a photographic mission to Greenland and studied the aviation potentials there. While we are talking, the door of the apartment opens without a knock, and Hermann Göring stands in the entrance, in the full-medaled uniform of Air Marshal.

His round pink face beams as he recognizes me—our first meeting since we were both in Sweden. He is fleshier than when I saw him last, but still robust and full of jovial humor. We chat about *elg* shooting in Scandinavia, which he loves, and after a few more brandies the talk gets around to military aviation. Udet brings up the recent visit of Charles Lindbergh, and quotes his statement about the growth of German air power, and Göring nods with pride. "The Luftwaffe could rule the skies of the world," he says, "if we were given a free hand."

This seems to be a sore spot with him, and over another bottle of brandy he and Udet discuss frankly Hitler's decision to freeze the present Messerschmitt and Heinkel designs, and go into mass production with what they have. At this time, Göring confides to me, he has in the blueprint stage a revolutionary new jet plane in which he places the greatest hope, but the project has been tabled by General Milch and *Der Führer* himself. Both Göring and Udet are hopping mad, I can see, and as we get well into our second bottle *Der Führer* is demoted to *der kleine Korporal*. Göring says grimly: *"Der Korporal's* mistake may be the difference to Germany between victory and defeat."

By midnight a third bottle of brandy is almost empty, and we sing some old Bavarian hunting songs, and wind up with a session of target practice in the apartment. Udet is a crack shot, and we use Walther .22 pistols; and later Göring hauls out his big 9-millimeter Luger, and we shoot out all the bulbs of the chandelier before I wander back to the Adlon in the small hours, with a spinning head but some sober thoughts.

"30 November, 1939. Hq., Finnish Air Staff, Helsinki."

All afternoon long, since two o'clock, Helsinki has been under aerial bombardment. The little Finnish Air Force has no modern planes to put up a defense, and only the clumsy marksmanship of the Russians has saved the city from total destruction. For a month the Red invaders have been advancing across the frozen lakes and forests in a bloody tide. These Russians are the lowest the human race can sink, lower even than beasts, and the refugees streaming along the country roads have tales of unbelievable butchery and rape.

Once again old Field Marshal Gustaf Mannerheim is at the helm in his country's dire emergency; and once again I am serving under him, this time as a consultant member of the Finnish Air Force. Finland has always been very dear to me: I have many friends here, and I know that if this peace-loving little nation falls Norway will be next, and all of Scandinavia will be neutralized, and the Axis or the Soviets will have control of the Atlantic seaboard for operations against the rest of the world.

We sit hour after hour in the headquarters building, pinned down by the bombs and with no planes to fly, and I think back to 1918 when I was fighting the Reds here in Finland. I was eighteen years old when I volunteered, a cadet in the war school in Oslo. To preserve Norway's neutrality, I enlisted under the name of Karl Nilson, like hundreds of other Norwegian volunteers. I think there were more Karl Nilsons in the Finnish army than any other name. Mannerheim was in his fifties then, tall and very striking with his square mustache and white astrakhan hat and polished black boots, and I followed him devotedly into battle.

Ten days of desperate hand-to-hand fighting in and around Tammerfors were climaxed by "Bloody Friday"—an Easter Friday, I remember. We lost more men than I care to think of, but our efforts turned the tide of the war, and afterwards we followed up with clean-up operations. At Sortevalla, my horse was shot out from under me, and I was down on the ground, and a Russian tried to run a bayonet through me. It just grazed my hip. I managed to pull out my revolver, a Nagant 7.5-millimeter, and plugged him directly between the eyes.

"April 9, 1940. New York."

Since early January I have been here in the States, representing Norwegian Airlines and Finland in negotiations with the United States Government and Pan American World Airways, to try to establish air passenger and mail service between the United States and neutral Norway. In conjunction with Swedish and Danish representatives, I have succeeded in concluding with Pan American an operating agreement whereby the air lines of the Scandinavian countries are to charter an S-42 Clipper, a second will be furnished by Pan American—and start on June 7, 1940, a regular air service into Bergen, Norway, well north of the combat zones in Europe.

I also have another mission in America: to help procure war materials for Norway, where the situation is becoming more and more tense. Still another job I was asked to do in returning to America is—unfortunately—over now. It was to assist in getting equipment for the Finns in their struggle against the Russians. Thanks to the understanding and aid of the United States Government, a hundred Brewster fighter planes were put at the disposal of the Finns. The hundred aircraft were shipped and got as far as Sweden, but before they could get into action little Finland surrendered to her mighty neighbor.

All the other members of the Norwegian military commission have gone back to Norway; but I am staying on to straighten out odds and ends. Today, my office phone rings, and the blow comes. The Norwegian Consulate is on the wire, and the news is stunning indeed—the Nazis have invaded Norway. The Norwegians, of course, are resisting; they have taken up the fight against the Nazi war machine with their small army, navy, and air force and what little equipment they have.

There is a terrible irony in the situation. Here I sit, alone in New York, with twenty million dollars' worth of military contracts for a nation unable to receive the arms and equipment and use them now, in its bitterest hour.

"April 20, 1940. New York."

I have been named Norway's military representative in the United States, and am to take care of technical arrangements in connection with the armaments contracts. But the situation is fluid, to say the least. The payments under the contracts will shortly become due, but not even the Norwegian Minister, Wilhelm Morgenstierne, knows yet what funds are available outside Norway, and whatever money there is seems to be needed everywhere.

Some Norwegian quarters in the United States want to get rid of the contracts; but this equipment, I know, will serve to arm the nucleus of a new Norwegian Navy, Army, and Air Force when the Norwegians start fighting from outside their borders to free their country from the grip of the Nazis. As long as I can, I want to hang onto the contracts.

The phone rings. It is Tom Morgan, president of the Sperry Gyroscope Company.

"I've been in touch with some of the concerns that you've entered into contracts with," Tom tells me, "and they're anxious to know if you are able to meet payments. On our searchlight contracts," he adds, "the payment of $28,000 is due in a couple of days, and I'd like to know what the situation is."

Now I am in a fix. I can get no money from the Norwegian Legation—and yet I cannot and will not let the contracts go.

An idea strikes me. Now that Norway is at war with Germany, England and France have automatically become her allies. I hurry to the offices of the Anglo-French Purchasing Mission, where Sir Arthur Purvis and René Pleven receive me with open arms.

Without hesitation Pleven says: "I'll give you a loan to meet the payment on the searchlights from the Sperry Company. Don't mention it! We'll have security in the searchlights, and anyhow, they'll have to be stored somewhere for the time being."

Before I leave, they even offer me an office in the same building.

A month later, I am still in New York, and still have my contracts. The British and French have examined them and found them very attractive, and are hot on my heels to buy them from me. The French have made a bid on the fighter planes, but I refuse to give them up, waiting and hoping for instructions from the Norwegian military authorities. With King Haakon and Crown Prince Olav, the Norwegian government is later forced to flee Norway and sail for England.

Finally a cablegram arrives from London. It instructs me not to sell anything, and to proceed to Ottawa to try to negotiate with the Canadian government for a suitable place for a camp for the training of Norwegian pilots. It is signed by Riiser-Larsen.

I call on my old friend Georg Unger Vetlesen to enlist his

assistance in establishing the new training camp, and then leave for Ottawa, where I reach an agreement with the Canadians to build the base at City Island in Toronto. It is decided to name the camp Little Norway.

"30 June, 1941. Nichols Field, Manila."

We arrive at Nichols Field this afternoon, after delivering another PBY flying boat at the United States Naval Base at Cavite, to be picked up there by the British RAF. Clyde Pangborn and I are flying together in the RAF Ferry Command, transporting planes from San Diego to Hong Kong and Singapore to bolster the crumbling defenses of the Far East. It is curious to see the complacency of Singapore, after half of Europe has already fallen to the Axis. The British are carrying on business as usual, ignoring the Jap armies marching steadily south through the jungles, and they assure us over a gin sour at the Raffles Hotel: "Nothing to be alarmed about, old chap— Singapore is the Gibraltar of the East."*

Manila is jittery by contrast, and Pangborn and I can sense the tension in the air as we sign over the PBY at Cavite and start for near-by Nichols Field. We are planning to have dinner there with my friend Colonel Lester Maitland, who flew a Fokker across the Pacific in 1927 at the same time I was flying Byrd's Fokker across the Atlantic, and who is on duty here with the United States Army Air Corps. As we arrive at the Air Force base a man in civilian clothes accosts me and shows his FBI identification. Washington has been trying to reach me, and wants to know if it is all right to give my location. I tell him, "*Ja,* sure," and put it out of my mind; and after a couple of Martinis at the Nichols Field Officers Club with Maitland, we all go to the Jai Alai in Manila for a late dinner.

We are just sitting down at the table when the same FBI

* It was taken within a year.

man shows up again, and hands me a red-bordered telegram from the British Air Attaché in Washington. The message is brief: "Report soonest." I think I have a hunch who has sent for me.

A number 1-A priority has been arranged for me on the Pan-American Clipper leaving Manila in half an hour. I have sent my clothes to the cleaners, and all I have is the rumpled white linen suit I am wearing. I rush out of the Jai Alai, and grab a bus to the airport.

"3 July, 1941. Munitions Building, Washington."

Dates and places crowd one another for my attention as I turn the pages of my diary, but this one stands alone above all the rest. In some ways, I think, it is the most important date of my life.

I enter the old Munitions Building on Constitution Avenue, escorted by RAF Group Captain Deboulay, of the British Air Attaché's office. We climb the iron steps to the second floor, to a reception room with flags and a sign over the door: "Commanding General, U.S. Army Air Corps." Major Gene Beebe, General Arnold's aide, beckons to me and smiles: "The Old Man's been waiting for you." We walk across the hall, and Miss Edna Adkins, Arnold's secretary, nods her head without even looking up from her typewriter: "Go right in." I am wondering, as I enter, whether Hap Arnold has changed. I met him first at a Quiet Birdmen meeting when he was just a major, about to be sent into exile at Fort Riley, Kansas, for testifying at the Billy Mitchell court-martial. Now he is a major general, head of the Air Corps, responsible for building America's feeble fleet of fewer than a thousand planes into the mightiest winged power in all history: the father of the United States Air Force today.

General Arnold looks up as I halt before his desk, ill at ease in my rumpled linen suit. He has the same curious half-moon grin, turned up at the corners, which earned him his famous nickname when he was a cadet at West Point. It is accented by a white scar on his chin, the result of a crash in a Jenny back in 1912 just after he graduated from the Wright brothers' school in Dayton. His eyes are steel blue, set wide apart, and deep, and suddenly I am thinking of Captain Amundsen's penetrating eyes.

"Where the hell have you been, Bernt? I've been looking all over Europe and the Pacific for you." His manner is still direct and brusque, relieved by a small boy's petulant pout. "What's a polar explorer doing in Manila? Want to go to work for me?"

He doesn't even wait for me to answer.

"Quit fooling around and join this man's Air Corps. We've got a job for you." His grin twitches at the corners. "What's your rank?"

"Flight lieutenant, Royal Norwegian Air Force, sir."

"Let's see. That would be captain in our army." He hits a switch on his squawk box. "Tooey? I'm sending Bernt Balchen down to see you. You can tell him what it's all about. Oh, by the way, make him a captain."

Brigadier General Carl Spaatz is on the phone when I arrive at his office, and his aide, Major Ted Curtis, motions to me to sit down. I listen as the General finishes his conversation. "Because the Old Man said so, that's why. Tell the British they'll have to find another ferry pilot. Get the paper mill working, and see that he's a captain in the Air Corps right away." He slams down the phone, swings around in his chair, and holds out his hand. "Welcome home, Bernt."

Tooey Spaatz hasn't changed, either. I knew him years ago, when I flew from Teterboro to McCook Field near Patterson, Ohio, to deliver the F-7 Fokker called the *Question Mark*, in which Spaatz and Pete Quesada and Ira Eaker set the world's endurance record. He plunges at once into a briefing on what

I am to do. I am to set up a base on the west coast of Greenland, for staging aircraft from the United States to the theater of operations in Europe, and for patrolling the coast of the island against an enemy attack. I have only one question: "But the United States isn't in the war."

Tooey Spaatz shrugs. "It will be."

EIGHT

BLUIE WEST EIGHT

1941–1943

General of the Air Force H. H. Arnold is the most exacting, the hardest-driving, the most understanding human being I have ever known. He is turbo-supercharged, working eighteen hours at his desk, flying back and forth across both oceans, making a day-long inspection of a new training base or a sprawling airplane factory at a dogtrot which wears out his staff in the first hour. He defines the impossible as something which hasn't been done yet. He completes a whirlwind tour of a bombsight plant, and turns to the manager. "Fine. Now double your output next month."

"But that's impossible, General," the manager gasps.

"I know," Hap Arnold answers with his most cajoling grin, "but that doesn't mean you can't do it."

In 1941 a steady stream of United States and Allied aircraft is already flowing from the American arsenals to the European fighting front. The longer-range bombers can go direct from Newfoundland nonstop over the Atlantic to the United Kingdom; but the medium bombers and fighters, limited in range to a thousand or fifteen hundred miles, must be ferried across the ocean by slow convoy vessels, losing precious time and facing the mounting peril of enemy torpedoes. Arnold's answer is:

215

Build a chain of bases and ferry the planes by air. There is no question whether they can fly the North Atlantic in the winter. They will fly it. There is no question whether we can build a base in the most inaccessible part of Greenland. We will build it.

A number of these staging fields have been started along the rim of the Arctic in Newfoundland, in Labrador, in Baffin Land, and in the south of Greenland at Narsasuak, from which the aircraft can be ferried to Iceland and thence to the United Kingdom. Task Force 8, of which I am appointed commander, is to create a link in this chain on the west coast of Greenland above the Arctic Circle: the northernmost American air base in the world. It will serve not only as a ferrying station, but as a communications base to transmit messages to our forces overseas, and report the weather for their air and sea operations; and my command is further charged with the responsibility of patrolling the entire coast and taking action in the event of enemy invasion.

We have very little to go on when we start looking for a site. Back in 1928, an expedition from the University of Michigan under Professor Hobbs established a scientific camp near the head of Söndre Strömfjord, a deep fjord of Davies Strait in the wildest part of western Greenland, and laid out a small airstrip. Later that year Bert Hassell and Shorty Cramer, on their attempted flight from Rockford, Illinois, to Sweden, made an emergency landing on the icecap near this site. In 1933 Charles Lindbergh scouted the Greenland coast for Pan American Airways, and mentioned Söndre Strömfjord as a possible commercial landing field. The United States Coast Guard has made some aerial photographs of the general area; and, with the aid of these, plus our own imagination, we come to the conclusion that Söndre Strömfjord can be adapted for our purposes. The site is approved by the War Department and given a code name: Bluie West Eight.

BAFFIN
BAY

ELLESMERE ISLAND

NORD

GREENLAND SEA

SPITZBERGEN

275 Mi.

THULE

Greenland

GREENLAND

Icecap

TAFELBERG MT.
Sabine Is.
HANSA BAY
CAPE WYNN
Clavering Str.
ESKIMONAES
Mackenzie Bay
Bonteko Is.
Ella Island
MESTERSVIK

Scoresby
Sound

EGEDESMINDE

Davis Strait

Sondre Strömfjord
BLUIE WEST EIGHT
HOLSTEINSBORG
Simiutak Is.
Lt. Stinston's B-17

ARCTIC   CIRCLE

Denmark Strait

ICELAND

BLUIE EAST TWO
IKATEK
ANGMAGSSALIK

REYKJAVIK
KEFLAVIK

Lt. Monteverde's
B-17
ATTERBURY DOME

GODTHAAB

SCALE OF MILES
0   100   200   300   400

BLUIE WEST ONE
NARSASUAK

N

NORTH ATLANTIC OCEAN

J. MACD

GREENLAND

Our first step is to draw up a blueprint of our prospective base, reduce it to scale, and superimpose it on the aerial photos to see if it fits the terrain. We shall need a runway at least a mile long to accommodate the military bombers, also hangars and machine shops, storage space for fuel, warehouses to hold our jeeps and trucks and bulldozers, docking facilities, and barracks. Our initial task force will consist of fifteen hundred men, trained Air Force specialists and radio operators and meteorologists, and civilian contractors to construct the housing and air field. The project is highly classified, and when the men volunteer they have no idea where they are going or for how long. I recall Captain Amundsen's remark once back in Kristiansand when I was a boy: "You go places where no one has ever been before, and you do not know what year you will come home."

We have on our list of requirements more than 150,000 separate items, a total of 50,000 tons, to supply a base that will be a hundred times the size of Little America. We must work in secrecy, without newspaper headlines or speeches or fanfare. This is not a race to fly the first plane over a mathematical point on the globe. From our base hundreds and maybe thousands of planes will fly east to the combat zones in a life-and-death race with the Axis, and the prize is freedom of all peace-loving peoples.

I am still new in the United States Air Force, and I do not know about government procedures and regulations in Washington, where civilian agencies still hibernate in a peacetime cocoon of red tape. Building materials will take half a year, the procurement department says, and some of the lumber will have to be shipped from the West Coast to our port of embarkation in Brooklyn. The only way we can be ready to sail in a couple of months on our estimated departure date, September 29th, is through a high priority order issued by General Arnold himself.

A single word from the Old Man is enough to blow up the

biggest log jam. For instance, I need at least three complements of war ammunition for our antiaircraft and other weapons, in case we have to protect our base from an enemy attack. When I give the Ordnance Department this requisition, the Colonel looks at me as if I were out of my mind. "We can't issue this to you, Captain. There isn't a war on." I reply meekly: "Would you please call General Arnold, sir?" He gives me a pitying glance and picks up the phone. I hear him say "Yes, sir," and then "Yes, sir" several more times, and he hangs up the phone, looking a little green around the gills and signs the paper with a shaky hand. "Take this, and get out of here quick."

Some of our equipment is not to be found in any government listing. One vital item is dog teams, for scouting and possible rescue work. General Arnold gives me carte blanche, and I send two men to Arthur Walden's old kennels in Wonalancet, New Hampshire. There they let us have thirty-five sled dogs, some of them descendants of the same huskies that went to the South Pole; and for good measure he throws in a couple of caged half-breed timber wolves that are too dangerous to run loose. They prove to be wonderful sled animals, tireless on several long rescue trips I make on the Greenland Icecap.

Also we need aircraft suitable for surveys and patrol. Ski planes are not available in the Air Force, and so I think back to my early days in Ontario. Bob Noorduyn, the Fokker expert, has just designed a high-wing single-engine plane called the Norseman. It is equipped with skis and wheels and pontoons, rugged enough for Canadian bush flying, and proves to be just what we need. Later the Norseman is purchased in quantity by the Air Force, designated C-64, and comes to play an important role in the development of our military bases all over the North.

One thing I cannot requisition, even with Arnold's help, is a Christmas tree. There are no trees anywhere in Greenland, and I know the importance of this traditional symbol of the Yule to youngsters far away from home. I go to New York to see my old friend Grover Whalen, and he explains the problem to the Wanamaker executives. When I leave I take along a dozen artificial Christmas trees, cases of gifts, and even tinsel and a Santa Claus outfit. I remember the need for recreation during the endless winter nights in Little America, and add athletic equipment and boxing gloves.

Even in a civilian organization there is a long time lag between ordering things and getting them, and I never really believed it would be possible in the government to have all our material delivered to the Brooklyn dock in time; but on September 29th everything is loaded aboard our cargo ships and the troop transport *Munargo*, ready to sail. We are on sealed orders, and the men look curiously at the holds crammed with lumber and cement and steam shovels and trucks, the sled dogs chained on the decks, the portholes of all the ships painted black. On our last night in port some of the civilians with the construction unit make a farewell tour of the Brooklyn bars, and a police officer brings them back to the ship in the morning a little the worse for wear. "Want me to toss 'em in the cooler?" he asks me. "Hell, no, toss them on board," I tell him. "They'll cool off where we're going."

After we are under way at last, I post a letter on the bulletin board of the *Munargo* for all the men to see. It reads:

No greater challenge to the pioneering spirit of Americans has ever been presented than the present vital necessity for the United States Army Air Forces to prepare themselves for operations in the Far North. The thin paths beaten in the snow by courageous explorers have been obliterated by time. It is up to us to establish detachments to serve as steppingstones to the far-flung areas we must reach.

To accomplish this task, we have hand-picked a small group of men of known qualities of leadership, of ingenuity, of initiative. On you depends the success of the job. Upon your shoulders rests the burden of keeping us informed of the weather, ships which may pass through your area, and the many other important incidents which may come to your notice or attention.

Communications and correspondence are sharply limited by the secrecy which of necessity surrounds your mission. Do not feel, on this account, that you are "forgotten men," or in any danger of becoming so. I have issued specific instructions that I be kept constantly informed of your activities, which are of the deepest concern to me.

I know your job is tough. I know, also, that your standards are high.

We are depending on you.

H. H. ARNOLD
Major General, U.S.A., Chief of the Army Air Forces

There is a significant ceremony aboard our troopship as we cross the Arctic Circle. For days we have been plowing through monotonous gray seas, and now for the first time we can make out a row of snowcapped mountains, like stationary white clouds, on the northern horizon. At noon, as our bows slice across the mythical line, a blast of bugles sounds assembly, and the entire company gathers on the afterdeck. With an appropriate fanfare of trumpets, and several impromptu wolf calls from the GI's, King Borealis and his royal court come aboard.

His Northern Majesty is an impressive figure. He wears a regal crown, consisting of a trench helmet liberally coated with white flour paste, and a sheet borrowed from the ship's sick-bay hangs from his shoulders clear down to the soles of his broad-toed Army combat boots. Behind his foaming cotton beard, the familiar features of the mess sergeant peer belligerently. One shaggy tattooed arm protrudes from the folds of the sheet, gripping a black dog whip, symbolic of His Majesty's authority in the Arctic. The other hand holds a cigar butt. Behind him are grouped his official staff, including the King's two regular helpers, Frost and Hunger, who bear a startling resemblance to a couple of husky truck drivers. One by one the enlisted men in

the crew are summoned before him, and King Borealis unfolds
a scroll, and reads aloud the oath of the Arctic Brotherhood:

"To all soldiers, sailors and civilians, to all seals and ptarmigans
and narwhals: Greetings. Know ye that this G.I. pioneer, having
crossed the Arctic Circle, is hereby accorded membership in our
ancient secret society of the frozen North, entitling him to shoot a
polar bear and sleep with an Eskimo squaw if he can find her. Now
let all my subjects henceforth treat him with the proper amount
of respect."

Two buglers blow a fanfare, the certificate is handed to the
initiate, and he bows low to the King and returns to his place,
grinning. I watch the men curiously as they take their oaths.
Many of them are farm boys from Alabama or Tennessee or
Georgia, and they have never seen snow before. Their conception of the Arctic is a romantic movie thriller, complete with
igloos and walrus and demure Eskimo maids in fur parkas and
feathers in their raven tresses, driving teams of reindeer across
the ice in the light of the Midnight Sun. I am sure that none of
them has any real conception of what we are heading into. I
am just as sure that none of them would turn back if he had.

They gaze open-mouthed as the coast comes into sight, the
jagged white peaks interlaced with perennial blue glaciers. As
far as the eye can see, there is only snow and ice. A young
corporal standing by the rail plucks my sleeve. "What do they
call this here dump where we're going to, sir?"

"Greenland."

"It's a hell of a name for it," he mutters under his breath.
Even the size of Greenland is a shock to most of them. One
enlisted man from Flushing wants to bet a month's pay that it
is not as large as Long Island. Actually Greenland is almost
half the width of the United States itself. With the exception of
Australia, which is generally classed as a continent, it is the
largest island in the world. It covers 840,000 square miles, and

is 1,400 miles long and 700 across at its widest point. It extends as far north as Latitude 82° 40', seven hundred miles nearer the Pole than Point Barrow, Alaska.

A rim of high mountains extends around the entire coast, and cupped inside them is a solid mass of ice, covering four-fifths of the island. Superimposed on the United States, the Greenland Icecap would blanket everything from New York as far west as Kansas City. Its average thickness in the middle of the island is believed to be about 10,000 feet. Scientists have measured the bottom of the Icecap at a thousand feet below sea level, and from these facts we know that there are deep subterranean channels running from one side of the island to the other. There is even the possibility that Greenland may consist of three separate islands, linked by the ice. Perhaps, as we build our future defense installations on the Icecap itself, our seismic soundings will disclose more of the secrets that are locked beneath this great relic of the ice age.

Eric the Red, who discovered the island about 985 A.D., gave it the optimistic name "Greenland" in order to lure settlers from Iceland and Norway. This first real estate promotion scheme was not a permanent success. The climate was milder a thousand years ago; there is evidence that the early Norse colonists had some herds of cattle, and along the coast near Julianehaab and Godthaab are the ruins of ancient farms and a stone monastery. But the winters evidently grew more severe, the food supply dwindled, the reindeer disappeared; even the tribes of nomadic Eskimos in the north and east died out. To-day in all of Greenland there are not more than twenty thousand inhabitants, natives and whites combined, most of them huddled on the lower part of the west coast.

Originally both Greenland and Iceland belonged to Norway. They were ceded to the Danes at the Treaty of Kiel in 1814, and Greenland is still a colony of Denmark, administered by the Free Danish Legation in Washington. It has been agreed that if the United States will take over the protection of the island, it will be allowed to install bases and landing fields on this vital Atlantic outpost, the key to tomorrow's weather in Europe.

From this enormous ice bowl in the Arctic flow winds and currents that generate the storm fronts for the North Atlantic, for England, for Norway, for the continent itself. Every bombing raid we make over Germany will be influenced by weather data from this remote island station. The Germans know the importance of Greenland, too. Nazi weather planes have been patrolling its coast, we know, and it was advance information from Greenland that enabled the trapped battle cruisers *Scharnhorst* and *Gneisenau* to slip out under cover of heavy fog and break through the Denmark Strait into the Atlantic. The timing, indeed the very success, of a future Allied invasion of Europe may hinge on the fact that we, and not the Nazis, hold Greenland.

We have picked up a ship's pilot in Godthaab, an Icelander named Eriksen who has lived in Greenland for a number of years, and he guides us through the narrow gap into Söndre Strömfjord. The fjord is a mile wide at its mouth, almost blocked at its entrance by a small island called in Eskimo Simiutak, which means "cork stopper," and runs inland northeast over a hundred miles. The mountains on either side rise straight out of the water to 5,000 feet, and as we steam up through the fjord we can see to the south the shining blue-green of the Sukkertoppen Glacier. A little further inside, the sedimentary alpine formations yield to rounded-off granite and glaciated hills. Here and there are patches of heather and willows in their autumn reds and yellows, a wild spectacle of color in the frozen landscape.

On October 9th, when we arrive, we find our two supply ships already anchored in the harbor and partly unloaded. We resort to a primitive arrangement to get our equipment ashore. Two barges are welded together, and on these we lighter our

Lincoln Ellsworth (*left*) and Bernt Balchen in the *Polar Star*.

Knut Vang

view of the Antarctic pack ice from the *Wyatt Earp* during the Ellsworth Expedition.

Returning four years later to the drifted-over camp at Little America,
I find only the tail of the *Floyd Bennett* rising above the snow.

The wreck of the Lincoln Ellsworth Expedition plane *Polar Star*.

supplies to the beachhead, across a half-mile of mud flat. Most of the flat is bare at low tide, so we must wait for full flood and float the barges as far as they will go, then build a tramway to hard ground. We take a shovel ashore on the tramway, and start unloading with its boom and winch. For the first few weeks we sleep on board ship, and cook our lunches outdoors on blacksmith forges while we work.

Fortunately the weather holds dry and clear. Everyone pitches in together according to plan, soldiers and civilian construction workers laboring side by side, to raise our first building. As soon as it has a roof on, we all move into it and sleep on the floor. A few days later a second building is completed. We transfer our gear into that, and the first building becomes our mess hall. We are building at the rate of three houses a day now, and we have more comforts. Our radio station is set up and operating. Stoves are installed in the new barracks, steel bunks are set in place, blankets are substituted for sleeping bags. We even make a Finnish steam bath out of an empty gasoline drum, and the delighted GI's strip off their clothes and sit by hot rocks and whip themselves in the Finnish custom with willow switches.

The first thing I do is reconnoiter a route to the airfield site we have selected on the basis of our aerial photographs. I take along the engineering officer, and select my two best dog drivers, Sergeants Dolleman and Healy, who have just come back from the latest Byrd Antarctic Expedition. We make our way inland over bare frozen ground, a distance of eight miles to the proposed location. We find there is ample room for a 6,000-foot strip and parking areas for the planes, and the surrounding mountains offer ideal locations for our antiaircraft defense. By the time I return, the men have roughed out a path more than two miles long, over which our heavy equipment can move. By the end of November, a temporary runway on the frozen ground is ready to accommodate the first plane.

I don't suppose the full realization of how utterly isolated we are here is borne in on the men until the *Munargo* sails back to the States, and they know there will not be another ship until next summer. Standing on the beach and watching it disappear, is like seeing home leave them. Suddenly they are alone, a few lives pitted against all the forces of the North. The darkness is coming on faster and faster, and every day the thermometer drops a little lower. The newcomers fight down a rising panic; it cannot get any colder; they cannot possibly survive if it gets any colder. And still the thermometer goes down a few more notches each morning, the shadows lengthen like a tightening noose.

Day after day the cold increases, the days grow shorter. At first the men put on every item of winter clothing that has been issued to them, bundling themselves in a half-dozen woolen shirts at a time. I do not interfere; I have found that the best way of dealing with a soldier is to let him experiment for himself. Presently they discover that this extra clothing only serves to cut off circulation; and by midwinter they are all dressed alike: a pair of shoe pacs with felt soles, regular ski-trooper pants with knitted cuffs to keep out the wind, a single woolen G.I. shirt, a wind-proof gabardine parka and pants, and—most important of all items of Arctic winter clothing—a one-piece union suit of long underwear. Two-piece underwear works apart on the trail or when you sleep; the shirt ends up around your neck, the pants sag around your knees, and your exposed kidneys are ice-cold. We discard the regular G.I. issue, and every man wears a suit of old-fashioned balbriggans.

I issue only one other order about personal appearances: no beards. Shaving every day seems an unnecessary ordeal in this Arctic wilderness, and one enlisted man suggests pointedly that I ought to tell Santa Claus; but thawing out a set of frozen whiskers, we found in Antarctica, can be more painful still.

Even the food tastes of the men seem to change. They devour

with relish foods they have never dreamed of eating before: codfish liver, codfish roe, ptarmigan, Arctic hare. I teach them to cook Greenland char in the Amundsen manner, cutting it into chunks and boiling it in sea water until it floats to the top; I think some families back in the States will be due for a rude shock when their sons come home after the war. At least, the diet agrees with them. The men at Bluie West Eight gain an average of ten pounds their first winter.

On Sunday, December 7th, the loud-speaker in our radio station suddenly blares the news that the Japanese are attacking Pearl Harbor. I call everybody out, soldiers and civilians alike, and inform them that we must consider ourselves as being at war with the Axis powers, and Söndre Strömfjord is henceforth on combat status. I read the articles of war to them, and announce that they are under military command and subject to martial law. Two days later I receive word from Washington that the United States has declared war.

Now the sun is only a red glow at noon, and with the darkness there's always a danger of depression. Exercise is one of the answers: if you get tired enough, you can sleep. But it is just as important to keep psychologically fit.

Duty hours are long for all hands—we work in three shifts daily, seven days a week; but we must allow time for rest and relaxation. I give the men instruction in skiing, and whenever the weather permits, they are out on the adjoining slopes practicing telemarks and christies.

When the storms drive us indoors, we put on impromptu entertainment in the crowded gymnasium. They are not very professional shows: a hillbilly quartet, a G.I. who juggles a half-dozen tin mess cups, a youngster from Georgia who tells stories in dialect. The jokes are old, the music is off-key; but I wish sometimes, as I hear about the bickering and complaints of rationing back in the States, that the folks at home could see this group huddled around the piano, arms draped over bulky shoulders, voices raised in loud harmony to drown out the storms and the relentless cold.

We have movies once a week, and we set up classes where different subjects are taught, the story of Greenland among others. Our large library is in constant use.

We have indoor gym hours when we wrestle, play basketball, and box. I have noticed around camp, a cauliflower-eared G.I. who seems to hold a grudge against all officers; and one afternoon, while I am refereeing a bout, he asks me very innocently if I will teach him how to box. As soon as we start to mix it together, I can see that he has fought before: he moves with professional skill and knows all the ring tricks. I acquire a fine shiner the first round, but to his evident surprise I manage to go the distance with him, and even get in a few good licks myself before we are through. He has a new look of respect on his face as we shake hands after the bout, and he tosses me a crisp salute: "Thanks for the lesson, sir."

I return the salute, and wink at him with my good eye.

The cold is not the only menace. One afternoon I am listening to a broadcast by Lord Haw-Haw, the English-speaking propagandist for the Nazis, and I sit erect with a start as I hear my own name: "I say, there, Bernt Balchen, how are you doing way up there at Söndre Strömfjord in Greenland? We know all about the new 6,000-foot airfield you have built, and we will be taking care of it in due time, old chap. Cheerio."

We pick up another broadcast, even more disturbing. It is a weather report in German. We monitor it with special equipment we have brought from the States, but we cannot pinpoint the sending station. All we know is that it is somewhere in Greenland.

When you fight the Arctic, you fight on the Arctic's terms. On the Icecap you fight blizzards and sudden williwaws—in Norway we call them *foehn* winds—which can build to a velocity of 200 miles per hour in a matter of minutes, roaring down the mountain side like snow sliding off a tin roof and wrecking buildings and installations. In the spring you fight thaws, and treacherous snow bridges that collapse under your weight, and hidden crevasses into which a sled and team of dogs may plunge, never to be seen again. In the air you fight ice that overloads your wings and sends you out of control; you fight eccentric air currents over the Icecap that rack a plane and drop it several thousand feet without warning; you fight the fog. Most of the time you win, but sometimes you lose, and the Arctic shows no mercy to a loser.

On March 14th a Royal Air Force Hudson bomber sits down on our runway, the first of an endless series of aircraft being ferried across the North Atlantic to the fighting front. Week after week they arrive in ever increasing numbers, despite the fog that builds steadily in the late spring, born of the ice pack and the cold current moving southward from the polar basin, to strike, at the southeast coast of Greenland, an arm of the warm Gulf Stream. In early June it has been stirred to life by turbulent winds blowing off the high plateau of ice in the center of the island, and it eddies and sucks around the jagged coast, flooding the narrow fjords, obliterating all the landmarks and navigational guides in a limitless white ocean. Here and there an uncharted mountain peak protrudes like a vicious reef; and the pilots of four B-17s, proceeding from Labrador toward Bluie West Eight, fight their way higher and higher in a desperate attempt to get above the stuff. Their gas is getting low, and radio contact is poor. Their SOS calls come through to us faintly all night as we try in vain to sweat them in.

At two in the morning, one Fortress finds our field and manages a successful landing. A second Fort is forced down in the water near Narsasuak in southern Greenland, and all of the crew are saved. The third pilot crashes his ship behind a small Eskimo village north of us; the plane is completely wrecked, but miraculously no one is hurt. We learn of their landing through the Danish radio, and I evacuate them safely, and dispatch a crew of our own mechanics to dismantle the plane and salvage as much as possible.

The fourth Fortress, with Lieutenant Stinson as pilot, makes a wheels-up landing on the Icecap itself, about one hundred and twenty-five miles southeast of our base. His crew shows the greatest presence of mind and ingenuity. No sooner has the ship skidded on its belly to a full stop than they set to work with hacksaws, cutting off the propellor blades from the engine which drives their electric generator, and digging out a space beneath it in the snow. Thus they obtain a power source to recharge their batteries in order to maintain constant radio communication. In addition, they clean out the hydraulic and heating systems and install a makeshift stove inside the plane, using engine oil for fuel. We get a radio bearing on them, locate them the following afternoon, and drop standard emergency supplies: sleeping bags, rations, a complete new set of wool uniforms for each man. We add some cartons of cigarettes and a bottle of whiskey, and I ask them if there is anything else they need. Stinson replies over the radio: "Drop us a couple of blondes and leave us alone. Everything's fine here."

The next job is to get them out. They have come down in a heavily crevassed area on the very rim of the Greenland Icecap. Evacuating them by boat would involve at least a month's travel by water and then by foot over the roughest terrain and up onto the Icecap, in order to get them to the coast. The best bet, I decide, is to try to land a plane near them on the Cap itself. On previous flights I have observed that shallow lakes of melting snow and slush form occasionally in depressions in the ice. A survey discloses a lake three miles long not more than a dozen air miles from the spot where the plane is wrecked.

I have assigned to me now a squadron of long-range reconnaissance planes, PBY 5-A Consolidated amphibians, under the command of Lieutenant Parunak and his executive, Lieutenant Sinkankas. In a PBY with Parunak I fly over the lake a couple of times, and decide that it is large enough for a Catalina to land on and, more important, take off again. This same evening the PBY drops me off at the lake with my veteran sled drivers Dolleman and Healy. We paddle our rubber boats ashore through the watery snow and land on a weird beach of sloping blue ice, as bare and smooth as the side of a porcelain tub. There we set up camp.

We wake next morning, the Fourth of July, to a drizzling cold rain that turns to sleet. We make ourselves as comfortable as we can, and wait out the weather. By noon it has stopped raining, with only light drizzle and fog, and squalls of sleet and snow. Healy and I leave Sergeant Dolleman at the camp and set out on skis, each with his own rucksack, a couple of days' rations, and ropes for crossing the crevasses.

In the spring the Greenland Icecap stirs with new life. The glaciers are more fluid, constantly moving and shifting as they work toward the sea, and break off into the ocean. The bending produces deep vertical cracks in the surface of the Cap. Some of these crevasses are virtually bottomless: you can drop an empty C-ration can into one of them and listen in vain for it to land. Most of the fissures are covered by thin roofs of snow, which vary in width and thickness. Snow bridges form natural booby traps in the trail; the only safe procedure is to test ahead of you with your ski pole every step of the way. In good light conditions, you can tell when you are over a crevasse because the snow bridge sags a little in the middle, and you must go roped at all times. A moment of carelessness may prove fatal.

The fog grows worse and worse and we proceed through the heavily crevassed area across the Icecap. The surface is so broken that sometimes, with only a hundred feet of rope, there are as many as three deep fissures between Healy and myself. We can hear water running constantly beneath the ice, eating

it away underfoot. Several times, as we feel our way blindly
forward, the rear ends of our skis drop sickeningly into an unseen opening. At last we give up, back-track into camp, put on
dry clothing, and wait to make another try this evening.

For our second attempt we avoid this hazardous area, and
make for a higher route. Swollen glacial rivers are running
down over the Cap, and we have to wade them knee-deep,
linking our arms together and fighting to keep our balance on
the slippery-smooth bottom. Occasionally a river is so large that
we have to detour many miles upstream before we can find a
place to cross. Altogether we cover more than thirty miles that
night, slipping and sliding; and once I plunge clean over my
head into a crevasse filled with slush. From my previous aerial
reconnaissance, I know that we are traveling in the general
direction of the plane; and at last, toward morning, we make
out the low throb of a motor running. We reach the plane about
nine o'clock, thoroughly soaked and exhausted, after fourteen
hours of steady traveling.

A PBY, flying over the wrecked ship, drops additional snowshoes and provisions for the trip out. Our plan is to travel by
night: with the lower temperature when the sun is low in the
north, the surface is drier and firmer, and the glacial streams are
less active. The thirteen men in the Fortress crew put on the
new clothing issued to them, adjust their snowshoes, and pack
their sleeping bags for the long march. I warn them they can
take only a day's rations, and that everything else will have to
be left behind; but they have no idea of the ordeal that they
are about to face, and smuggle into their bags various personal
belongings they want to salvage.

Our caravan starts out single file across the ice, all the men
roped together. I lead the way, and Healy, like a loyal sheep
dog, brings up the rear to herd any stragglers along. For the
first couple of miles the men are enthusiastic; but gradually
their ardor begins to cool. One by one they discard items they

have tried to bring back, and presently our trail is marked by an increasing succession of cameras, electric razors, fountain pens, wallets, uniform caps, a pair of officer's dress shoes, a girl's picture in a leather frame. By midnight most of them want to drop their sleeping bags as well; but this is a risk we cannot afford to take. The PBY has dropped a storm warning, and I try to urge them along a little faster: "See that hill over there? The lake's just behind it." But they can only shuffle at a dead walk, faces set, eyes half closed in utter weariness.

By five o'clock in the morning we make out the lake in the distance. An hour later we reach camp, where Sergeant Dolleman has a steaming pot of pemmican waiting for us. The men are too tired to eat. They flop down where they are and do not move until Lieutenant Parunak lands in his PBY an hour later to take them back to the base. The next morning Lieutenant Stinson comes over to headquarters to thank me for the help. "I thought a couple of times while you were taking us through those snow crevasses that you were the most ornery and mean and tough goddam colonel I'd ever run across," he says frankly. "I still think you're the toughest, but I'll take back the rest."*

Our rescue is none too soon. Two days later I happen to fly over the same area, and look in vain for the lake on which we landed. A large fissure has opened in the ice directly under it, and all the water has poured down through. The entire lake has disappeared overnight.

Now the sun is shining day and night, and we are getting the full effects of the thaw. Our roads become quagmires, and the buildings we have erected on the permafrost start heaving, their foundations rippling up and down like a snake's back. Some of the barracks are so warped we have to pull them down to keep them from collapsing. Only one building does not budge, a storage plant which is located on a gravel slope, with

* After the war I learned that he had named his son for me.

a foundation of loose rocks. This is the answer to our problem. Henceforth our housing is bedded on a layer of gravel, and eventually this type of foundation proves to be the solution for all construction in the Arctic permafrost.

Our construction work is now ahead of schedule, and we can work in shifts that aren't so hard. With the warmer weather, the men enjoy the outdoors to the fullest extent.

One enlisted man finds three peregrine falcon chicks and manages to train them, learning all about it from a book about falconry he finds in the library. He looses them on a long string and teaches them to return and perch on his gloved wrist.

We get three ravens the same way, but they are no match for the falcons when it comes to training; they do just as they please, stealing, making a racket, and always getting into mischief. One favorite pastime is to tease the sled dogs, placing a piece of fish or meat just where the dogs cannot reach it. They howl and growl and strain on their leashes, and the ravens fairly laugh with delight.

Out on the coast we get hold of a sea eagle. She has a wingspread of eight feet and tips the scales at twenty pounds. She is gentle and docile, and sits quietly watching the ravens' antics. But the second we turn the ignition key of the jeep, she comes shooting through the air and settles on the back, spreads out her wings and floats leisurely along.

The birds are great morale factors for the men; and since we have a rule that nothing is to be killed within three miles of camp, it soon becomes a sanctuary. Blue and white foxes romp around, and the freshest find their way right into the mess hall, where they play around the tables while we eat.

During all the summer of 1942, the possibility of enemy attack is never out of our minds. Since the outbreak of the war, long-range Nazi planes—Focke-Wulfs, JU-88s, and Blohm and Voss 135s—have been patrolling Greenland's east coast, and once a Focke-Wulf Condor flew directly over our base. So far no actual installations have been discovered in Greenland; but we know that on at least one occasion Nazi operators disguised as seal hunters were picked up off the coast by the United States Coast Guard cutter *Northland* on its Greenland patrol. I remember that Ernst Udet had mentioned to me in Berlin once that he had reconnoitered the Greenland coast and studied its air potentials; and whenever there is a lull in our operations I scout the shoreline north and south as far as my fuel supply will carry me, looking for any sign of an enemy landing.

Also as I fly I keep an eye out for possible sites for new American air bases, even closer to Europe. Mackenzie Bay and Scoresby Sound, I think, might be good locations for forward installations to cover our convoys to Murmansk, and also to support a possible Allied offensive through Norway. But there is another idea in the back of my mind. Years ago I talked with Knud Rasmussen, the great Danish explorer, who in the early twenties had made a trip by dog team from Greenland around the Arctic rim to Nome, Alaska. In our library here at Bluie West Eight I come on Rasmussen's book "Across Arctic America," and I recall as I read that he told me once of an ice-free harbor on the northwest coast of Greenland, a place called Thule.

On August 24th I make an aerial survey of Thule with two of my PBYs, the first reconnaissance flight that far north along the coast. I see that everything Rasmussen said is correct: Thule has all the potentials for a great air base, extensive gravel flats for long runways, plenty of room for hangars and barracks, and, in North Star Bay, a deep-water harbor, open two to three months a year, that could handle any cargo ship. One bare stretch I drag with wheels down, tempted to land.* When I get back to my headquarters, I write a lengthy recommendation to

---

* From what I know now, I could have landed without any difficulty on this stretch, later called B-site.

General Arnold, the first report ever submitted on Thule's possibilities as an air base.

All this summer of 1942 the Bolero movement—code word for the prelude to the Allied invasion of Western Europe—has been in full swing. Aircraft in an endless stream have been pouring across Greenland, most of them refueling at Narsasuak, called Bluie West One, but a number of them coming in here at BW 8. It is a tribute to Yankee training and skill that these young Air Force pilots, fresh from civilian life and inexperienced in long-range flying, have so few accidents and forced landings—less than one in a thousand. But now the summer phase is coming to an end, and we are getting into the fall, with its storms, darkness, heavy icing, high winds, and must be prepared for bad luck to strike any day.

It strikes early in November when a B-17 Flying Fortress, engaged in a routine search mission for a missing transport plane, makes a wheels-up landing on a heavily crevassed section of the Cap, in one of the roughest and most inaccessible parts of Greenland. The ensuing rescue effort, the biggest ever attempted in the north, goes on for half a year and involves a number of aircraft as well as Coast Guard and Navy vessels and dog teams and motor sledges. A total of five men are killed before the evacuation is completed, and one of the crewmen, Lieutenant O'Hara, loses both legs. I make three belly landings in the snow with a PBY, the only ones ever accomplished, to bring out the last survivors. The whole operation is called by the Air Force one of the great sagas of the Arctic, an unparalleled story of suffering and sacrifice and human endurance during almost six heartbreaking months on the Greenland Icecap.

The missing C-53 transport which set this chain of events in motion ran into engine trouble on a flight from Iceland and was forced down somewhere on the east coast of Greenland. The first word at BW 8 is confusing. They report by radio that they are at 9,200 feet altitude, and give their position as Lat. 61° 30′ N. and Long. 42° 30′ W., which would place them out over the water. Three days later comes another message from the C-53 giving the same position but 2,000 feet altitude. Atterbury Dome, one of our chain of weather stations on the east coast, reports seeing flares shot in the air to the north; but our search flights over several hundred miles of the area are without result. No further word ever comes from the downed plane; it vanishes forever.

Meantime a hundred and twenty planes from the Bolero movement have been called on to intensify the search, combing the Cap in grid patterns whenever there is a break in the increasingly bad weather. We are nearing the winter solstice, and shall have no sun left at all in another three or four weeks. The crews take off before dawn and land after dark, with flare pots for runway demarcation, in order to utilize the few remaining hours of daylight.

On November 9th comes word that one of the Bolero planes, a Fortress with a crew of nine, has failed to return. The big bomber was assigned to the northern sector of the search pattern, which would place it somewhere on the west leg of the Curio Range, a radio range we had set up at Angmagssalik, and in the area of the Atterbury Dome weather station. Now with two planes down, and the sun sinking lower toward the horizon each day, we must redouble our efforts before darkness closes in. I commandeer a civilian C-54 from T.W.A., to extend the range of the search, and day after day we comb the Cap in vain.

The freezing winds are building to gale force, and always as we fly there is the threat of a sudden williwaw. Once I am at 12,000 feet over the Icecap when we hit a violent downdraft, the down-roll of a williwaw curling off the Cap, which drops us to 8,000 feet with our plane still in climbing attitude, throwing us on our side with the rudders full out opposite in an effort to counteract. Then we hit the reverse draft, and shoot upward

again to 15,500 feet, in descending attitude. I estimate the wind
velocity at about 175 miles at this time, and with an indicated
air speed of 215 m.p.h. our groundspeed is only 37 m.p.h. For
twenty minutes our four-engine ship is tossed like a leaf in a
cyclone. It's the severest turbulence I have ever encountered in
an airplane, and I think in all my flying this is the narrowest
escape of my life.

On November 24th, after two weeks of futile search, I follow
a hunch and make a long sweep to the southward. Ahead I see a
little red star climbing the dark sky, and then another flare and
another, and I alter course and drop down. The wrecked Fortress is lying in a valley of a glacier, at an altitude of about 4,000
feet, like a crushed dragonfly on the ice. It has hit in the worst
possible area of the Cap—an active part of the glacier, scored
with crevasses and bottomless canyons in the ice. I see from the
air that the impact has broken the fuselage behind the wing,
and the tail end of the plane is hanging down into an abyss.
Held on the level ice only by the weight of its front end, the
bomber is obviously in a precarious position.

It is a miracle that any of the crew are alive. They were
flying low over the Icecap in heavy overcast, we learn later,
and suddenly one wing tip struck the ice, and the plane flipped
and then leveled again, skidding and cartwheeling to a halt at
the very rim of the crevasse. Lieutenant Monteverde, the pilot,
was unhurt, but one crewman, Sergeant Spina, had broken his
right wrist, and another was badly cut by safety glass when he
was thrown through the nose. The navigator, Lieutenant
O'Hara, helped carry Spina back into the plane, and some snow
sifted into his boots, but he gave it no thought at the time.

The crew lashed canvas over the shattered nose, and huddled
inside the unheated plane, with icy gusts blasting through the
cracks in the twisted fuselage. The blizzard let up after three
days, but when they crept out they discovered that the ice
around them was so badly fissured it was dangerous to move in

any direction. They needed medical help for the two crewmen, and their radio was not operative, so O'Hara and Spencer, the copilot, volunteered to make a try for the coast. They were still within sight of the plane when a snow bridge gave way, and Spencer plunged out of sight. He slid a hundred feet down a hidden crack in the glacier and, by one chance in a million, landed on a block of ice wedged in the fissure. His crew-mates lowered a parachute shroud line to him, and inch by inch he worked his way back up the slippery wall, only to be stopped by an overhang at the surface. They passed down a machete to him, and he clung to the shroud line with one hand as he chopped his way over the protruding rim.

Now O'Hara noticed for the first time that he had no feeling in his toes, and realized that the snow inside his boots had frozen both his feet. Monteverde tried to thaw them with the heat of his own body, holding them against his bare stomach, while the other crewmen redoubled their efforts to get the radio going. At last they managed to pick up signals, but the transmitter still could not give out their position. The glacier was active, the ice fissures around them widened, and bit by bit the sagging tail of the plane settled deeper into the crevasse. They had almost given up hope when on the 24th they heard the far-away drone of my engines.

I take one look at the crumbling glacier, and instruct them not to leave the plane unless roped together. I have on board emergency supplies—stoves and sleeping bags and clothing and first-aid equipment—and my first couple of drops are made with cargo parachutes. The howling wind whips them past the plane before the crew can grab them, and the bundles slip over the rim of the abyss. I decide to try free-dropping without chutes, and warn the men to stay under cover inside the wreck. I come down to about fifty feet over the glacial valley, bucking the violent air that boils off the Icecap, and kick out the remaining bundles, actually hitting the fuselage several times. The wind is so strong that the drifting snow streams from the B-17's wing tips as I pull up after the drops and head for the auxiliary station at Atterbury Dome, eighty miles away.

I rip out a page from my diary and make a sketch as I fly, showing the location of the wreck and distances and routes, and weight it and drop the instructions to the station. Here they have dog teams and motor sledges, and in command is Lieutenant Max Demarest, one of the best young glaciologists in the States. He is experienced in Arctic travel, and I feel certain that the crew will be evacuated without further difficulty.

I am back four days later, as soon as there is another break in the storm, to drop additional medical supplies for O'Hara. While I am circling the wreck, I pick up a radio call from an approaching Grumman, a Coast Guard amphibian piloted by Lieutenant Pritchard, who was with me last year at BW 8. I tell him he can make a wheels-up landing with his little amphibian on a level area near the downed Fortress, and I will drop him rope and bamboo poles and snowshoes for crossing the crevasses to the wreck. An hour later Pritchard reaches the stranded party. O'Hara's feet have started to become gangrenous, and he cannot be moved back to the Grumman without a sled, so Pritchard guides the two other injured crewmen across the glacier to his rescue-plane and flies them out safely. From the air as I circled I have already spotted two motor sledges from Atterbury Dome, with Lieutenant Demarest and Sergeant Tetley, only twenty miles from the wreck, making good time across the Cap. They should reach the Fortress by late tonight, and take out O'Hara, and Pritchard will return in the morning for the rest of the crew. I head back to BW 8, confident that our troubles are almost over.

The Arctic is an unscrupulous enemy. It fights with any weapon that comes to hand, it strikes without warning, and it hits hardest just when you think the fight is won. The following morning, November 29th, it strikes a double blow. First comes a report that Demarest's motor sledge has broken through a snow bridge, only a hundred yards from the Fortress, and he has fallen to his death in a crevasse. Less than an hour later I hear that Pritchard and another Coast Guard crewman have taken off on their second evacuation flight with the B-17 radio operator, Howard, and failed to return to base. It is not until the following March that the remains of the Grumman are discovered, flattened against a mountain side in the blinding snow. All three men were killed instantly.

Now begins the Long Wait. The Arctic winter has closed in, and the violent storms have reached their peak. Every day when the weather allows us to fly, our planes make supply drops over the wreck, despite severe icing conditions and intense gales. O'Hara's gangrenous legs are getting worse, and he must have medical attention. Sergeant Tetley with the second motor sledge has remained with the Fortress crew since Demarest's death, and Monteverde decides that the only chance to save O'Hara's legs is to make a desperate gamble for the coast. Tetley estimates that he can make the trip in two days. He wraps O'Hara in his sleeping bag and puts him on the sledge, taking along a tent and emergency rations for three days. With him go the two strongest members of the B-17 crew, Spencer and Wedel, the flight engineer. Spencer knows only too well the danger of hidden crevasses, and he walks ahead on snowshoes to test the trail, and Wedel follows behind.

About two miles from the wreck they come to a smooth slope on the glacier, and Tetley decides they can all get on the sled and ride to make better time. As Wedel comes alongside to climb aboard, a concealed snow bridge collapses beneath him, right beside the sledge. He makes one desperate grasp, his fingertips sliding off the sled runner, and vanishes from sight. Tetley guns the motor, and they hurtle the gaping hole just in time. There is no chance of ever finding Wedel's body, they know, and they push on across the Cap with O'Hara. A couple of miles farther, the oil line to the motor congeals and breaks, and without Wedel's engineering ability they cannot repair it. Tetley and Spencer set up the tent and carry O'Hara inside, just as another heavy blizzard strikes.

There they are discovered three days later by Captain Pappy Turner, flying out of the 6,000-foot landing strip at Ikatek (Bluie East 2) only a short hour by air from the wreck. He drops food and medical equipment and also a walkie-talkie, so we can keep in touch with the survivors at the sledge camp as well as the three crewmen at the wrecked Fort six miles away. Another rescue caravan sets out from Atterbury Dome with thirty-five dogs. They are within ten miles of the sledge camp when bad weather forces them to retreat, and they struggle back to the Dome with only eight dogs left. Two months have gone by, and hope is beginning to fade that any of the survivors will be alive by spring.

Late in December I am called to BW 1 for a conference with Colonel Wimsatt, commanding officer of the Greenland Base Command, and Admiral Smith, commander of the Greenland Naval Patrol, to discuss whether anything else is left to try. I have one last trick to outwit the Arctic. Back in 1925, when Amundsen and Ellsworth were forced down on their first attempt to fly to the North Pole, I remember that Riiser-Larsen and Dietrichson took off the heavily loaded Dornier Wal flying boats by skidding them on their bellies across the floe ice, and I propose a belly landing on the cap with a PBY.

But the Navy, disposing of the PBYs, doesn't see it my way. I'm given a glacier-cold shoulder. No planes for me for such a lunatic purpose.

I tell them if I'm to crawl in on my hands and knees, I'll get the boys off the Icecap. I'm boiling hot under the collar, and Wimsatt and I go out for fresh air. Soon afterward we have a wire on the way to General Devers, our commanding general stationed in England, in which we request a plane. He cables right back that I may have the plane, but it must be manned with volunteers.

And now, at long last, the Navy wakes up and gives me two of their PBYs.

I poll the crew members of the planes to see who will volunteer for this mission. Every man steps forward. I select a skeleton crew consisting of Lieutenant Dunlap, the pilot of one PBY, and his radio operator and crew chief, and also Dr. Sweetzer, the medical officer at BE 2. We strip the armor plating and all machine guns from the plane to make it as light as possible, and wait for the first available weather. Just as I am about to start, on February 5th, a message is handed to me:

Factory indicates forward bulkhead of PBY too weak for landing on snow. What are you plans?

COMMANDING GENERAL, ARMY AIR FORCES

I scribble my answer and hand it to the messenger: "Going ahead as contemplated."

"5 February, 1943."

I have sent a couple of B-17s ahead to the rescue area, to scout conditions, and at eight o'clock this morning they report the weather fair and calm, the ground temperature about 10 below zero. I have decided to evacuate the group at the sledge camp first, because of O'Hara's critical condition. We have had no time to make a test landing, but I figure that if anything is going to happen it will happen anyway, test landing or not.

The area at the sledge camp has a slight upslope of about 2 per cent only. I tell Dunlap to bring the plane in at normal landing speed, like a power stall letdown on a glassy sea. We set the air speed at a fixed 80 knots, sinking about 200 feet a minute, and hold the plane in this position until the hull grazes the snow. Dunlap cuts the throttles, and the PBY slides smoothly

right up to the camp. Spencer is standing in front of the snow
hut they have built over the tent, and Tetley scrambles out as
we halt. Dr. Sweetzer and I crawl inside.

O'Hara is lying in his sleeping bag, his face a waxy yellow,
emaciated and weak, but he forces a little grin. I carry him to
the plane in my arms, as light as a bundle of rags. He weighed
180 pounds when he landed on the Cap three months ago, and
now he is only about 80 pounds. Spencer and Tetley crawl
aboard the PBY, and I give it the gun. The hull of the flying
boat has already frozen to the snow, and it will not budge.

The men scramble out onto the wings and rock the plane
back and forth until it is free, but before they can climb back
inside it has frozen tight again. I order the crew to get out and
stand at either wingtip float, wiggling the plane up and down
until it breaks loose, and I start sliding. I taxi slowly in a wide
circle, and the men line up on the snow outside this circle, and
wait for me to come around. As soon as the right outboard engine has passed over their heads, they dive for the blister one
by one, like jumping aboard a merry-go-round, and the radio
operator and Dr. Sweetzer grab each man in turn by the scruff
of his neck and the seat of his pants, and haul him inside. I
shove the throttles forward, and after a few seconds of eternity
the hull breaks the snow's grip and we are airborne.

"*17 March, 1943.*"

This morning the B-17s report favorable weather conditions
at the sledge camp once more, after over a month of unending
storms, and I am ready to attempt the second phase of the rescue. O'Hara has been flown back to the States to Walter Reed
Hospital, where both legs have been amputated just below the
knee, and we hear his condition is good. Now we will try to
bring out the last three members of the B-17 crew.

My plan is to land again at the sledge camp, and set down

a dog team to travel to the wreck, and I bring along Sergeants Dolleman and Healy, and also Captain Harold Strong, an old Alaska hand and experienced polar traveler. Everything looks good from the air as we bank over the site, but as we come in for our landing, we run into an opaque sheet of driving snow particles, whipped up by the wind. Our visibility is no more than fifty feet, and the blowing snow is so thick that we can barely see our tip floats as we slide to a halt. We planned to land 100 yards to the left of camp, but drift in the blinding snow, and are 400 yards to the right of the sledge camp. The dogs and sled are unloaded from the PBY, and the drivers shake the frozen hull free by rocking the floats. We take off blind, wobbling from one side to the other until we have enough speed to get rudder control. Our windsheld is completely iced over, and we are on solid instruments until we climb above the ground drift into the sunlight.

The vertical visibility is perfect, but on the ground the wind churns the snow up and it is impossible to see more than a couple of yards ahead. The B-17 guides the dog teams through safely, by radio, and the next day they are at the wreck. Now at last the Long Wait is almost over.

"5 April, 1943."

Spring is coming fast, and three days of unbroken rain, with thunder and lightning in the mountains, turn our field at BE 2 into a sea of mud and slush by the later part of March. I am afraid that the snow will be sticky now at the sledge camp, but we decide to take a chance with the weather opening again this morning. Captain Strong has reported by walkie-talkie that it is warm, with no wind, and I tell him to dismantle the sled and be ready to load everything aboard fast. With nine dogs and six added men and equipment, we shall have a much heavier load than on either previous try.

Monteverde and his crewmen and rescuers and dogs all climb aboard the PBY in silence, still unable to believe that their ordeal is ending. We make one long run, but the wet snow clings to the plane, and we cannot get up flying speed and get off uphill as we did before. I try a run downhill and halt just in time as a crevasse looms ahead. We make a third try uphill again, but the engines have been overheating, and as we gain speed the right engine catches fire. We manage to get it extinguished, but the vacuum pumps are damaged, and everything is black with soot. We unload the passengers, and roll up in sleeping bags for the night.

The engine is still capable of running for some time. Next morning there is a little breeze and it is colder. I decide that the PBY might get into the air with a lighter load, and I tell Dunlap to take the three B-17 crewmen back to BE 2. Strong and Dolleman and Healy and I will try to make it by dog team across the eighty miles of the Icecap to Atterbury Dome. The PBY disappears uphill, in a cloud of snow, and then I see it emerge into the sunshine above us. Dunlap climbs until he has altitude, then feathers the bad engine to conserve fuel, and sets his course back home.

I have no instruments along for land navigation, and I have to guide the party by dead reckoning. With a prismatic pocket compass and a protractor, I make computations in pencil on a diary page, and clock off our mileage on a distance-measuring wheel fastened to the runner of the sled. For five days we hole up in a williwaw, staking our dogs securely. and digging under the snow ourselves to ride out winds up to 150 miles an hour. Ten days later we have worked our way to the coast, through drifts and sastrugi as high as three feet, and arrive safely at Atterbury Dome on April 18th. Here a PBY picks us up, and takes us back to BE 2.

Colonel Wimsatt is waiting for me, with a top-secret telegram he has just received from Washington:

You are hereby directed to annihilate the Nazi-occupied station at Eskimonaes on the east coast of Greenland.

MARSHALL

War in the Arctic is a silent war, and in the silence and vast distances an enemy may move undetected. A man is only a dot in all that whiteness; huts and radio towers are invisible from the air amid the boulders and uneven patches of snow; the drifts cover an intruder's tracks as fast as they are made. It was three scouts of the Sledge Patrol, traveling by dog sled up and down the barren shore, who had stumbled on the Germans' secret hiding place.

The members of this unique patrol are former Danish and Norwegian trappers, as well as a few Eskimos, who used to make their living running traplines during the winter along Greenland's east coast. Their tiny cabins are scattered at intervals along the trail, and their knowledge of the country cannot be duplicated. In the fall of 1941, Admiral Smith of the United States Coast Guard and Eske Brun, Danish Governor of Greenland, had organized these civilians, and they were hired by the United States Army to form a regular military patrol of the east coast of Greenland, as far north as 77°, working out of various stations along the coast, visiting all the unoccupied huts along the trails, and reporting any signs of enemy occupancy.

On March 11th, the way I hear it, three members of the patrol were approaching Sabine Island in northwestern Greenland, and observed a couple of tiny figures moving along the ridge of Tafelberg Mountain. Realizing that no human beings were supposed to be in that area, they made for a near-by trapper's cabin at Cape Wynn, on the south side of Clavering Strait, planning to investigate further in the morning. In the hut they found two strange sleeping bags and a green uniform tunic with a swastika on the sleeve. As they were searching for further evidence, their alert ears detected someone approaching. They had no time to harness up their dogs, but set out on skis for the nearest patrol station at Eskimonaes, some sixty miles south.

Their precipitous flight gave the enemy two good dog teams. On March 23rd, a small party of Germans commanded by Lieutenant Ritter arrived at Eskimonaes in the sledges abandoned by the patrol. They attacked the base with rifles, automatics, and hand grenades, firing a machine gun into the air to give the semblance of being in force. The occupants, equipped only with hunting rifles, evacuated in a hurry. Fortunately they had a portable radio transmitter, and were able to send out word of what had happened. The Germans seized three additional dog teams and sledges, confiscated a number of soft-nose cartridges which the trappers used for hunting game, and placed all personal effects of the Danes in one hut, together with the Danish flag and about a hundred fox skins. Everything else they destroyed. Beside the flag they left a characteristic note:

March 23: The U.S.A. protects its defense interests here in Greenland. We do the same also. We are not at war with Denmark. But the administration on Greenland gave orders to capture or shoot us, and besides that you gave weather reports to the enemy. You are making Greenland into a place of war. We have stayed quietly at our posts without attacking you. Now you want war, so you shall have war. But remember that if you shoot with illegal weapons (dum-dum bullets) which you have at hand here in the loft of the radio station, then you must take full responsibility for the consequences, because you are placing yourselves outside the rules of war. Note we have put all personal effects of the hunters and all pelts in this hut, while we have destroyed the radio apparatus operating for the U.S.A.

COMMANDANT OF THE GERMAN WEHRMACHT DETAIL IN ESKIMONAES

On his way back to Sabine Island, Lieutenant Ritter and his men encountered three more members of the Sledge Patrol, returning to Eskimonaes after a reconnaissance to the north. The driver of the lead sled, Eli Knudsen, did not hear the

German command to halt. One of the Nazis killed him outright, and he was later buried in a stone shelter beside the trail, with a cross and a Danish flag to mark his grave. Ritter took the other two sled drivers as prisoners to Sabine.

Now our own preparations are going on to carry the attack to the enemy. Iceland offers better facilities for the mission, so it is decided that I shall proceed to Iceland to undertake the bombing of Eskimonaes and Sabine from there. In view of the distance involved—the round-trip flight from Iceland to Eskimonaes is as long as from London to Africa—we realize that the fuel supply of the Fortresses we are using will give us a close margin for bombing and strafing. Consequently we use one bomb-bay to carry 300-pound demolition bombs, and place an emergency fuel tank in the other.

We take off from Iceland about eleven o'clock in the evening of May 13th, in the strange twilight of an Arctic spring night. As we head north, the midnight sun begins to appear over the horizon. By the time we reach Eskimonaes, about three o'clock in the morning, it is shining brightly as at noon. The sun is in the northeast. Eskimonaes, on the south slope of the island, lies in deep shadow, the small buildings and radio station almost lost amid the rocks and splotches of snow.

We make several preliminary passes at low altitude to orient the bombardiers with the target. We can see how completely the Germans have destroyed the station: doors swing open loosely, windows are broken and vacant, there is no sign of life around the half-burned and wrecked buildings. Scratches made by sled runners are still discernible on the ice, leading both north and south, but in the Arctic it is difficult to tell how old a sled track may be. Although we assume the station is deserted, we carry out our orders, dropping our bombs and strafing the buildings, and leave them burning as we head back to Iceland.

Our fuel supply is barely sufficient to get us home. For our

mission to Sabine Island, I realize, we shall need Liberators
with long-range tanks. We will use the Fortresses to cover us
in case we are attacked en route by German aircraft, which are
still patrolling the east coast of Greenland and northern Iceland. While the Liberators are on their way from the States, we
lay our plans for our coming raid on Sabine: the first bombing
of German installations on this side of the Atlantic, the northernmost bombing ever attempted by the Army Air Forces.

On May 25th, the weather breaks favorably for the flight.
The Liberators are loaded each with ten hundred-pound demolition bombs. In view of the distance, the two Forts carry no
bombs, but place auxiliary fuel tanks in their bomb-bays, giving them greater capacity for combat maneuvers. The Forts start
half an hour ahead of the faster Libs, about four in the morning; and the flight makes its appointed rendezvous at nine over
Bontekoe Island in eastern Greenland. There the B-24s and one
of the B-17s wait for five minutes. Accompanied by another
Flying Fortress, I head toward Sabine to reconnoiter the target in hopes of drawing some anti-aircraft fire and thus deter-
mining the amount to be expected. The other ships have been
instructed to assemble fifty miles southeast of Sabine and await
our return.

The morning light is brilliant as we approach the target. The
sun glints on the icy hills, and the white snow patches and
black rocks make a striking checkerboard pattern beneath us.
The elevation of Sabine is about twelve hundred feet; the island is heart-shaped, some twelve miles in length, with a bight
on the eastern side where the German base is located. As we
fly over this area at 5,000 feet, I make out two main buildings:
one a two-story affair which I judge to be the radio station,
and the other a one-story shack several hundred yards away
which seems to be a storehouse. In the middle of Hansa Bay,
a German supply ship is frozen in the ice. It is a 300-ton traw-
ler, its mast and smokestack sawed off to make it as inconspicu-

ous as possible, and the sides of the ship banked with snow to camouflage it further. There is a ledge of rock behind the camp area, about a hundred feet high, on which their antiaircraft emplacements are located. We can see people running toward the guns, but we encounter no ack-ack fire as we bank.

Over the radio, I brief the Liberators on the target, and order them to attack at four thousand feet. The supply ship and the two main buildings are to be the primary targets. The Libs come out of the sun, right over the station, but owing to the confused pattern of dark boulders and white snow the bombardiers cannot identify the target accurately. I order them to stand at one side; and Captain Turner and I circle in our Fort and come down from the north through a valley, diving into the main building at about fifty feet. As we approach, we give it everything we have with our forward machine guns, and the tail gunner takes over as we complete our pass. Pulling up over the station, abreast of the ledge, we are met by a burst of machine guns and cannon fired horizontally at point blank. No hits are scored. Looking back, we can see smoke from our incendiary bullets pouring out of both buildings, making them easy targets for the Libs.

Now the big B-24s come around, scoring several hits and causing considerable damage to the surrounding area. We follow the bombing with low-level strafing, both armor-piercing and incendiary ammunition, giving a thorough hosing of lead to any object we can see on the ground, and also firing over thirteen hundred rounds into the supply ship in Hansa Bay. We stay over the target as long as our limited supply permits, about twenty minutes, and then the bombers are pulled off and we set a direct course back to Iceland.

As soon as the Coast Guard vessels with the landing parties arrive at Hansa Bay, we return to Sabine to cover their landing, and fly low over the German station. There is no sign of life. The buildings are gutted, and the ship in the bay caught fire from our strafing and melted the ice as it burned; there is only a black circle of open water through which the charred hull has sunk.

The Coast Guard cutter *Northland* is standing by, with troops from the Greenland Base Command. We radio that the station appears to be abandoned, and the cutter makes for the island beach. Led by Captain von Paulsen, a landing party of helmeted Coast Guardsmen and United States and Danish ground troops with rifles and automatics heads for shore.

In the cove as they approach they can see twin lines of telephone cable, trailing from the sunken German supply ship shoreward to the main buildings of the station. Frozen into the snow are life jackets, bits of wreckage, the splintered ribs of a lifeboat. The bomb craters in the ice look for all the world like craters in the moon. The camp area is littered with the exploded 50-calibers with which we had strafed the station, some of the slugs flattened against the flint-hard ground.

What the bombers hadn't destroyed, the Germans had. Every building on the island is reduced to charred rubble. In the blackened piles the men find ruined Lugers, exploded ammunition, parts of 20-millimeter guns, tools, wrecked weather instruments. Behind the base lie the frozen bodies of two complete dog teams; the retreating Germans had killed the animals in their harness. At the foot of the ledge, another scouting party discovers several cargo parachutes, made of red cloth, their attached bundles open but not destroyed. Inside are complete German uniforms, arctic clothing of excellent manufacture, and metal boxes of food, including some delicious Danish butter. Evidently the Nazis were supplying the base regularly by air with equipment, perhaps even with men. The landing party finds a newspaper dated May 15, 1943, indicating that the last visit of the supply plane was either shortly before or just after the installations were bombed.

Later an Army patrol, climbing a small hill on the south side of the island, comes abruptly on a lone German crouching in the rocks. Several hand grenades lie on a ledge beside him, but he surrenders without a struggle. He gives his name as Dr. Sensse, and claims to be a lieutenant in the German Medical Corps and medical officer of the expedition. He is a short, thick-set, surly Nazi, somewhere in his early thirties, the crisscross dueling scars on his face almost hidden by a scraggly brown beard. Apparently he was on a reconnaissance mission when the bombing took place, and returned to the destroyed base just as our landing party arrived. He is wearing a Norwegian parka; questioned by a Dane in the party, he admits casually that it belonged to Eli Knudsen, the driver of the Greenland Sledge Patrol who was ambushed and killed. The Doctor seems proud of the fine grave they made for Knudsen, and describes his personal efforts to heap tundra and rocks over the body, and set up a respectable cross with Knudsen's name and the date lettered in thumb tacks.

Dr. Sensse is taken into custody aboard the *Northland,* and the landing party renews the search along the south side of the island. Presently it locates an aircraft-type rubber life raft, in which the Doctor evidently planned to make his escape. A steel case beside it contains a number of neatly packed German hand grenades. Attached to the case is a scrawled note left by the fleeing Germans:

Dear Dr. S:

We have been bombed by U.S. four-motored bombers and therefore will disappear to the home country after we have destroyed what is left. K., P., M., H., and N. have already left; the others will follow soon, I hope. I shall give exact reports about you in Germany. Everything else you will find here with the letter. You know what the plans are. I cannot speak more plainly in case an accident should allow this note to fall into the wrong hands. You will find a sketch on the inside of this sheet which will make it possible for you to bear life here. Many greetings sent you.

The sketch on the reverse side shows the hill, a hut called "New Hut" and a path to the summit of the pass, where a tent is shown, marked "Here are petrol and cooking utensils." Four stone heaps are indicated on the map, and beneath them is lettered: "Four little stone heaps here. Below is your equipment and further down in the direction of the arrow are two boxes of provisions buried in the snow. Again, thousand greetings. Your comrades."

The landing party spends a day digging out the booty. Radios, hand grenades, rifle and pistol ammunition, tinned food, and more clothes are found concealed in the rocks. So busy are they with these operations that they fail to notice the ice jams which have formed around the *Northland* at her anchorage. The oversight nearly proves fatal. Early in the afternoon a black German Junkers drops out of the sky, and makes a run over the ice-locked cutter. The guns on the trapped ship bang steadily, and the Nazi plane shears off and goes away without dropping its bombs. Hurriedly the shore party comes aboard, the cutter works its way free, and with the lone German prisoner begins its struggle back through the fast-closing ice pack toward Iceland.

Late in July I am in Iceland at the headquarters of General Bonesteel, commanding general of the Allied forces there, and I learn that Lieutenant Ritter has just been brought in from Scoresby Sound. They cannot get any information out of him, and I volunteer to talk to him. As I enter the stockade, he introduces himself in a relieved manner: "How do you do, Colonel Balchen? I have known about you from Spitsbergen." He speaks fluent Norwegian, and soon he is telling me the whole story of the German landing at Sabine; in exchange I get him some books on glaciology and polar science that he desires.

Lieutenant Ritter says he was an Austrian officer in the First World War, a student of geology, teacher and author of several books of his own on the Arctic, and formerly the master of a German whaling ship. He was commissioned in the German Navy early in 1942, and placed in command of an expedition to Greenland to set up a weather reconnaissance station. Its purpose was to supply weather observations to the German Luftwaffe, and to the German submarines for their warfare in the North Atlantic. In addition, according to Ritter, Greenland was used regularly to send advance weather information to Nazi merchant ships which enabled them to run the gantlet of the Allied navies, in the straits between Iceland and Greenland, and carry Axis supplies from Norway to Singapore and the East Indies and Japan.

Ritter's ship, the *Hermann*, bought in Denmark and fitted out in Kiel, left for Norway in August of 1942, proceeding from there to the east coast of Greenland. No specific instructions were given to Ritter as to where to locate the weather station; he picked Sabine Island as the farthest north he could get, and landed there on August 26, 1942, erecting the base on the shore of Hansa Bay. The station functioned all that fall and winter, making ground observations five times daily and sending radio sonde pilot balloons aloft once each afternoon. The results were radioed in code to the German Naval High Command in Berlin. The radio was operated by Diesel-powered motors and dynamos, and sent its report twice daily.

When the members of the Danish Sledge Patrol discovered the Nazi uniform which had been carelessly left in the trapper's hut along the trail, Lieutenant Ritter advised Berlin at once that they had been detected. He was ordered by the German Naval High Command to proceed to Eskimonaes and destroy that installation. The escape of the Eskimonaes garrison convinced him that it would be only a matter of time before the base at Sabine would be attacked; and he recommended to Berlin that they evacuate Sabine and transfer their men and equipment to a more remote location in the north. His capture and

our subsequent bombing upset these plans. The remaining
Germans fled north along the coast to an appointed rendezvous,
where they were picked up by a German seaplane from Norway.
I can tell as he talks that he has no love for the Nazis, and he
concludes frankly: "I'm glad to be out of the whole damn
mess."

I am still in Iceland on September 7th when General Arnold
and his staff stop over in Keflavik, on their way to England, for
a conference with the Iceland commander. While Arnold is at
the Hotel de Gink (the Air Force nickname for VIP quarters
all over the world), I have an opportunity to talk to him about
my work in Greenland. Arnold nods as I talk, and looks at me
for a long moment with his penetrating blue eyes. "There's something else on your mind. What do you want to do now?"

"Get into the fighting in Europe, sir."

His lips twitch a little. "Haven't you had enough fighting
yet?"

"Well, sir, I was talking to Colonel Turner, our air attaché
to Sweden, when he came through BW 8 on his way to Washington a couple of months ago, and I'd like to do something to
help the Norwegian resistance movement. Way back when I
took out my first U.S. citizenship papers, I made up my mind
that some day I would try to justify belonging to Norway and
America both. Maybe this would be my chance."

When General Arnold grins, I am not sure whether he is
smiling or just thinking, but if he is thinking, I can always be
sure he is way ahead of me.

"You better come back to Washington," he says, "and talk
to Bill Donovan at OSS."

(*Top, left*) The belly landing of the PBY on the Greenland Ice-cap during rescue operations there.

(*Top, right*) After our long journey across the Greenland ice fields following the rescue of the B-17 flyers. *From the left*: Sergeant Dolleman, Colonel Balchen, Captain Strong, Sergeant Healy.

(*Right*) General "Hap" Arnold (*center*) visits us in Iceland.

Official U.S. Air Force Photo

A USAAF plane delivers an air drop to underground forces in occupied Norway, near Oslo. (From a watercolor painting by Bernt Balchen.)

NINE

VE DO IT

1943–1945

Last night in London there was another heavy air raid; but this morning the broken show windows of Selfridge's Department Store on Oxford Street are all boarded up and business is going on as usual. A very proper clerk in the men's clothing department greets me, polishing his hands, but his smile grows frosty when he sees some sixty American G.I.s clumping into the store behind me in their thick-soled brogans. "You wish something, Colonel?"

"Ja, some civilian suits," I reply. "No two alike."

His Adam's apple bobs up and down a couple of times. "I'm afraid I don't understand, sir. You mean two different suits for yourself?"

"I guess you don't get the American lingo. I mean two suits apiece for all these men here with me—shirts, ties, shoes, socks—the works."

The clerk gulps so hard that his Adam's apple wedges in the inverted wings of his celluloid collar. "But that is quite impossible, Colonel. Clothing is rationed."

"I've got the coupons," I shrug, and dump a whole bale of them on the counter. "Just make sure all the labels and identification marks are taken out."

By this time he is convinced that we are the crew of a Nazi submarine, at least. "Send the clothes around to the American Embassy on Grosvenor Square," I tell him, as a finishing touch, "marked 'Ambassador Winant—Personal.'"

The Air Force crewmen with me are almost as puzzled as Selfridge's clerk. They are all well seasoned "carpetbaggers" as we call them, men who have been flying B-24 Liberator bombers on drop-missions to the Free French underground, but they have no idea what their new assignment will be. All they were told was to come to London to meet the Cold Weather Man. They also know they will be flying as civilians, because they had civilian passport photographs taken yesterday and visas were issued to them for Sweden, Finland, and the Soviet Union. They know they are mixed up in another OSS project, but I cannot tell them any further details.

Our operation is known only by the code name Sonnie. Back in Washington, on my return from Greenland, I reported to the hush-hush headquarters of the Office of Strategic Services, on a back street behind a brewery. There General "Wild Bill" Donovan himself briefed me on this mission. As soon as I arrived in England, I contacted Colonel David Bruce, head of OSS in London,* and Allen Dulles, who was also in the top echelon of secret operations. In charge of the Norwegian desk in the London OSS offices I found my old friend Commander Georg Unger Vetlesen, who once dug deep into his own pockets to help set up in Canada the Royal Norwegian Air Force training base called Little Norway.

In the OSS war room on Baker Street, hung with wall-size maps of all the fighting fronts, they went over with me the whole situation in Scandinavia to date. In occupied Norway, the long arm of Axis power stretched clear up to the Arctic Ocean. To the south Denmark was overrun, and south of Denmark lay Germany proper. East across the Baltic was Finland,

---

* In 1958, United States Ambassador to Germany.

ARCTIC OCEAN

NORWEGIAN
SEA

TIRPITZ   BANAK   PETSAMO
KAAFJORD   KIRKENES
KARASJOK   MURMANSK
KAUTOKEINO

NARVIK
KIRUNA

ARCTIC CIRCLE
BODÖ
Bodö Saltdal

BODEN
LULEÅ   KEMI
KALLAX

ATLANTIC OCEAN

NORWAY

SWEDEN

FINLAND

Gulf of Bothnia

TRONDHEIM
HOLTAALEN
BOLLHÖE
Jotunheimen
Sognefjord JORSTAD HASLEMOEN
Glacier
Lake Loen
BERGEN
Herdla Is.   SANDUNGEN
OSLO
SELJORD HORTEN
STAVANGER
TVEIT
CRISTIANSAND

SUNDSVALL

Tammerfors

HELSINKI

Gulf of Finland   LENINGRAD

MULLSJÖ

STOCKHOLM   TALLIN
ESTONIA

NORTH SEA   SKAGERRAK   KATTEGAT
GOTHENBURG

DENMARK
COPENHAGEN
MALMÖ

BALTIC SEA

RIGA
LATVIA

LITHUANIA

U. S. S. R.

U.

HAMBURG

GERMANY

BERLIN

N

SCALE OF MILES
0   50   100   150

J.MacD

THE SCANDINAVIAN COUNTRIES

whose traditional enmity with Russia had forced her into an alliance with the Axis. The Nazi grip on the north was tightening, and as Grand Admiral Raeder of the German Fleet once told Hitler: "Who controls the coast of Norway, commands the North Atlantic."

Only Sweden had been by-passed in the Axis invasion—leaving that country a peaceful eye in the hurricane of war all around it. The neutrality of Sweden was a great advantage to the Nazis. Without expending a single soldier for occupational duty, they could transport strategic materials across the country, and exchange coal for Sweden's lumber and steel in order to reenforce their war machine. For generations there had been trade agreements between the two nations, and many Swedish and German families were interrelated; but lately, as the Swedes saw the behavior of the Gestapo in the occupied countries, public sentiment had been growing more and more in favor of all-out aid to their Norwegian and Danish neighbors.

Actually there was a tremendous advantage to the Allies also in Sweden's neutrality. Here was a safe haven for 80,000 Scandinavians who would otherwise have wound up in Nazi concentration camps, and for another 150,000 refugees who had escaped from Latvia, Estonia, Lithuania, Poland, and parts of Germany itself, fleeing both the Nazis and the Communists. Norway had no sooner been invaded in 1940 than refugees started streaming into Sweden. Then arose the serious problem for the Norwegian government-in-exile of getting the able-bodied men out of Sweden and into active service against the Nazis.

For a time some refugees managed to get back into the fight by traveling from Sweden through Finland, across Russia and Siberia to Japan, and across the Pacific Ocean to Canada. But when the Finns joined the Nazis in the war against Russia, even this long and difficult route was shut off.

Now, as the anti-Nazi feeling increased, the OSS briefing officers told me, Sweden had declared herself willing to defy Berlin at last, and had authorized Norway to have 2,000 trainees of military age flown from Stockholm to London. The Norwegian government-in-exile had bought two Lockheed Lodestar planes for flying some of them out; but these transport operations were controlled by the British, who, curiously, rejected all pleas to purchase more airplanes so that the ferrying service might be expanded. Consequently, the evacuation amounted to a mere trickle.

The new American program, Operation Sonnie—my job—was to set up an adequate air transport service, and first of all to bring the 2,000 trainees to London, from which some could be sent on to Little Norway, near Toronto, for flight training, others to Nova Scotia for naval training, and still others could be assigned directly to Norway's merchant marine.

That same night, at United States Strategic Air Force head-quarters in Widewing, a suburb of London, I had dinner with General Tooey Spaatz and his deputy, Major General Frederick Anderson, and we discussed the problem of where to find the airplanes for the new project. Available planes were scarce, because everything was tied up with the big push starting in France soon. Also at the table was Jimmy Doolittle, hero of the Tokyo raid the year before, who had just replaced Ira Eaker as Commanding General of the Eighth Air Force. "How about Colonel Heflin's carpetbaggers?" Jimmy suggested. "They're already under OSS orders. Intelligence has cleared them, and we could pull some crews out of that group."

"Can you handle it, Bernt?" General Spaatz asked, and I replied promptly: "Sure, ve do it."

Tooey Spaatz grinned a little; he liked what I said, I think. "Okay, Freddie, you and Bernt can write out the directive. Ve'll do it."

On January 27, 1944, I receive orders designating me as special representative of the Commanding General, United

States Strategic Air Force, with authority to make all decisions and take such action as I deem necessary to execute the mission. Now I am attached to the European Division of the Air Transport Command, and assigned to me are five B-24 Liberators from Colonel Heflin's group. While the crewmen are being camouflaged in their new civilian clothes, the Libs are out at Bovington airfield, also having their military insignia removed, and being painted a mysterious dark green. Each plane is equipped with a Gee-Box, an accurate radar navigational aid to guide it through the blind weather that we shall need for our clandestine missions. Operation Sonnie is ready to go into battle.

Our first battle is with British red tape. To my consternation, the British civil authorities refuse us permission to operate out of their landing fields. A round of endless discussions ensues. From the British General Staff to the British Air Ministry, from the Home Office to God knows where, always I get the same official run-around. They pretend they have no knowledge of the project, and when I tell them it has been requested by the Norwegian government and okayed in Washington, a top-ranking officer loftily demands to know how the Norwegians have dared to go outside the chain of command. "As a matter of fact, isn't Norway one of our colonies?" he says. The general feeling seems to be that we have no damn business in that neck of the woods. The British have been charging the Norwegian government for each refugee the Norwegians bring out from Sweden with their own equipment, and the U.S. Army Air Force would make no charge and would operate on a far larger scale. But the final authority is at such a high level that I cannot fly up to it with my Colonel's wings. I am told it simply cawn't be discussed. I shall just have to wait and see.

I wait and see, day after day, until the middle of March. One afternoon at Kingston House, headquarters of the Norwegian government-in-exile, I explain the whole situation to my friend

Trygve Lie, Norway's Foreign Minister, adding that if we are ever going to do any good, somebody will have to slash through this red tape.

Lie has an idea. "Tomorrow I am having luncheon with King Haakon and Crown Prince Olaf. Winston Churchill and Anthony Eden will be there, and before we sit down I will drop a flea in His Majesty's ear."

The following afternoon Trygve Lie phones me. During the luncheon, he says, the King asked Churchill point-blank: "Why are the Americans refused the right to fly into Sweden to take out the men we need for our Air Force and merchant marine?" Churchill, perplexed, replied that he had no idea what had been holding up the operation; of course they could fly. He turned to Anthony Eden, who was very red-faced and embarrassed, and ordered him to give us permission at once. Two days later I have the clearance from the British, crank up my five war-weary B-24s, and head for our future air base at Leuchars in Scotland.

No more suitable place could have been found for our project. Leuchars Field is situated at sea level a few miles from St. Andrews; and its runway, extending almost to the water's edge, is ideal for take-offs and landings in thick fog. It is an RAF Coastal Command Station, where a group of the Royal Norwegian Air Force is now stationed. The commanding officer is Colonel Finn Lambrechts, a second cousin and former flying mate of mine, and there too are many of my old comrades from Horten. They are operating Catalina flying boats, supporting the Norwegian Underground, and Mosquitoes against Nazi convoys along the Norwegian coast; and we have the advantage of their special facilities and weather information. Our line of flight will be up the North Sea to our coast-in point, then a dash over occupied Norway to Swedish territory, and a final dog-leg down to Bromma Municipal Airport at Stockholm. To confuse the enemy, our entry point will vary all the way from Trondheim down to the extreme southern tip of Norway.

On March 31st, the very day we arrive, the weather reports are just what we have been hoping for. There is solid overcast all the way across Nazi-occupied Norway. At midnight, eleven hours after landing at Leuchars, I am airborne again on the initial flight of Operation Sonnie. With me as copilot is my new executive officer, Lieutenant Colonel Keith Allen, who is dark-skinned like an Indian and almost as taciturn. He is one of the finest instrument pilots I have ever known, both skillful and courageous. A large part of his life has been spent in airplanes and he is destined to die in one. Along as crew members are Captain Dave Schreiner and Lieutenant Robert Durham, both veterans of many carpetbagger operations with the Maquis in France.

For this first flight across Norway, I follow the course of the Sognefjord Glacier, because I know there are no Nazi defense guns there. We encounter no enemy flak, even when the clouds start breaking up at the Swedish border. A tail wind brings us to Stockholm ahead of schedule, and I see the golden spire of the City Hall sticking up through the fog. We are told to circle Bromma Airport, but after a while our gas gets low, and I come into the regular traffic pattern for a landing. Parked on the ramp is a Swastika-marked DC-3, which the Nazis have seized from the Dutch KLM, waiting to take off for Berlin. The German crew gazes curiously at our green-painted B-24, the first such aircraft to land here at Bromma, as we are hurried into the passenger terminal.

Here, suddenly, I find myself face to face with a man I have known as press attaché in the German Embassy in Oslo before the war, Dr. Grassman of German Intelligence. I know he has spotted me, so I greet him pleasantly: "Guten Tag, Dr. Grassman. Wie geht's bei Ihnen zu Hause?"—"Good morning, Dr. Grassman, how's everything at home?" The Doctor is so flabber-

Opening a container of American-made plastic explosives and other sabotage
equipment dropped by Operation Sonnie to Norway's freedom fighters.

A container drop is received by Norwegian resistance forces.

Supplies and equipment stacked high on the beach at Thule, Greenland, during construction work on the airfield in 1951, and ships at anchor in the iceberg-filled harbor.

gasted he can only sputter, and I step into a waiting car and
drive with my crew to the Grand Hotel, fronting on the canal
across from the Royal Palace.

Allen, Schreiner, and Durham have brought along K rations
and pup tents; but we are ushered into a palatial suite, and after
a hot bath I take the three of them downstairs to a breakfast
they could not find in all of war-rationed England: fresh orange
juice, pitchers of real milk, steaks with fried eggs on top, hot
rolls, and all the country butter we can eat. The dining room is
full of foreign agents chatting in their native tongues, and I
lean back and listen with great interest, understanding some of
these languages. I think my ears have never been so busy.

Sweden in 1944 is a sort of honest broker for all the wartime
intrigue going on. Stockholm is like a curb exchange for the
espionage and counter-espionage trading of all the belligerent
powers. Under-cover operators and mysterious diplomats without portfolio shadow one another in endless circles around the
revolving doors of the Grand Hotel. Sweden shuts its official
eyes to these fast transactions taking place across the international board, and the thrifty citizens adopt a practical attitude
toward the situation. I should not be surprised to see a corner
shop advertising masks and false whiskers.

The Grand Hotel is a house of all nations, with Japanese and
Russians and English and Germans living on various floors, and
bowing politely whenever they meet. We have a few cocktails
before dinner the first night, and Dave Schreiner is in high
spirits. As we come out of the lounge, I see a group of high-
ranking Nazi officers walking toward us, and I warn him
quickly to act very friendly and put on a cordial front. We pass
in the corridor, and Schreiner makes an all-out effort to comply.
He waves a hand cordially. "Hello, enemy!" I grab his arm, and
he confides in a stage whisper: "I guess we fooled 'em that
time."

Here in Stockholm I start laying plans for our future operations. First I pay my respects at the Embassy to the American Minister, Herschel Johnson, and tell him about the official project to evacuate 2,000 Norwegians out of Sweden. He warns me sternly to remember my obligations as a guest in a neutral country, and not to make any contacts that would embarrass the State Department. "As the highest American official here in Sweden, I want to know what is going on at all times. If I ever catch you doing anything illegal here, I'll have you deported."

"Don't worry, Mr. Minister," I assure him, "you'll never catch me."

Now I establish my most important contact in Stockholm, a man I have known for years in the old country. He is Dr. Harry Soederman, chief of the Criminal Institute in Sweden and a great friend of Norway. He and other prominent Swedes have set up many training camps for Norwegian refugees, where more than 12,500 Norwegian youths are now receiving instruction as what the Swedes call "police soldiers." They wear Swedish uniforms with Norwegian patches on the shoulders, carry Swedish guns and ammunition, and participate in maneuvers with the Swedish armed forces. It is a tremendous asset to have all this manpower of Norway trained and ready, and I think nothing speaks more clearly for the attitude of Sweden during the war.

Dr. Soederman is working closely with the Norwegian resistance movement, and he puts me in touch with the leaders of the Norwegian underground in Stockholm, and also the secret radio operators assigned to official positions in the Norwegian legation. Through these contacts, I can secure information about German fighter activity and flak battery installations along my lines of flight, and I am given secret radio codes and call letters so that my planes can communicate directly with the underground stations behind the lines in Norway. I also establish connections with OSS in Stockholm, and finally with the British Overseas Airways Corporation. The BOAC chief,

Douglas Grey, gives me office space for my official headquarters.

Because of Sweden's neutral status, our operations must be as inconspicuous as possible. The Swedish Air Authority is worried, and Carl Jungberg, director of the Swedish Air Ministry, tells me I must have some numbers on my aircraft. "Okay," I say. "What size?" He shrugs: "Oh, big enough so you can read them." The side of my plane is a dark green, so I paint on a number in black. It is four inches high, and in bright sunshine you can read it almost ten feet away.

Still I have one more problem. In accordance with Swedish civil aeronautic rules, we will be obliged to file our flight plans in advance, and the manager of the German air transport station at Bromma airport, named Schaeffer, is a recognized Nazi agent. We know he will relay my flight plans promptly to the German Command and thence to all the fighter bases along the route. Dr. Soederman wants to arrest Schaeffer on some trumped-up charge, to get him out of the way, but we figure that a man we can watch is safer than some unrecognized Nazi agent who would replace him. I decide instead to post fake flight plans, and this arrangement satisfies the aeronautics authorities and saves my flights from being molested.

In the months that follow, some of our relations with the Germans in Stockholm have all the aspects of comic opera. One of my Liberators cracks a cylinder-head on a flight from Leuchars. Knowing that the DC-3s the Germans are operating between Berlin and Stockholm use the same kind of engines, I ask my friend Captain Carl Florman of the Swedish Air Line to borrow a spare cylinder from the Lufthansa representative at Bromma. The German replies that he does not have one on hand in Stockholm, but will arrange for one to be sent up from Berlin on the next plane. The following day the air transport delivers a cylinder from an American B-24 which has crashed in Germany, and I install it in my Lib and fly back to Leuchars.

There I get a spare cylinder and take it to Stockholm the next day to replace the one we borrowed from the Nazis.

Our agreement with the Swedes allows us a maximum of three planes daily, but whenever the weather is right—that is, bad—we not only use our full quota, but expand it to as many as twenty-two flights in a single night. One day I am sitting in a B-17 on the Bromma field, and in front of me on the other side of the field, a long line of my Liberators is parked. A German DC-3 lands on the runway and the three members of the crew climb out. They start toward the terminal, then suddenly they do an about-face and stare at the Libs incredulously. I see their three forefingers move up and down in unison as they count "Ein, zwei, drei . . ." and so on to nineteen.

Each Liberator can carry thirty-five passengers, and by the end of the war Operation Sonnie will have evacuated more than 5,000 men from Nazi-occupied territories—Norwegians, Czechs, Belgians, Russians, Danes, and Italians—as well as a number of marooned Britishers and French and Hungarians and Canadians and Swiss and Brazilians and Poles and Icelanders and Cubans and Finns. Before the operation is over, my little air force of five war-weary Liberators has expanded to sixty airplanes—a good-sized air line—and to house my Stockholm detachment of 250 men I have to rent two large apartment houses, with additional hotel rooms and small apartments scattered all over the city.

Late in May of 1944, Sonnie takes on a new and even more delicate assignment. Through Dr. Soederman, I learn of a critical situation that is developing in the Norwegian resistance movement. More than 40,000 young men have taken refuge in the mountain forests of Norway to avoid falling into the hands of the Gestapo and being conscripted as workers for the Nazis. They are being trained for guerrilla operations, and are in desperate need of everything—weapons, ammunition, food, clothing, and medical supplies. The RAF has been dropping some equipment to them, but now, with the coming of almost continuous daylight during the summer months, the British have decided the hazard is too great. If the drops cease, Soederman fears that the discouraged guerrilla units may disband and filter across the border into Sweden, and a potentially powerful striking force for use against the Nazis will be dissipated. His pleas to London have been of no avail, and he asks me if I can do anything about it when I return there.

As soon as I am back in Leuchars, I fly down to London and see General Spaatz. He listens, poker-faced, as I describe the plight of the Norwegian resistance, and then leans back in his chair and fits his fingertips together.

"What do you want to do about it?" he asks.

"If we had armed planes," I suggest, "we could handle the drops ourselves."

"Sounds like a hell of a ticklish business if the RAF won't tackle it." He takes a long hard look at me. "Think you can handle it?"

With me it is the same as General Hap Arnold likes to put it: the impossible is something that hasn't been done yet. *"Ja,* ve do it."

General Spaatz has that little grin of his. "From now on, you're the Ve Do Its."

About a month later, on June 22, 1944, his Majesty King Haakon and Crown Prince Olaf pay an official visit to Leuchars Field, accompanied by my old friend Admiral Riiser-Larsen, now head of the Royal Norwegian Air Force. The King is to present his personal guidon to the Norwegian Air Force unit stationed at Leuchars; and before the ceremonies he expresses a wish to inspect the American aircraft and personnel flying to Stockholm.

My flight crews are lined up in uniform in open formation

for the review, and behind them on the line are our B-24s. Half of the planes are dark green; but the others have just come from Bovington, painted a cold shiny black, so that the rays of any enemy searchlights that may catch them will bounce off and make them tricky targets. There is no mistaking the nature of their mission.

I try to steer the King toward the green planes, but he seems to be drawn, as if by a magnet, to the black ones.

"Such a nice shine," he murmurs, "so different from the planes we generally see, with their drab colors."

I have no choice but to follow him as he mounts the steps of a newly converted B-24. His face is expressionless as he notes the exhaust pipes fitted with dampeners to conceal their red glow at night, and the flame arresters on the muzzles of the machine guns.

"Running into neutral Sweden with armed planes, Colonel Balchen?" the King asks in mock surprise. His eyes take in the drop racks in the open bomb bay, and the plexiglas greenhouse that has been substituted for the regular nose turret in order to give the navigator a clearer view of the drop zone. The bottom turret has been removed, and the King gazes thoughtfully at the padded opening, called Joe Hole, through which saboteurs will be parachuted. In silence he rips out a page of his pocket notebook, scribbles a few words, and hands it to me.

"Will you deliver this message to my countrymen?"

I fold the page and tuck it into the pocket of my blouse. "It will be in Norway tonight, Your Majesty."

At eleven o'clock we take off on our first drop mission, bearing the code name Fetlock I. Keith Allen and Dave Schreiner are to alternate with me at the controls. As we leave the Scottish coast, we come right down to the water to avoid being picked up by the German radar screen, and skim the wave tops to the Norwegian coast. We pick up the coast after two and a half hours. Just south of us is Herdla Island outside Bergen, where the Nazis have a fighter field; but they do not detect us. With their guns safely behind us, we zoom up to 7,000 feet, past the bright slopes of Jotunheimen Glacier, and I look down on the pine forests where I hunted *elg* and capercailzie, and the salmon streams I fished as a boy. To our left now is Lake Loen, and just ahead, in a pocket of darkness in the mountains, is our drop-target for tonight, Bollhöe.

We are carrying three and a half tons of guns and explosives for the Underground to use in a big sabotage operation they are planning against the Nazi heavy-water industry. A couple of miles away the three beacon fires of the reception committee suddenly flame up in a row in the valley, and we coast down to an altitude of 500 feet, and lower wheels and flaps to reduce our speed almost to stalling point. We line up on the three beacons, ready to drop over the first light so that it will land on the middle one.

Below us in the gray dawn we can see the men on the ground, and a flashlight giving the well-known signal: "V . . . V . . . V . . ." Now our intercom begins to chatter: "Bomb-bays open." "Dispatcher ready." "Three—two—one—*drop*." The plane jerks a little when the twelve containers leave the drop racks, and as we bank and turn I can see the packages landing in a cluster around the center fire, the men running to strip off the parachutes and hide the containers, and then get the supplies on to their destinations. The three bonfires are quickly doused, and the valley is dark again as we head back to the coast.

King Haakon is still at Leuchars when we return, and I am invited to a luncheon in his honor. As I am sitting down at the table, I receive an acknowledgment from the reception committee at Bollhöe, transmitted by underground radio. I hand it to the King without a word, and he reads: "Everything received, also message H.M. Thanks to the Yanks." We look at each other, and our eyes blur for a moment.

By now we have two more urgent supply drops scheduled in

rapid succession. I fly the second one, three days later. There
has been considerable discussion as to whether this mission is
feasible. Our destination is near the village of Holtaalen, in the
Trondheim area, and because of the midnight sun at this high
latitude the flight has to be completed in full daylight. It is a
beautiful trip. We come in across the mountainous coast between one and two in the morning. There is fairly good cloud
cover over the coast, but as we get farther north it burns away.
Coming into Holtaalen, we can see the smoke of the reception
committee's fires, rather than the fires themselves, below us. To
the north and west the mountains are bathed in the light of the
low sun, which glitters like gold on their snowcapped peaks—
an unforgetable sight. On the ground, as we come in at 700
feet, we can see the men clearly, and we even photograph them
as they receive the drop.

On the return we fly down to the interior of eastern Norway,
near the Swedish border, where it has been reported that the
Germans are building a large new airfield at Haslemoen, apparently to defend the region in case of sudden troop movements from neutral Sweden. It is about four-thirty on a beautiful sunlit morning as I fly over the town, just above the treetops. Many of the houses down there are the homes of friends
of mine. My men ready their cameras as we approach the site
of the rumored airfield, hugging the treetops. Just before we
burst out over the field I go up to 800 feet, and we snap photographs right and left. Down below us, Germans are running
across the field in their underwear, some of them buttoning up
their coats as they try to reach the antiaircraft guns. Before
they can fire a round we are out of sight. We have a beautiful
homeward flight across Norway and out over the coast, seeing
no enemy aircraft. We have verified that a field of considerable
dimensions is being built, though it is not yet operational.

Now the Ve Do It Group goes into full-scale operation, supplying new hope and strength to Norway's mounting resistance.

Expert OSS men are attached to our unit, and trainloads of food and medicine and sabotage materials are shipped to Leuchars from the OSS packaging stations near Birmingham, sealed in special containers to which we attach colored parachutes. The shadow army hiding in the hills is reenforced with hundreds of tons of weapons, ammunition, TNT, and high-explosive plastic which can be molded undetected into keyholes, and triggered with tiny detonators to blow up a power plant or munitions factory. In addition to our night drops behind the lines, we fly armaments and explosives directly into Stockholm. It is arranged with Dr. Soederman's police that when we come into Bromma with a contraband load, we give the call-word "Flygvapnet" which means "air force," and they throw a cordon of police around the plane. Later a truck shows up and moves the secret cargo to one of my apartment-house cellars, where it is stored until another truck can smuggle it over the back mountain roads into Norway, the guns concealed in hollowed-out logs under piles of timber. In all our operations into Stockholm, not one single ounce of equipment is ever lost.

Each sortie into Norway has a separate code name, which is communicated to the underground by the British Broadcasting Company. Into the regular program is inserted an innocent phrase like "The finch has laid three eggs," which means that the reception committee called Finch will receive three drops. The next evening BBC may announce, "Two sea gulls are flying," and that night Project Sea Gull gets two plane loads over. On all their drops, the men of the unit add personal gifts of their own, cigarettes from their rationed supplies or a bottle of liquor or the latest magazines. At the time of the Normandy invasion, the drop crew includes today's newspapers with pictures of the successful Allied landing, and next morning these are on the tables of all the hotels in Oslo for the Nazis to see. Always we attach a little note with our gifts: "This is the American Air Force. We are with you all the way. Best regards from the Yanks," and sign our own names. Later, long after the war, when I go back to Norway, total strangers will come up to me— a waiter at the hotel in Oslo, maybe, or a bus driver, or a lumberjack, and pull a worn slip of paper out of his wallet and shake my hand.

Already the effects of our drops are being felt all over Norway, in stepped-up guerrilla activity and sabotage, and Nazi security efforts are redoubled. On several occasions our signals are intercepted, and we arrive at a drop zone to find German troops waiting there like ferrets at a mousehole. Our maps are supplied by OSS, with fighter stations and antiaircraft batteries pinpointed in red; but in spite of the best underground intelligence we sometimes run into unexpected interference. One night I am going in over a corridor that is supposed to be secure, and as I come out of a break in the clouds at low altitude, my black B-24 is trapped by searchlights from a flak ship, and the sky is full of ack-ack around me. I pull the plane almost inside out in violent evasive action, and escape with a few holes only.

Everywhere the Luftwaffe has been alerted for the Ve Do Its. On my way back from a drop mission near my boyhood home in Kristiansand, I encounter a German Heinkel 177, a reconnaissance plane armed wtih two cannons. He is right on my course, and I decide my only chance is to carry the attack to him, despite my inferior armament. Luckily he refuses the challenge and turns tail and flees, and I fly right down over the water and get out of there in a hurry. The Nazis sometimes even follow us all the way to England. Captain Withrow is returning to our auxiliary base at Metfield-in-the-Wash, bringing refugees from Sweden in an unarmed green Lib, and just as he is coming in for a landing with wheels and flaps down, the air explodes with 20-millimeter shells. A German JU-88 has swooped down on him from the rear. Withrow groans, "No, no, not on my own field!" and pulls sharply into a climbing turn,

and the Nazi fighter, trying to avoid a collison, dives into the
ground and explodes in flames.

One of my drop missions takes me to Sandungen, just north
of Oslo. On the outskirts of the Norwegian capital, on top of
the high hill called Holmenkollen, is my own home in Norway.
I am curious to see what condition the house is in, so flying
back from the drop at Sandungen, about five o'clock of a beautiful clear morning, I find myself jumping down over the hills
that I know so intimately. In a little while I pass my house,
perched high on a steep, wooded hillside that falls away nearly
a thousand feet to the valley. As I roar past on a level with the
windows, I can actually look inside some of the rooms. To see
your own home a hundred yards away, in time of war, and to
know there are friends whom you've known all your life within
shouting distance, yet to be shut off from all this because of
enemy occupation, is a cruel and terrible thing to experience.
Even the fact that, so far as I can see, the house has not suffered
any physical damage, does not make me feel much better.

Turning off just before getting down to the antiaircraft
batteries in front of Oslo, I set my course westward across the
mountains, then down a long fjord and out over the open sea
at an altitude of about 500 feet. It is a safe flight home, without
any difficulties.

After the capitulation months later, when again I come back
to my house near Oslo, my next-door neighbors and close friends
will tell me how they were awakened that fine morning by the
din from a big, black, four-engined aircraft that flew right by
their house and on which they could see the white American
star.

Many of our drops include radio equipment, and the clandestine network is spreading rapidly through occupied Norway
to every village and mountain hide-out. Laborers conceal tiny
units in their lunch boxes, anglers carry secret transmitters in
their creels with steel fishing-rods for antennae, and one in-

genious agent wears in his mouth a set of false teeth which is
actually a receiving set, the two back molars pivoting on swivels
for tuning. One sending station is set up in a hospital attic
behind clotheslines hung with diapers, and operates for months
until the Nazis get a bearing on it. In the midst of pounding
out a message, the agent is surprised by two Gestapo men; he
shoots them both, and rushes through a maternity ward, filled
with screaming nurses and babies in cribs, and down a back
stairs to the street. There two more SS guards are waiting, and
he kills them also, climbs a wall into an adjoining building and
sheds his working clothes, and steps outside. A German officer is
strolling with two streetwalkers, and he nonchalantly links arms
with one of the girls and walks with the German officer through
the cordon of Gestapo guards. A week later he is back in
Stockholm.

Now the resistance movement is growing bolder, encouraged
by the German reverses in France, and leaders travel back and
forth by rail between Oslo and Stockholm, right under the noses
of the Gestapo. Some of them put on diving suits, and make the
trip submerged in the water tenders of locomotives, and others
seal themselves in empty oil tanks and arrive in Sweden nearly
unconscious from the fumes. To divert Nazi suspicion, one of
the leaders of the Norwegian resistance, Jens Christian Hauge,
later Norway's Minister of Defense, has been writing an impressive tome entitled *Cultural Improvement in Norway Under
the Germans,* and this literary pursuit has taken a surprisingly
long time to complete, and has involved a great deal of research
all over Scandinavia. In Stockholm he informs me that some of
our signals are being intercepted by the Nazis; and I decide to
go to Oslo myself and talk to my friends in the underground
there and set up a new code.

I drive to the Norwegian border, hike over an old moose-
hunting trail I have followed many times through the woods,
and am picked up on the other side by the underground at a

prearranged rendezvous and taken into the center of Oslo. It is strange to be in my old home town again, unable to communicate with anyone I know. My mother and sisters are living in the city, but I dare not even telephone them for fear of reprisals. I see several of my friends in the street but cannot speak to them. One old friend recognizes me as I am sitting at a table in a restaurant. He turns white as a sheet and chokes over his coffee, but does not speak to me. Coming down the street as I step out of the restaurant is a prominent local Quisling, who I know would betray me at once, and I duck into the lobby of a nearby hotel—the same one in which I was an honored guest after the Atlantic flight. The clerk looks at me sharply, and I step quickly into an automatic elevator; but before I can close the door I am joined by a Luftwaffe general. I ask him in German what floor he is going to, and he tells me the third, and then remarks: "You speak a very good German. Where did you learn it?"

"All Norwegians with a little education speak German," I reply.

He nods, pleased. "What kind of work do you do in Oslo?"

"I'm a repairman. Some communications have broken down, and I'm here to fix them."

I let him out on the third floor, and get out at the next and walk back downstairs and out through the service entrance. Twenty-four hours later I slip across the border into Sweden, and fly to England.

In London next morning I meet my friend Ted Curtis, now a Brigadier General and Tooey Spaatz's chief of staff, who invites me to lunch with Air Marshal Sir Trafford Leigh-Mallory, over-all commander of the Allied Air Forces.

Sir Trafford wants to have a talk about the whole business of flying over Norway and dropping supplies there.

"How are things going?" he asks, sipping his Martini.

"Fine, thank you, sir." I try not to show too much satisfaction. "As you know, we've been operating only a comparatively short time, but already we've evacuated a thousand Norwegians from Sweden, and we have made ten drops to the underground in northern Norway."

"Well," he says, "you seem to have a horseshoe in your pocket." Then he becomes serious. "I feel rather embarrassed about this—here my man in the RAF refused this job. I don't know whether you are quite aware of the risks you are taking for your crews, flying in there. I think it's just good luck, myself, that you've gotten away with it so far."

"Well, sir," I say, "I think I'm quite well acquainted with Norway."

"You may think so," says Sir Trafford, "since you have made a couple of flights over there. What do you know about Norway?"

"After all, sir, I'm not a native-born American. I was born and raised in Norway and have done quite a little flying there."

"But, Colonel," he says, "the situation is different today. How long since you've been back to Norway? Not just over it but on Norwegian soil."

"I was there yesterday, sir."

Sir Trafford gulps his Martini. "Hm-m. Shall we go in to lunch?"

During my visit I tell General Curtis about the downed American airmen interned in Sweden—now over a thousand pilots and crew members. Early in October he himself flies in one of our B-24s to Stockholm to confer with Swedish and Allied officials about getting these internees back. He arrives at Bromma Airport in uniform, probably the first American general to enter neutral Sweden in full war regalia, and confuses local security officers still further by neglecting to carry a passport. That night at the Grand Hotel he asks me to join him for dinner in uniform, and there are some startled faces among the hotel staff when I show up in my true colors. At the very next table is a group of Nazi intelligence agents. They cannot take their eyes off our Air Force wings and ribbons, and I suspect they are secretly wondering whether the war is lost already.

The American internment camp is at Mullsjö, in Sweden's beautiful lake country, and the men are treated like honored guests, with the finest food and lodging and two-week passes into town every month. Most of them are the crews of bombers crippled in raids over Germany, who could not get back to England and had made forced landings in Sweden. A few had parachuted into Norway, and they tell us some hairy tales of their escapes. One flak-riddled Fortress caught fire over Larvik, and the pilot ordered the crew to bail out. The right gunner's parachute had been ripped by a shell fragment, so he climbed on the navigator's shoulders and rode piggy-back to the ground. The whole crew were gathered in by the resistance forces, and hidden for a week in a church steeple, while the Gestapo scoured the neighborhood in vain. All over Norway the underground movement is on the lookout for downed Allied fliers, they report. Four British Lancaster crews had been marched in full uniform, escorted by an underground agent, right through the German lines to the coast, where they were picked up by submarine. Another agent dressed himself in the uniform of a Wehrmacht officer and brazenly escorted a downed Spitfire pilot by train to Oslo, where both "prisoner" and guard mysteriously disappeared.

Gradually the Ve Do It group is getting to be known as Ve Do Everything. Before the war is over, we are supplying the reception committees with dynamite and TNT, winter underwear, sectional houses, fishhooks, even bales of hay for their horses. Once a bale breaks open as it is dropped from the plane ahead, and I fly through a haystorm. The entries in my logbook for these days are hard even for me to believe when I read them afterward:

"Drop 2,500 lbs. radio equipment and agents near northern

Norwegian border, round trip 2,700 miles over enemy territory in beautiful summer daylight."

"Deliver gas depot and pumps in town of Malmö on S.E. coast of Sweden, for refueling motor torpedo boats operated by American Commander Raymond Guest, planning to run sabotage equipment into Denmark."

"Hauge and Vetlesen discuss with me a plot to kidnap Quisling by drugging his wine and deliver him to Allies in London. We decide Nazi retaliations against the civilian population would be too severe."

One mission is so secret I do not even enter it in my diary. In Stockholm Dr. Soederman informs me that the Germans have fired into Sweden two of their latest V-2 guided missiles, evidently in an experiment to trace their trajectory and determine the deflection caused by rotation of the earth. One of the giant rockets has scarcely been damaged, and Soederman's people have concealed it from the Nazis, and Ve Do It is asked to smuggle the secret weapon to London for detailed study by the Allies. My problem is to find a plane large enough to carry it. The rocket comes in three sections, a total weight of four tons, and our B-24s cannot fit them inside. Back in London, I know, is a battered old C-47, an antique bucket of bolts affectionately called "The Bug," which the Air Transport Command maintains at the field for local hops. Without divulging my real purpose, I persuade General Earl Hoag, in charge of the European Division of ATC, to let me borrow the aged crate.

Keith Allen, Bob Durham, and a Norwegian radio operator fly the Bug through the gantlet of German coastal defenses to Stockholm, and the three sections are crammed inside, and it is locked and sealed. Somehow the Nazis have gotten wind of the project, and on Allen's return trip, as he reaches the Norway coast, they open up with all their ack-ack batteries. Through masterly piloting, Allen wheels the lumbering Bug and its precious cargo in and out between the flak bursts, skims low

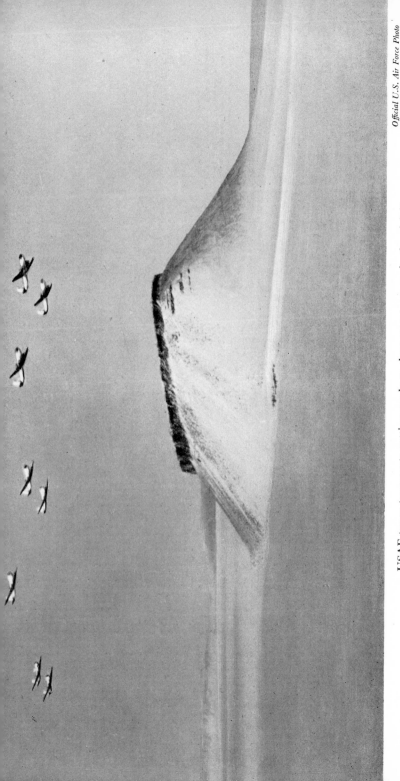

USAF troop transports getting ready to drop paratroopers in the vicinity of Thule, Greenland, during Operation Windchill, March, 1954.

Don C. Kn[...]

Pack ice at the North Pole, as seen during my 1949 flight from
Fairbanks, Alaska, to Thule, Greenland.

At the White House, October, 1953: presentation of the Harmon International
Trophy by President Dwight D. Eisenhower to Colonel Bernt Balchen. *From the
left:* Ansel E. Talbert; Alexander de Seversky; Lieutenant-General James H.
Doolittle, USAF Reserve; the President; Harry Bruno; Colonel Balchen.

over the North Sea to evade pursuing fighters, and rolls to a safe halt on the Leuchars strip. I fly the Bug the rest of the way to Farnsborough to deliver the cargo. The only way to get into the cockpit is to squeeze in along the big boxes in which the machinery of the V-2 is packed. I have no sooner landed at Farnsborough than the doors of a big secret hangar open, and a crew comes and pushes the plane inside and closes them again. Professor Alexander, head of the Research Department investigating enemy missiles at Farnsborough, is elated over the booty we have brought back from Sweden. He says it is one of the most important seizures of the war. Now the British can study a defense against the new V-2s, which will be raining down on London less than two months hence.

Ve Do It is still officially attached to the Air Transport Command, and General Hoag is becoming increasingly perturbed at all these mysterious goings-on. I am always requisitioning more combat crews, more machine gunners, more ammunition, and it does not sound to him much like an ATC operation. He is like a setting hen that has had an egg slipped unsuspected into the nest, and finds she has hatched an osprey. In September we have two fatal crashes, one when Captain Bullock's B-24 is lost in heavy weather, and the other when Lieutenant O'Hara flies into a mountain top at Seljord in Norway, and the whole crew is killed. This is enough for General Hoag and he asks me for an explanation. I am not at liberty to answer, and I suggest it would be best for him to see General Spaatz at Widewing.

"I'd like to find out what's going on in my own command," he complains to the general. "I don't know what Colonel Balchen is up to."

General Spaatz tells him something of the story, and explains why it is necessary for my planes to be camouflaged as part of the ATC. "Besides that," he adds, "Balchen has a lot of activities that even I don't know anything about, and I'm much better off without knowing what they are. You just take it in the same

vein, and just give him anything he asks for within reason, and
don't ask any more questions."

I am grateful that General Spaatz has again supported us, and
from then on I have no better friend and supporter of my whole
operation than General Hoag. With our operations constantly
growing, we need such support.

Sometimes it happens that I am not too sure myself just how
an operation will turn out. One night, just outside Oslo, I am
making a drop in a large swampy area between two ridges. In
the middle is a shallow lake, but the darkness makes it hard to
tell the difference between land and water. I see three bonfires
nicely lined up, and some blinking going on that I cannot make
out clearly. Our challenging signal is fired, and somebody blinks
with the light again, and I drop our supplies and get out of
there in a hurry. Later I find out what happened. The lake was
full of fresh-water crayfish, a great delicacy in eastern Norway,
and an old fisherman had set out a series of stakes baited with
cat meat. He had built three bonfires along the beach, to attract
the fish, and was wading in the shallow water from stake to
stake, holding a bobbing lantern as he gathered the crayfish in
his dipnet. Suddenly he heard the roar of an airplane directly
overhead, and down out of the darkness came a huge container
with a parachute attached, landing with a splash right in front
of him. "You goddam Nazis!" he muttered, shaking his fist at
the sky. "Can't you even let a man fish in peace?"

Other containers were dropping all over the lake, and he
gathered up his stakes and cat meat sullenly, and started for
home. On the trail he met the local reception committee, and
they asked him guardedly if he'd seen any parachutes falling.
"Damn right," he growled. "They scared all my crayfish away."

Most of the containers were recovered by the consignees.

In September of 1944 the tide of war is running stronger and
stronger against the Axis, from the Mediterranean all the way
to the Arctic Circle. Finland has just withdrawn from the Nazi

alliance, and German troops are beginning to trickle out of the country, across Finnmark, down to Norway. Vetlesen needs to establish underground radio stations to keep track of the German troop movements, all along the subarctic coast to Kirkenes near Petsamo, Finland—a round-trip flight of 3,000 miles, the absolute maximum capacity for our Libs.

On September 20th, Keith Allen, with Dave Schreiner as his copilot and Bob Durham as navigator-bombardier, takes off from Leuchars on one of these long-range missions. They are planning to drop an agent en route at Kaafjord, where the great German battleship *Tirpitz* is hiding in a deep narrow fjord, safe from aerial attack. This observer will hide out in the hills, as part of the so-called Operation Wet Nurse, and report whenever the *Tirpitz* is ready to slip out to sea, so that the waiting British Barracuda bombers can go into action. Allen and his crew have been thoroughly briefed on Russian radio codes and equipped with Russian recognition flares, in case they have to make an emergency landing inside the Soviet Union.

They encounter heavy Nazi flak as they cross the coast of Norway, and one engine is hit and catches fire. Allen feathers it, but soon the second one on the same side begins to sputter. He and Schreiner have great difficulty keeping the plane on course with two engines, but they manage to parachute the agent only thirty miles from the intended drop zone, then nurse their faltering plane to the nearest field at Murmansk, where the Soviets have given our planes permission to land.

As they reach the mouth of Kola Inlet, approaching Murmansk harbor, three Russian searchlight cones of three each are turned on, indicating the airfield ahead. Previous to this, they have been picked up by a blue beacon and also by a searchlight which is subsequently turned off, evidencing identification by the Soviets of the approaching aircraft. The harbor is crowded with the entire Russian northern fleet, including eight American destroyers given to the British early in the war and sold by them in turn to the Russians; and in their midst is the Soviet's particular pride, a former British battleship which has been renamed the *Archangel*. The rest of the story I quote now from the official Counter Intelligence report:

"In attempting to make a 360° turn, the crippled B-24 flew, without knowing it, over the battleship *Archangel*. During all this time, Russian recognition flares were being fired by the Americans, in addition to their running lights, passing lights, and landing lights which were turned on in order to identify their plane as friendly. Altitude at this time was 1,400 feet, and radio-calls were being transmitted on the W/T international distress frequency. While the plane was in the turn, Russian shore batteries and naval forces opened fire, hitting the number two engine and the left wing, and shooting off the left rudder. The plane caught fire and the pilots agreed to abandon ship. Lt. Col. Allen ordered Capt. Schreiner to bail out with the rest, explaining that he would follow. Firing from the ground continued while the plane descended. The interior was ablaze, flames rushing past the bomb-bay door and rear camera hatch, and the crew bailed out by jumping through the flames. Despite the fire on the command deck, the engineer pulled down and inflated two life-rafts and dropped them through the bomb-bay. The left waist gunner was hit with flak after he bailed out.

"During these events the navigator, Lt. Robert Durham, accomplished the burning of all classified material, and completed detonation and destruction of all secret radio equipment. The nose of the plane had been shot off, and he escaped through the well of the navigator's compartment. Before he left, as did two others, he had looked into the pilot's compartment and seen no one. It later developed that the fire prevented the evacuation of Lt. Col. Allen. The navigator was pinned by searchlights as he descended. When he reached the ground, he threw away his gun and called for help, with the intention of organizing the rest of the crew. This appeal for help was answered by machine-gun fire, which increased in intensity as minutes passed.

"The tail-gunner landed in the water and also shouted for help, and his appeal was likewise met by machine-gun fire, whereafter he maintained silence. Knowing that the left waist-gunner was hurt and could not swim very well, he stayed in the water until he located his crew-mate, after which he swam to shore and both men were apprehended by an armed Russian girl. Capt. Schreiner and the radio operator also landed in the water. Capt. Schreiner was picked up by a dinghy, and the radio operator was seized on the beach.

"Both ankles of the right waist-gunner were fractured on landing, and machine-gun fire was aimed at him and maintained so effectively that his parachute, still attached to him, was thoroughly riddled. He stated that he was picked up bodily by Russian soldiers, and let fall again because of his injured feet. Thereafter he was laid face down on the ground, a heel placed on his neck, and a rifle muzzle held against the back of his head, while he was searched."

Bob Durham is captured by a Russian lieutenant, who takes him to headquarters for questioning. After they are convinced of his identity as an American, a Soviet staff officer lets him view the plane, which is entirely demolished, and then he is moved to a cabin to wait deportation. Hours later a body is found in the wreckage and brought to the cabin for Durham to identify. It is Keith Allen. "You want to take it with you," the Soviet officer asks, "or throw it away?"

In Norway the German army of occupation is on the defensive now, fighting a force without substance. The shadow lies cold and silent across every Nazi installation. An unseen hand closes on a sentry at his post; there is a flash of steel, the crunch of a revolver butt, and only a few ski tracks lead away into nothingness in the white winter hills. A troop train is mysteriously derailed in a steep canyon. An unexplained avalanche roars down the mountain side onto the SS barracks. A harassed general calls an emergency meeting of his staff, and while they are drawing up plans to combat the shadow army, an explosion in the main power plant plunges the headquarters into total darkness.

Nazi guards are strengthened, and leaves canceled; rewards are posted in shop windows, savage reprisals are threatened. Still the Undergrounders slip through the Gestapo net like Norwegian sardines. At Banak, on the Barents Sea, a group of Norwegians attach magnetic mines to a German munitions ship, and the blast obliterates the cement dock and hurls the forepart of the ship two hundred yards through the air to a rocky mountain side, where it still hangs to this day.

Norway's secret war records, released after the hostilities, tell the crippling effects of some of our drops. "At midnight on August 13th," the official *Linge* report states, "seven Norwegian saboteurs met at the bus depot in Korsvoll, on the outskirts of Oslo, where the Nazis had a large warehouse full of airplanes and spare parts. The Undergrounders carried suitcases loaded with 250 pounds of American plastic high explosive and 60 pounds of dynamite. Picking the lock of the bus depot, they waited for the German guards to make their rounds and disarmed them one by one, capturing their keys and making their way through connecting basements to a point directly below the stored aircraft parts. Expertly and quickly they placed the explosive charges, lit the fuses, and made their escape undetected. Minutes later there was a terrific blast: 25 Messerschmitt planes, 150 airplane motors, and the largest spare parts depot in all of Norway was completely destroyed."

"*January 13, Operation at Jorstad Bridge.* The railroad bridge at Jorstad was being used daily by great numbers of troop trains carrying Nazi soldiers from Norway south to shore up the crumbling defenses in France. The Norwegian Under-

grounders overpowered four German guards in the darkness of
a bitter-cold night, appropriated their sheepskin coats and fur
caps and guns, and continued to walk guard as if nothing had
happened, while placing explosives under the structure. Their
job finished, the Norwegians slipped away on their skis, and
when the next German troop train moved across the bridge it
was blown sky-high. Ten cars were destroyed completely and
more than 300 Nazis killed and wounded. At a time when re-
enforcements were critically needed to bolster their sagging
front lines along the Rhine, it took the Germans a week to
repair the bridge."

"*January 15, Operation on Troopships.* No part of Oslo was
more closely guarded by the Germans during their occupation
than the steamship piers. No fewer than 35 armed sentries were
on duty alongside the Nazi transport *Donau,* bound from Oslo
to Copenhagen, Denmark, with troops being ferried to the front
lines in Germany. Two Norwegian saboteurs appeared on the
scene, dressed as stevedores and equipped with false identification papers, and were passed through the guards and allowed to
enter an elevator at the edge of the pier, where the *Donau* was
just finishing loading. On their way down the elevator, the two
Undergrounders slipped through a hole previously prepared,
made their way along the hull of the *Donau,* and fastened explosive limpets. For good measure they paddled a rubber boat
around to a sister ship, the *Rolandseck,* and used up the re-
mainder of their limpets. The *Donau* departed with 1,500
troops and 300 motor vehicles, and out in Oslofjord at eleven
o'clock that evening it exploded with such force as to rock the
entire waterfront. The *Rolandseck* also sustained heavy damage."

By the end of 1944, the steady string of Allied victories on
the continent are driving the Wehrmacht back to their homeland, and the Allied Chiefs of Staff fear that when the Germans

are finally beaten in Central Europe, they may attempt a final stand in *Festung Norwegen*—Fortress Norway. It is decided to give the Undergrounders all-out aid in their struggle to rid their country of the Nazi invaders. Many Swedes would like to join their Norwegian neighbors and declare war, but the Allies persuade them that they can help best by remaining neutral; and Stockholm becomes the spearhead of the new northern front.

Our latest project, called Where and When, is to transport Norwegian police troops and a field hospital from Kallax on the Gulf of Bothnia in northern Sweden to Kirkenes in northern Norway, from whence they will follow up the retreating Nazi troops. We will also deliver food and clothing to the scorched-earth areas.

Our advance base of operations is at Kallax. During the winter, Ve Do It flies 1,442 men and 2,456,000 pounds of equipment to the far north, and the entries in my logbook read like a shipping manifest: "450 tons supplies and 265 military personnel to Bodö." "70 Norwegian engineer troops to Kautokeino." "40 tons hospital equipment from Kirkenes to Banak."

This winter flying reminds me of Antarctica and Greenland together, but with ack-ack and fighter planes thrown in for good measure. We have no equipment for preheating our engines, although the temperature drops as low as fifty below zero. Instead we use a system, developed in Alaska, by which we dilute the oil in the engines with gasoline, right after they are stopped, thereby keeping them crankable regardless of the cold. This method works fine, and the Swedish Air Force, to which it is new, is much impressed by it. Trained Swedish snow-removal battalions work constantly to clear the fields so that we can take off on wheels. This is an integral part of Swedish military training, and I think the idea could well be adopted by our own Air Force for northern operations. Our pilots have had little experience in cold-weather flying, but I am able to show them some of

my old bush-pilot tricks. Also I teach them skiing, in case they
are forced down in the snow, and I even have some classes in
Swedish. One youngster asks me why he must learn such a difficult language. "So you can talk to these pretty Swedish girls," I
tell him, and he becomes one of my best pupils.

Sub-zero weather is not our only problem in northern Norway. When Finland sued for peace with Russia a year ago, she
was forced to cede to the Soviet Union a long strip of territory
at the top of the Scandinavian peninsula; and as the Nazis re-
treated, the Soviet occupation forces pursued them north,
ravaging the homes of the simple Finnish woodcutters and the
camps and houses of the Lapp reindeer herders as they advanced. The Russians had halted at the Norwegian seaport of
Kirkenes, taken it over lock, stock, and barrel, and destroyed all
but two houses of the city in conformance with their scorched-
earth policy. Although Kirkenes is officially under Allied Command, Colonel Lukim Grigge, Soviet Commandant at the field,
reigns like a Russian czar.

When I sit down at Kirkenes on January 12th, we are the
first Allied air unit, except for Russians, to land in occupied
Norway. The Soviets have established complete censorship of
the field, I find, and Colonel Grigge demands that the Norwegian commanding officer furnish him with a passenger list
two days in advance of all our arrivals. Without clearance from
the Russians, nobody is allowed to step off the plane.

The Norwegian air attaché in Stockholm is deeply concerned,
but I assure him I'll take care of everything from Kallax. I have
a Norwegian liaison officer in my outfit, and I put him to work
writing out lists of names taken at random from a phone book.
We give these lists to the Soviets, and their slow-witted intelligence service is completely satisfied.

Soon comes another regulation from the Russians: no Norwegian who has come to Kirkenes may return to Sweden without their clearance. As the campaign moves along, we get the

field at Banak cleared. For some reason the Norwegians are forbidden to fly from Kirkenes to Kallax without Soviet permission, so I tell Grigge I will fly them as far as the approved field at Banak—but from there I take them wherever they want. Surprisingly, the Russians never catch on.

One of our tightest operations comes in February during our push westward across Finnmark. At Kautokeino, a small Lapp settlement in the mountains near the Finnish frontier, a company of about 150 Norwegian ski troops have come to grips with the Germans holding the main road running northward to the coast. A liaison officer has gone in to them with a reindeer train, and now he sends out word to us that the Norwegians' ammunition and medical supplies are running low, and that there are some casualties to be evacuated. He asks whether a plane can fly in for these purposes, informing us that he has marked out a landing strip on the ice of the river near Kautokeino.

I decide that we can probably handle it with one ship; but, not being too sure of the situation, I decide to make the trip myself, with one of my pilots, Captain Holdiman. On the way we get a radio signal that the Germans have landed a paratroop unit on the mountain ridges near Kautokeino in order to outflank the Norwegians. Therefore, I first fly over these ridges to take a look, and am pleased to see that the snow conditions where the Nazi paratroops have been landed are such that they are slowed up in the drifts, which will give us a little leeway.

As I come around on my pass over the place the Norwegians have staked out on the river ice, we have to turn just above the forward German positions. Evading their fire, we look over the landing strip and decide to make a stab at it. No sooner do we touch down, however, than the plane sinks into a foot and a half of snow. It rolls only a few times its own length before it is jerked to a violent stop, luckily without doing a flip-flop. Safely down, we turn over our cargo of ammunition and medical necessities to the Norwegians; but now the question is how we are to get out of here.

There is only one thing to do: to get as many men out of the firing line as possible and turn to to make a more adequate runway on the ice during the night. Hour after hour we work together in relays, tramping down and shoveling out the snow, and by ten o'clock the next morning we have a runway about a thousand feet long by sixty feet wide. It is bumpy and dangerous, of course, but we just have to get the plane off. I keep hoping for a helping wind, but what little there is blows right across the runway. Holdiman and I decide to make a try anyway. Lowering half wing flaps, we hold the plane with our brakes at the end of the strip and then let her go with full power. As we hit the end of the runway, we are making just about sixty m.p.h. We have barely enough speed to pull out just clear of the snowbank ahead and keep the plane airborne. Once again, we have to make our turn right in front of the German firing line. They come at us with everything they have, but fail to hit us. Both Holdiman and I let out sighs of relief as we gather sufficient flying speed and clear out of that area. From then on, we have a beautiful flight back to Kallax.

As spring comes on, the Norwegian ski patrols that have taken over from the Russians at Kirkenes push south and west on the heels of the retreating Germans. The front becomes constantly more fluid, and the troops advance through devastated, burned-out country, their movements further hampered by the Germans' grim legacy of mines and booby traps everywhere.

On May 3rd a terrible explosion occurs near the little Lappish settlement of Karasjok, where Norwegian troops are demining the road from Finland to Banak. A truck is being loaded with defused Teller mines when one of them explodes and sets off about fifty more, killing twenty-two men instantly and severely injuring nine others. At Kallax I receive an urgent radio appeal from one of my agents in the Karasjok area, for immediate aid for the sufferers. Getting in touch at once with the Norwegian authorities in Stockholm, we learn that they have available there a field hospital and two doctors—the chief of the Norwegian medical services, Colonel Semb, and one of his aides, Dr. Wergeland. I immediately dispatch a plane to Stockholm, and seven hours later it returns with the field hospital and the two medical men. We also pick up a Norwegian nurse who is available at the village of Sundsvall, and fly her to Kallax. The air is turbulent on that spring day, and the nurse, who has never been in the air before, becomes violently airsick. Our plan now is to fly the hospital equipment over to Karasjok and parachute it in, in containers, and also to parachute the doctors and nurse. This is, to say the least, news to them—especially to the nurse, who has just made her first flight.

In a parachute training school which has been set up in a gymnasium at Kallax, we give the doctors and nurse all the instruction we possibly can that morning, showing them, with the help of our training apparatus, how to jump from the plane and roll on landing. Then we give them lunch and take them out to the plane. The flight to Karasjok is hair-raising for them, as we have to pass through a front and fly contact through some narrow mountain valleys. When we arrive over Karasjok we find that the spring thaw has rendered the runway on the ice in the river there useless; but on the river shore is a large snowbank which seems to be the logical place to drop the personnel. Dr. Wergeland jumps first. He lands beautifully, rolls over in the snow and stands up. Next the nurse goes out, and when she hits the snowbank she does not even fall over, but stands there calmly unstrapping her chute. After conferring with a medic on the ground, Dr. Wergeland signals to the plane that they will need all the medical help they can get, and it is decided that Dr. Semb will also parachute in. Although he is in his fifties, he jumps without the least hesitation, as neatly as the others.

When they have been delivered, we drop the medical supplies
and equipment right in front of the village church in Karasjok,
the only building left standing in the town. An hour later they
are operating in the church, which also serves as a hospital. All
the injured are saved, and as soon as possible we fly them out in
two small Storch ski planes, placed at our disposal for the occasion by the Swedish Air Force, to Kiruna and thence to the
hospital at Boden. The two doctors, the nurse, and the field
hospital equipment are evacuated the same way.

The Soviets have decreed that the Norwegians may not possess
radios or firearms; but these I continue to supply. I remember
the White War under Marshal Mannerheim back in 1918, when
we in Norway joined the valiant Finns against our mutual
Communist enemy, and I think the people need guns to protect
themselves from the Reds, even more than from the Nazis. In
Kirkenes the Soviet troops have no tents, but sleep in a circle
in the snow with their felt *katinka* boots to the fire, and in the
morning they shake themselves like dogs and get going again.
Telephone poles are dug up during the night and carted away
for firewood. Russian soldiers steal watches and personal pos-
sessions from the Allied barracks, and if a thief is caught his
superior officer shoots him and leaves him lying in the street.
They have no concern for their men. Once I see some Russian workers clearing an airstrip with a bulldozer. I warn the
colonel in charge that the field has been mined by the retreating Germans. He pays no attention, and a few moments later
the bulldozer and soldiers are blown into the air by a violent
explosion. The Soviet colonel shrugs his shoulders. "Nothing
to worry about," he says. "We have plenty of men, and we can
always get more bulldozers from America."

I am flying to Kirkenes on May 8th when I hear Churchill's
broadcast that Germany has surrendered. The war in Europe is
over, but there is no time for Ve Do It to celebrate. Now we
must start flying relief supplies at once to the starving inhabi-

tants of ravaged Norway. From the former Nazi stronghold at
Bodö our advance units radio an appeal for food and medicine
and Swedish Red Cross supplies. We fill ten C-47s to capacity
and take off. The Bodö strip, as we fly over it, is lined with
JU-88s and Messerschmitt 104s in trim military rows. A German follow-me jeep escorts my lead plane to a parking place
and as I dismount the German commandant salutes smartly
and announces that a fleet of staff cars is at my disposal. You
would think the Luftwaffe had been doing nothing for years
but greet American aircraft.

The residents of Bodö have recognized our planes flying over,
and by the time we arrive in town the buildings are flying
Norwegian flags that have been kept hidden all through the
war. All the Norwegian ships in the harbor have broken out
the national colors, and a thousand men, women, and children
march down the main street, singing for the first time in five
years the Norwegian national anthem. In the leading hotel,
where the high Nazi officers stayed, a special banquet is waiting
for my crews. It is the best that Bodö can offer: thin barley
soup, a small piece of whale meat with a sort of gravy, and one
potato apiece.

In the Bodö-Saltdal area we discover, to our surprise, that
there are some 150 prison camps where 70,000 Russian soldiers
are penned up behind barbed wire, living in their own filth.
When one of the prisoners is sick, his comrades steal his bed-
ding and push him outside to die; corpses lie all over un-
buried. The gates of the first stockade are thrown open, and
within an hour there have been two murders, several fires
have been started, and shops are being broken into all over the
city. We have to rearm the Germans with the guns they have
just surrendered, and I order them to herd the Russians back
into the stockade again and stand guard over their conquerors
until I can notify the Russian authorities. Later I report to
Colonel General Shcherbakov, commander of Russia's Arctic

Army, that he can reclaim his countrymen. He grunts with con-
tempt, and replies in German: *"Sie sind verbraucht!* Used up.
Expended. They have surrendered, they are not Russians any
more."

A few days later I am in Oslo at the Grand Hotel, the same
one where I took refuge in the elevator a year ago, and in the
lobby I meet the Luftwaffe general who shared the elevator
with me. He stares at my uniform in surprise: *"Ist es möglich?"*
(Is it possible?) "Yes, general," I say, "I met you in this hotel
a year ago." He shakes his head. *"Es ist fantastisch!"*

He walks away with a laugh.

About a month after the capitulation, King Haakon arrives
in Oslo.

Outside my hotel I hear the sounds of a band and of heavy
ski boots striking the cobblestones in cadence, and I step out
the door. Down the street are coming lean, hard-faced, proud
young men, carrying on their shoulders the American rifles and
carbines we had dropped to them. They are men of the underground forces, back from their mountain hide-outs, parading
before the King. They see me on the hotel steps, and someone
in the line recognizes my uniform and shouts, "Thanks, Yanks!"
My throat is so tight I cannot answer. Now I know in my heart
that it is possible to love two countries.

Comes in July a letter of commendation to the Ve Do It
Squadron:

With the cessation of hostilities, it is but right and fitting that
the Office of Strategic Services should express to you its sincere ap-
preciation of the outstanding cooperation you have given. Your
supply-drops have been one of the outstanding operations of the
war, and you have transmitted intelligence of inestimable value to
the Supreme Commander, Allied Expeditionary Forces. This headquarters is fully cognizant of the fact that the operations you have
been called upon to fulfill have been both difficult and hazardous,
and, on many occasions, above and beyond the call of duty. Your

command has at all times reflected credit both upon the Air Forces and upon the American spirit that is so deeply engendered in your officers and men. You have carried out a task which at no time has had a precedent in the annals of American air history.

WILLIAM J. DONOVAN
Major General, Commanding

Today, as I look back over my diary of the war years, a casual event comes to my mind, an incident which has even more significance now than then. Here in my logbook is an entry written just before the war ended: *"3 May, 1945. Dinner Russian Hdq., Kirkenes. Drink cod liver oil first."* And a chance remark made to me over a glass of vodka keeps turning over and over in my mind.

That morning I had noticed increased activity among the Russian troops, and Colonel Grigge informed me that a delegation from Moscow was arriving at Kirkenes, and he would like me to come that evening for dinner. General Shcherbakov would be there, he said, and three or four important visitors from the Kremlin. I had been warned about this Russian ruse to get information out of guests, when drinking has loosened their tongues, and before setting out for Soviet headquarters I took the old-country precaution of swallowing a big cupful of cod-liver oil. The flow of vodka progressed with the dinner, and a Moscow official beside me began to show the effects. I pretended I was well in my cups also, and he became very confidential and nudged me.

"We push to Narvik, Zhukov to Denmark. Come together. You understand?" He joined his hands in a gesture like a pincers closing.

I understood, all right. To hold the coast of Norway was as important to the Soviets as it had been to Hitler, and I recalled Admiral Raeder's remark: "Who controls Norway controls the North Atlantic." As soon as the party was over, I flew back to

Kallax and got on the phone to headquarters in Stockholm; and, when the war ended, it was Marshal Montgomery and not Zhukov who won the race to be first in Denmark. Had the Russians grabbed Norway and Denmark as they planned, the entire Scandinavian Peninsula might still be behind the Iron Curtain today.

The little remark that lingers in my mind came just at the end of the dinner. Colonel Grigge, seated opposite me, was getting maudlin, and he lifted a glass of vodka and reached across the table.

"Colonel American Balchen, we drink to you," he said thickly. "But one day in the Arctic we will be fighting you." And he clinked his glass against mine.

TEN

TRUE NORTH

On May 23, 1949, when I was in command of the Tenth Rescue Squadron in Alaska, I flew over the North Pole from Fairbanks in Alaska to Thule in Greenland. I had not seen Thule since 1942, when I made an aerial survey in a PBY from Bluie West Eight and reported to General Arnold that here could be one of our main ramparts of defense in the Arctic. Now, seven years later, this conviction was stronger than ever in my mind, and I wanted to visit the site once more.

We took off from Ladd Field in one of the four-engine C-54's assigned to Tenth Rescue for our long-range search program. Air Force B-29 weather-profile ships called Ptarmigans were flying regularly over the Pole now, and our squadron was extending its rescue operations in case of a forced landing on the polar ice. It was a beautiful spring evening when we left Fairbanks, and the scattered lights of the gold camps pricked the twilight as we crossed the Tanana Valley and the winding Yukon River and climbed over the Brooks Range, packed with clouds. We broke out on top at 12,000, into the full rays of the midnight sun. Below us the tundra was shrouded in darkness—still two hours until dawn down there—and in a few moments we picked up the sleepy lights of Barter Island.

We took a heading of true north, across the unbroken whiteness of the Arctic Ocean. East toward Herschel Island the ice was solid, but forty miles out we came on the first open leads, and a hundred miles from the coast were giant ice floes on which a C-47 on skis could set down safely. From here on there was a low cloud layer a couple of hundred feet high, covering thousands and thousands of square miles. This is a common condition in the Arctic during the summer, and I made a note that our search planes would need reliable radar for rescue operations here. The undercast extended from 76° to about 80° north latitude, and from then on we had good visibility all the way to the Pole.

Spread out before me, as I sat at the controls, was an ever-moving ocean. North of 85° the ice was definitely drifting toward the Greenland Sea, looser to the east of us, with more big leads than on the Alaska side. Even at the Pole itself I could see patches of open water, the floes grinding together and throwing up pressure ridges, constantly shifting as the ocean currents carried the pack over the top of the world. This ice is getting thinner each year, as the whole Arctic grows warmer. Since Dr. Nansen's ship *Fram* drifted across here in 1896, it has decreased in thickness more than twenty feet, and in the same period the level of the Atlantic Ocean has risen nine inches. Cod and other fish of temperate regions are moving steadily northward into the milder waters, and leading scientists like Professors Sverre Petterssen and Hans Ahlmann predict that if the present rate of warming up continues for another thirty years, we shall have an ice-free ocean over the North Pole in the summertime.

I looked north as I flew, and beyond the north to the future, and in my mind I could picture commercial vessels plying some day over this vast new sea, opening up the riches of all the hitherto inaccessible lands within the Arctic rim: Prince Patrick Island and Grant's Land and the whole Canadian Archipelago. Perhaps a gold strike bigger than the Klondike would be made here, or the greatest oil sinks of the northern hemisphere would be found where now ice covered all. We should have a short cut to the Far East that would alter our present steamship routes and create new industrial areas, with incidental population movements. More important from a military standpoint—and my mind kept turning over and over the little remark that Colonel Grigge had made to me at Kirkenes at the end of World War II—we should have another ocean to defend.

I banked a wing and circled the Pole, flying around the top of the world in two minutes, and then set a straight course for Thule, where a joint U.S.-Danish weather station had been established. We landed on a gravel strip at the base of the mountains, but not in the same area I had recommended to General Arnold for a runway. As I was filling out my Form I, a sergeant of the crew scratched his head. "Look, Colonel, weren't you pilot on the South Pole flight, too?"

I nodded absently as I was writing. "*Ja,* sure. Why?"

"Well, then, don't that make you the first man who ever piloted a plane over both Poles?"

"I guess it does," I said. It hadn't occurred to me until that moment.

Han skal leve til han dor. A man lives until he dies, and as he lives he grows. I look back through the entries in my diary, and what was important once is not so important any more. One day's headlines are forgotten the next, and there is nothing but confetti in the gutters after a parade is over. Once at Kings Bay I was eager for Captain Amundsen to win the race with Commander Byrd; but now I understand what Amundsen meant when he said: "We are not competitors. We are partners in a joint assault on the polar regions." It is not for headlines that a man explores the lonely ends of the earth, but for the knowledge he will bring back of places that no man has ever seen before.

All my life I have asked the question: What makes an ex-

plorer, a man like Amundsen, a man like Byrd? Now as I look
my own life over I ask myself the same question: Why am I an
explorer? I have lived from adventure to adventure, but is it
only to look back now on the adventures I have had? I think an
explorer does not belong to yesterday only, but also to tomorrow. His importance is in helping shape the future, in pioneering new trails across sea or land or sky that the world will
follow. The great contribution of men like Amundsen and Byrd
lies in the vision they had, the concept of tomorrow's air age,
and they belong to the great company of pioneers who helped
to usher in the new era of polar flight.

As a man lives he grows, and as he grows he must change,
because the world is changing. The old Mercator projection
map which hung on the schoolroom wall back in Kristiansand,
picturing the polar regions as exaggerated waste lands stretching across the top and bottom of the world, is as obsolete as the
child's slate on which I chalked my early geography lessons.
Long-range air transportation, following the shortest route between two points regardless of underlying terrain, has shrunk
the Arctic Ocean to its true perspective. Roald Amundsen
clearly saw this coming, and that is why he learned to fly back
in 1912, and held in Norway the No. 1 private flying certificate.
Today the only true map is the globe, and the airplane has
turned it on its side. In Roman times the Mediterranean Sea
was considered the center of the world; but our new Mediterranean is the Arctic Ocean, and the North Pole is the crossroads
of tomorrow's travel.

Three of the earth's continents, North America and Europe
and Asia, form the ice-covered beaches of the Arctic. The large
industrial areas of these continents are virtually all situated
between latitudes 35° and 50° north. Not only will commercial travel follow this polar route. In time of war, enemy aircraft and missiles may be expected also to use the great circle
course, bringing all these areas within range of strategic attack.

"Across the Arctic," General Spaatz has said, "any industrial target is within reach of our Air Force, and by the same route the United States is in range of the enemy."

The Soviets realize the importance of operational control of the Arctic Ocean, and for at least five years they have been conducting a training program to meet this requirement. We have the same requirement, which will increase in importance with new weapons. It is our responsibility to keep these vast polar regions under constant surveillance, and make our Arctic defenses and our retaliatory offensive strong enough to keep the enemy from war.

Late in 1948, as the Air Force extended its operations in Alaska, I was called back into active service. After my war duties ended I remained in Norway, helping to establish an all-Scandinavian Airlines System, SAS; but now came the request from Washington to assist in developing an Air Force program of operations in the Arctic. On my departure for the States, I was paid a glowing tribute by the Soviet newspaper *Literaturnaja Gaseta*.

"During the last three years, Colonel Bernt Balchen was the President of the Norwegian 'civil' airline DNL. He built large flying fields from government funds designed for landings of heavy American planes. His construction activities were of such an extent that even Sweden was included, also playing with 'civil' aviation. After Sweden the turn came to Finland, to make it ready to receive American bombers.

"The brave colonel was a very popular personality in the pages of the Scandinavian military press. But beware, just recently this very active Bernt Balchen resigned and disappeared from Norway, to be discovered—in the American Department of Defense! An astonishing change: the former president of a 'civil' airline reappearing as a coming commanding officer of the American Arctic military aviation.

"Really, this is not astonishing at all. The American military spy Balchen has completed his mission in Scandinavia. He has equipped the flying fields after directives from the American Army, and coordinated Norway to the demands for U.S.A.'s 'polar strategy.' Now he is coordinating the defense of the North states with the plans of the American militarists."

On November 11, 1948, I arrived at Elmendorf Field in Anchorage, Alaska, and reported to General Nathan Twining, then head of the Alaskan Command, and today the Chairman of the U.S. Joint Chiefs of Staff. The operations of the Tenth Rescue Squadron, which I would now command, covered the entire territory of Alaska, an area as wide as the United States from the Atlantic to the Pacific Ocean and from the Gulf of Mexico to Canada. Here was every variety of weather and terrain, from the williwaws of the treeless Aleutians to the drenching rains of the southeast Panhandle, from the moderate temperature of the swampy Susitna flats around Anchorage to the sub-zero of the Arctic seaboard and the polar ice beyond.

Our planes were B-17s and C-54s on wheels, C-47s on ski-wheels, and Cessnas on skis and floats. Whenever the range permitted, we used helicopters and three-quarters of our rescues were performed by these reliable workhorses. Whirlybirds are superior even to dog teams and, I think, would be of tremendous importance in any Arctic warfare, particularly during the summer thaw. Our crews were on the alert twenty-four hours around the clock all year, and we averaged a rescue every two and a half days.

Our officers and men were drawn from every Air Force outfit, SAC and TAC and MATS, and most of them were what they call in Alaska "cheechakos"—new to the north country. I set up a rigorous training program, and each week led the crews on a hike of twenty miles, carrying thirty-pound sacks. We slept out on the Aleutian muskeg, or on the frozen Arctic tundra, so the men could learn by firsthand experience how to survive in the cruelest conditions. I had not forgotten what Captain

Amundsen said to me once when I was only twelve years old: "In the Arctic you must always be prepared for the worst, and then whatever happens will be easier."

Bush flying was equally new to these cheechakos, and there were no Air Force directives for operating on skis, or preheating engines in cold weather. Now what I had learned in thirty years of Arctic flying came to good use, and I was able to hand down my experience to these apprentice youngsters, and create new pilots who will be flying the North when I have hung up my headset for the last time. All my crews were trained in polar navigation, and by the end of 1950 the Tenth had made 150 landings on the pack ice, and had maintained for two weeks a station on a drifting floe, the forerunner to T-3.

This natural aircraft carrier, called T-3 by the Air Force, is nothing but a great slab of shelf ice broken off from Ellesmere Land, and caught in an eddy of the Beaufort Sea. It is moving in a clockwise direction, which should take it from eight to ten years to travel from Ellesmere Land past Point Barrow, then up the International Date Line between Alaska and Siberia to the Pole, and east and south past Ellesmere Land once more. The Beaufort eddy is inside the polar circular flow, which moves counterclockwise, carrying driftwood from Japan and Siberia to the Arctic coast of Alaska, and on to Greenland and Iceland and even Spitsbergen. Actually the Soviets were the first to establish such a station on the pack ice, when Professor Otto Schmidt's Russian expedition from Franz Josef Land flew to an ice floe near the North Pole in 1937 and drifted southward on the east side of Greenland. We must assume that the same type of floating airfields are being used as observation posts by the Soviets today.

The ice of T-3 is 120 feet thick and about nine miles long by four wide. It contains some dirt and gravel from Ellesmere Land. A weather station is maintained on it, and here scien-

tists probe the secrets of the polar basin, and Air Force planes
can land and take off on their patrols of the Arctic frontier.

The newest scientific methods of snow compaction are used,
creating runways as smooth and hard as concrete during the
cold season. But during a couple of months in the summertime, the "icecrete" runway gets too slushy to be used regularly.

Our Arctic frontier extends far beyond our own continent.
Because of our membership in NATO, our northern defense
line stretches for 3,000 miles, from the tip of the Aleutians off
Kamchatka clear around the rim of the world to the western
boundary of Russia. Today the Russians have one half of this
Arctic coastline, NATO has the other. Part of our global defense is to develop and maintain operational control over the
5,500,000 square miles of polar sea between us and the Soviet
Union.

Near the middle of this perimeter is our new base at Thule.
Back in 1950, Air Force Secretary Stuart Symington read with
interest a paper I had submitted proposing a central search and
rescue organization for all our northern military operations, a
sort of Arctic NATO. Thule in Greenland would be one of
the pivots of this project. Later that year his successor, Secretary
Thomas Finletter, came to Alaska and discussed this plan with
me; and in February, 1951, I flew to Greenland with the first
party of construction engineers. Now at last my big dream of
ten years was coming true. Between the first of July and the
end of August, I watched a great modern air base spring up on
Thule's frozen flats. The Air Force and Army and Navy worked
as a team together, more than 300,000 tons of equipment was
brought to Greenland by plane and ship, and the amphibious
landing was equal to four fully equipped combat divisions. An
hour after the first vehicle rolled ashore, a beachmaster had set
up traffic controls, and Operation Thule was under way. A
force of 13,000 men, ten times what I had at Bluie West Eight,
completed the base in record time. I was with General Curtis

LeMay, commander of SAC, when he made the first landing on
the new runway, and my faith in the site was justified when he
said: "Bernt, here's a place I can fight from."

Not only is Thule a strong rampart in the path of any enemy
invader. In effect, the entire 700,000 square miles of the Greenland Icecap is one vast potential air base. Thanks to the ingenuity and skill of American and Canadian engineers, we can
use the natural resources of the Cap itself to create permanent
runways anywhere above the melting line. Heavy compacting
machines flail the snow inside closed compartments, re-forming
the ice crystals and packing them together before they have
time to turn into water, and producing "icecrete," which is
rolled out and cured by cold. These runways can be built at
comparatively small cost, and are subject only to normal maintenance and snow removal. Fuel storage tanks and even housing
can be hollowed out in the ice. These can be connected by
tunnels within the Cap, free from weather, secure from possible
enemy bombing, and difficult to detect, carrying fuel pipe lines
under the ice to forward installations. Once the Greenland
Icecap was considered as a liability. Today it is one of our
greatest military assets, a 1,400-mile defense line for the North
American continent.

Shortly after World War II ended, General of the Air Force
H. H. Arnold died of a heart attack, brought on by overwork
during the war. He was as much a combat victim as any bomber
pilot shot down in battle. Just before his death he made a
prophetic statement: "If World War III should come, its strategic center will be the North Pole."

This is the direction in which our eyes must be ever turned.
Today our Distant Early Warning line in Canada and Alaska
scans the northern skies with radar day and night, ready to alert
our defense centrals if anything like trouble shows on the
screens. We are prepared for intruders flying ten miles high and

with speeds up to six hundred miles an hour. But what will happen when planes and missiles fly twenty miles high, and their speeds reach the two-thousand-mile mark? Any additional minute we can gain is vital, in order to keep the intruder under attack on his way to the target, and to give us time to destroy an atomic weapon while it is still over the polar wasteland.

I believe our only security is another DEW line at least a thousand miles farther north. Faced with the reality of supersonic manned aircraft and guided missiles, the Congress must provide funds to establish an advance Arctic warning system on the extreme perimeter of the continent, equipped with even more sensitive radar, searching the skies as far forward as the Pole itself.

Our allies in Europe are protected by a radar line which goes from Southern Europe up through Scandinavia. In northern Norway, this line comes to an abrupt stop at the edge of the Arctic Ocean, making it a simple matter for Soviet bombers taking off from Arctic bases in Russia to bypass this line by flying north of it and to proceed unnoticed down the Norwegian Sea and the North Atlantic, if they have sufficient fuel to dogleg this way for an attack on the Atlantic seaboard of the United States.

From both a NATO and an American standpoint, the logical step is to see to it that this gap is closed as soon as possible, so that we have one continuous radar fence from Europe across the Arctic to the tip of the Aleutians. The United States, with its industries and retaliatory capabilities, is obviously the prime target for the Soviets, who will want to reduce the warmaking capabilities of their opponent.

By carrying out these proposals of mine, we could have radar stations two thousand miles beyond the existing radar fence operating eatward from Norway to the present DEW line, giving us precious additional time for warning and also time for interception and destruction of invading forces. We would eliminate the present holes in our warning system.

To my way of thinking, the complete radar fence system should look as follows: 1) the Scandinavian-cross-Arctic radar fence; 2) along the east coast of Greenland to Iceland, from where an extension of the present DEW line will go over to England; 3) the present DEW line; 4) Pine Tree line; 5) Mid-Canada line.

The new fences mentioned could be established more easily and at less cost than the present DEW line, and with the speed of present aircraft we would gain four hours' warning time. By the time the extended fences could be completed, we shall most likely have to figure on the basis of aircraft flying at 2,000 miles an hour. With such speeds, we would have one hour's additional warning. The only way we can get this precious hour is to build out our radar defense. Our communication system from one side of the Arctic NATO line to the other—from Alaska to Norway—must also be made more effective, to transmit traffic dispatches fast enough to be of value. Two minutes' delay may be too great.

But our defense is more than cocking our ears like a frightened rabbit, listening for the first growl of the Russian bear. Along with our radar must be anti-missile stations and launching sites in the remotest Arctic. Here also belong forward fighter defenses to meet any intrusion. Coupled with all this, we must operate from stations on the pack ice—as the Soviets are doing—to take care of various and secret needs.

From the east coast of Greenland and the Arctic Ocean we can cover most of the Soviet Union with our intermediate range ballistic missiles. We can cover their ICBM sites with our IRBMs from the Arctic, and we should not waste any time in taking advantage of what nature has provided for us here.

The Soviets have announced ahead of us that they now have the ICBM. It is regrettable that they have this jump on us, but from the time this announcement was made, to the time when they will have an operational weapons system, is a long and hard road. Generally it takes several years from the test flight of one of our new bombers to the day when it becomes a part of our operational forces. An entirely new weapons system, with countless new problems, most of them involving new concepts and systems for their solution, will take the Soviets at least as long to complete as it would take us—five to ten years.

Our Strategic Air Command's manned bombers, with their nuclear bombing capability, will in my opinion for quite some time to come be the real deterrent from an attack on NATO and our shores.

With our knowledge of the northeast American Arctic, we know that we can install there IRBM sites, which could also be our anti-missile sites, in comparatively short order and at reasonable cost. These sites would also be the logical places from which to start the interception of an enemy ICBM, and the wastes of the North American Arctic can be used for the destruction of these deadly machines.

Perhaps my Russian admirers have already surmised that the Tenth Squadron in Alaska was engaged in more than search and rescue while I was there, and during our missions we kept our eyes open for such defense sites. It is the Soviet's suspicion of our ability to strike back, I think, that is the greatest single deterrent to attack today.

We must look north, but like a good pilot, we must be able to see to the west and, more important, to the east. The Soviet's only entrance to the North Atlantic is between Norway and Spitsbergen. If we can block this Dardanelles of the Arctic, we can turn the Atlantic into a NATO lake where our shipping can move free of naval interference. "Who controls Norway commands the North Atlantic" is as true for the Communists as it was for the Nazis once. The Russians themselves must realize that their Achilles' heel is in the Arctic, and that their occu-

pancy of Scandinavia would close this exposed flank. Here is
where the next brush war is most likely to flare up, I think,
and our defense of the Scandinavian Peninsula is vital for the
security of all the world's democracies.

The growing Soviet capability of delivery by air is an ac-
cepted fact. We can no longer ignore the warnings of our military leaders, and sacrifice security for economy. Already there
is a widening gap between what is expected from air power in
the Arctic, and what our air power can actually do with the
funds allotted. We must develop the proper type of equipment,
and we must train our men to operate this equipment and to
live in the far North all year round. On a strong Arctic depends
peace in the air age.

We are in the Arctic to stay. Back in 1949, General Frank
Armstrong and I made the first nonstop flight from Fairbanks
to Oslo, a distance of 3,900 miles. Early in 1957 the Scandinavian airline SAS, which I helped found, inaugurated a passenger service along this same route, and today several commercial
companies are getting ready to fly regularly over the Pole. The
low temperatures encountered in the Arctic are no more severe
than in any other operation in high altitude, and modern elec-
tronic aids make polar navigation routine.

The network of radar stations, air bases and weather stations
that has been built up in the Arctic for defensive requirements
has to be considered as a permanent installation. For the safety
of navigation of the airways of tomorrow this net must be an
integral part of the worldwide traffic control which will, especially in the Arctic, receive an increasing workload as our
air age develops and mankind requires more airlift. Already
contrails mark a traveled highway across the top of the globe,
and passengers sip cocktails matter-of-factly over the North Pole
and complain to the stewardess that the cabin is too warm.

Soon will come the day when heavy cargo planes make their

début, transporting a hundred tons or more at 500 miles per hour. Then will come even bigger carriers, with even greater ranges, and their economical operation will make possible freight rates with which they can compete successfully with our present basic transport vehicles, ships and railroads and trucks. Giant cargo carriers are to my mind the most important development of modern aviation, both for commercial and for military use. At the end of the war, General Arnold visualized an airlift by civil airlines, if an emergency arose, capable of transporting an entire Army corps to Alaska or Iceland. Development of the heavy cargo transport for the Air Force was stopped for lack of funds. Today more than ever we need this type of plane for the mobility of our armed forces, as well as for maintaining a commercial fleet able to compete for world trade in the age of tomorrow.

Today goes fast, and tomorrow is almost here, and maybe I have helped a little in the change. So I go on to the next adventure, looking to the future but always thinking back to the past, remembering my teammates and the lonely places I have seen that no man ever saw before, still hearing the crunch of skis and the howl of Malemutes carrying far away and forever through the thin air.

INDEX

Acosta, Bert, 88, 89, 91-92, 94, 95, 100, 102, 103, 105, 106, 108, 109-12, 114, 115, 119, 121, 123, 126-28
Across Arctic America, by Rasmussen, 235
Air Pioneers, 301
Air Transport Command, 262, 281
airways, future, 310-11
Alaska, 302, 303-06, 308-11
Alexandra Mountains, 169
Allen, Keith, 264, 265, 270, 280, 283-85
America (plane), 79, 85, 87-91, 93-95, 97-102, 128, 129
  flight across the Atlantic, 102-22
American Transoceanic Company, Inc., 91
Amundsen, Roald, 14, 16-20, 22-27, 29, 33-36, 38-40, 43, 45, 46, 48, 49, 54, 59, 60, 78, 127, 128, 131-33, 135, 146, 163, 165-67, 178, 183, 188, 189, 192, 212, 218, 242, 300-01, 303-04
  death, 146
  discovery of South Pole, 191-92
  last Viking, 123-47
  My Life as an Explorer, 133, 134, 146
  The South Pole, 127
Anchorage, 303
Anderson, Frederick, 261
Andrée, Solomon August, 32
Angmagssalik, 237
Antarctica, 148-92
  icecap, 16
  See also South Pole
Archangel (battleship), 284
Arctica; air routes, 301-02
  aviation in, 76
  defense, 302, 305-11
  See also True North
Arctic Aviation, 80-82

Arctic Barren Lands, 79
Arctic Brotherhood, 221
Armstrong, Frank, 310
Arnold, Henry H., 60, 195, 212-13, 215-16, 218-21, 235-36, 256, 269, 298, 300, 306, 311
  death, 306
Atlantic Aircraft Corporation, 68
Atlantic Ocean; flight over (New York-to-Paris Air Derby), 65, 66, 87-122
atomic weapons, 307
Atterbury Dome, 237, 240, 242, 246
aviation; Arctic, 76, 80-82
  blind, 107
  instrument flying, 109
Axel Heiberg Glacier, 182, 183, 189

Banak, 286, 288, 290
Barents Sea, 286
Barren Lands, Arctic, 79
Bay of Whales, 163, 165, 167-69
Beaufort Sea, 304
Bennett, Floyd, 23, 25, 37, 41, 42, 45, 47, 48, 54, 55, 58, 61-64, 66, 79, 85, 87-89, 94, 95, 100-01, 133-37, 139-42, 186, 191, 201
  death, 144
Berge (photographer), 35, 42-43
Bertaud, Lloyd, 94
Biddle, Tony, 201
Blériot, Louis, 125
Bluie West One (Narsasuak), 236, 242
Bluie West Two (Ikatek), 242
Bluie West Eight, 215-56, 298, 305
Bolero Movement, 236, 237
Bolling (S.S.). *See Eleanor Bolling*
Bonesteel, General, 254
Bontekoe Island, 250
Borealis, King, 221

Braathen, Chris, 165-67, 191, 197, 198
Branch, Harllee, 201
Bremen (plane), 138, 139, 142-44, 194
Brennan, Mike, 37, 50-53, 55, 57
British Broadcasting Company, 273
British Imperial Airways, 202
British Overseas Airways Corporation, 266
Bruce, David, 258
Bruno, Harry, 56, 59, 60, 61, 63, 65, 66, 99
"Bug, The," 280
Byrd, Richard Evelyn, 15, 22-28, 36, 38, 40, 42, 45, 46-49, 53-63, 65, 66, 87-94, 97, 99-105, 108, 110-12, 114, 115, 117-19, 121, 123-28, 133, 134, 145, 149, 152, 162, 177, 179, 181, 184-86, 300-01
    Antarctic expedition, 148-92
    Atlantic flight, 87-122
    Skyward, 61

C. A. Larsen (S.S.), 149, 151, 155, 156, 158-62
Cache Lake, 79-81, 82, 84, 85, 87
Carmen Land, 183
Chamberlin, Clarence, 89, 91, 92-94, 99, 112, 127, 128
Chantier (S.S.), 13, 15, 16, 21, 25, 27, 28, 34, 37, 41, 42, 45, 47, 48, 50, 52, 54, 55-57, 61, 65, 139, 140
Cheeseman, Al, 80-82, 84, 85
Christmas, 163, 219-20
Churchill, Winston, 263
Churchill. *See* Fort Churchill
City of New York (S.S.), 148-92
clothing for winter, 133, 226
Cold Weather Man (Balchen), 258
Coli, Major, 89, 92, 93, 138
Colonial Airlines, 95
Columbia, plane, and flight to Germany, 93-94, 127
Cook, Captain James, 145
Coolidge, Calvin, 128, 194
Coste (aviator), 92
Counter Intelligence Report, 284
Cramer, "Shorty," 145, 216
Cuisnier, Louis, 139, 143
Curtis, Charles, 194

Curtis, Ted, 213, 277, 278
Curtiss Field, 91, 93, 138

DNL. *See* Det Norske Luftfartselskap
Danish Sledge Patrol, 255
Date Line, International, 155, 161, 304
Davies, "Taffy," 161, 163
Davis, Noel, 89, 93
Dawn (plane), 136-37
Deboulay, Captain, 212
defense, Arctic, 302, 305-11
del Priete, C. P., 145
Demarest, Max, 240, 241
Demas, Pete, 198
deportation notice to Balchen; and granting of citizenship, 194-95
Det Norske Luftfartselskap, 200-02, 204, 205, 302
Devers, General, 242
Dietrichson, Leif, 130, 146, 242
Dietrichson, Olaf, 18
Discovery Inlet, 164-65
Distant Early Warning, 306-08
Dolleman, Sergeant, 225, 231, 233, 245, 246
Donovan, William J., 256, 258, 296
Doolittle, Jimmy, 60, 261
Drouhun (aviator), 92
Dulles, Allen, 258
Dunlap, Lieutenant, 242, 246
Durham, Robert, 264, 265, 280, 283-85

Eaker, Ira, 213, 261
Earhart, Amelia, 145, 195-97
Eden, Anthony, 263
Eielson, Carl Ben, 37, 146
Eleanor Bolling (S.S.), 151-56, 169-71
Ellesmere Land, 304
Ellsworth, Lincoln, 14, 16-20, 23-25, 35, 38-40, 48, 197, 199, 242
Elmendorf Field, 303
Eskimonaes, 247-49, 255
Europe-to-America; first flight, 138
exploration, Arctic, 32
explorers, 24, 300-01

Fairchild plane, 168
Fanefjord (S.S.), 197
Farley, James, 201, 202

Farnsborough, 281
fauna, Arctic, 29-30, 51
Fédération Aéronautique Internatio-
    nale, 125
Ferrarin, Arturo, 145
ferrying planes across the Atlantic, 216
Finland, 207-09, 282-83, 289
Finletter, Thomas, 308
Fitzmaurice, James, 138, 139, 141, 142
Florman, Carl, 267
Floyd Bennett (plane), 144, 183-85, 187
Floyd Bennett Bay, 197
Foch, Ferdinand, 125
Fokker, Anthony, 28, 61, 68-72, 76, 79,
    85, 88, 90, 94-97, 100, 112, 125, 136
Fonck, René, 93, 102
food in Greenland, 226-27
Ford, Henry and Edsel, 134, 135, 136
Ford plane, 134, 135
Fort Churchill, 79-82, 86
Foulois, Benny, 60
Fram (S.S.), 299
Framheim, 132, 135, 165, 167
Franklin, Sir John, 16
Franz Josef Land, 204, 304
Friendship (plane), 145
future airways, 310-11

Gates Flying Circus, 91
Gatty, Harold, 145
General Aviation, 144
geology, Arctic, 31-32
Germany, 199-201, 205-06
    supplies on Sabine Island, 253-54
    war planes, 234-35
Gjoa (S.S.), 16
Gneisenau (warship), 224
gold rush; airplane use, 71
Goldsborough, Brice, 137
Göring, Hermann, 206, 207
Gould, Lawrence, 37, 151, 161, 167, 171-
    77, 180, 182, 186-88, 190
Grant's Land, 299
Grassmann, Doctor, 264-65
Grayson, Mrs. (aviator), 136
Great Britain; red tape, 262-63
Greenland, 214-56, 304, 305, 308
    icecap, 230-33, 236-38, 306

Greenland Base Command, 252
Greenland Sledge Patrol. *See* Sledge
    Patrol
Grigge, Lukim, 289, 290, 296, 297, 300
Grosvenor, Gilbert, 194
Guest, Raymond, 280
Guggenheim, Harry, 62
Guggenheim Foundation, 61, 65

Haakon, King, 131, 210, 263, 269-71, 295
Haines, "Cyclone," 161, 168, 172, 186
Hamilton, Leslie, 138
Harlem, Olaf, 18
Harmon, Clifford B., 125
Haslemoen Field, 272
Hassell, Bert, 145, 216
Hauge, Jens Christian, 276, 280
Haw-Haw, Lord, 28
Healy, Sergeant, 225, 231, 232, 245, 246
Heflin, Colonel, 261, 262
Heimdal (S.S.), 13, 14, 21-23
helicopters, 306
Helland Hanssen, Mount, 183
Herdla Island, 270-71
Hitler, Adolf, 195, 205, 206
Hoag, General, 280-82
Hobbs, Professor, 216
Holdiman, Captain, 290, 291
Hoover, Herbert, 194-95
Hudson, Ontario, 72-81
Hudson Bay, 80, 82
Huenefeld, Guenther von, 138, 143
Hump, Antarctic, 188-90, 199

icebergs, 148
icecap. *See* Greenland
"icecrete," 305, 306
Iceland, 223, 249, 250, 254, 256
Ikatek (Bluie West Two), 242
instrument flying, 109
Intercontinental Ballistic Missile, 308
International Date Line, 155, 161, 304
International Ski Derby, 30

Johnson, Herschel, 66
Jorgensen, Captain, 156-58

Jorstad Bridge, 286-87
Josephine Ford (plane), 28, 33-36, 39-45, 59, 61, 62, 65-67, 89, 97
June, Harold, 144, 168, 172-75, 177, 184, 187-90, 194
Jungberg, Carl, 267
Junkers, Erhart and Herta, 139

Kallax, 288-92
Karasjok, 291-93
Kautokeino, 290
Keflavik, 256
Kimball, Doctor, 97, 101
King Edward VII Land, 169
Kings Bay, 14-15, 34, 37, 41, 46
Kingsford-Smith (aviator), 145
Kinkaid, Doc, 29
Kirkenes, 283, 288-91, 293, 296, 300
Knudsen, Eli, 248-49, 253
Köhl, Herman, 138, 142, 143
Köppen (mechanic), 141, 143

Labrador, 229
La Guardia, Fiorello, 195
Lappland, 289
Larsen. See C. A. Larsen
Leigh-Mallory, Sir Trafford, 277
LeMay, Curtis, 305-06
Leuchars Field, 263, 264, 269, 271, 273, 281
Leviathan (S.S.), 126-27
Levine, Charles, 93, 94, 97, 99, 127, 128
Lie, Trygve, 263
Lindbergh, Charles A., 89, 92, 94, 97-100, 112, 144, 206, 216
Little America, 132, 164, 167-68, 171, 172, 175-77, 180, 197-98
Little Norway, 211, 258, 261
Liv Glacier, 185, 198
Lockheed-Vega plane, 196
Longyear City, 32
lost fliers, 138
Löwenstein-Wertheim, Princess, 138
Lufthansa, 267

Mackay, Elsie, 138
Mackenzie Bay, 235
MacMillan (Donald) Expedition, 25
Magnetic North Pole, 16

Magnetic South Pole, 155
mail carrying by air, first transatlantic, 120
Maitland, Lester, 211
Mannerheim, Gustaf, 204, 207-08, 293
Marshall, George C., 247
McIntyre, Ross, 202
McKinley, Ashley, 146, 184, 187, 188, 194
Messerschmitt fighters, 200-01
Milch, General, 206
Minchan, Friedrich, 138
Mitchell, Billy, 60, 61, 212
Monteverde, Lieutenant, 238, 239, 241, 246
Montgomery, Marshal, 297
Morgan, Tom, 209-10
Morgenstierne, Wilhelm, 209
Mulloy, Thomas, 139, 144
Munargo (S.S.), 220, 226
Murmansk, 235, 283
Murphy, Charles J. V., 139, 141
My Life as an Explorer, by Amundsen, 133, 134, 146
Mussolini, Benito, 38, 40

Nansen, Fridtjof, 18, 299
Narssasuak (Bluie West One), 216, 229
Narvik, 296
National Aeronautic Association, 101
National Geographic Society, 194
navigation, air, 64
New York City, 58-59
  celebrations for Byrd, 128, 193
New York-to-Paris Air Derby, 87-122
New York Times, 161, 191
New York *World*, 139, 146
Nichols Field, 211
Nilsen, Oscar, 149, 156
Noah's Ark, 184, 198
Nobile, Umberto, 14, 35, 38-40, 43, 46, 48, 49, 146
Noorduyn, Bob, 69-70, 219
Norge (dirigible), 14, 15, 22, 27, 33, 35, 38, 39, 40, 43, 46, 48, 131, 146
Norseman (plane), 219
North Atlantic Treaty Organization, 305, 307, 308, 309
North Pole; crossing of, 45, 48

Northland (U.S.S.), 235, 252-54
Northwest Passage, 16
Norway, 199-200, 202, 209, 210, 262-64, 285-90, 297, 309
  honors for Balchen, 129-31
  resistance movement, 268-78
Norwegian Airlines, 208
Norwegians; bringing out of Sweden, 262-68
Noville, George, 23, 24, 79, 85, 87, 88, 91, 92, 100-03, 105, 106, 109-12, 114, 115, 119-21, 123, 127, 128

Oertell, Robb, 23, 24, 35
Office of Strategic Services, 256, 258, 260-62, 266, 273, 274, 295
O'Hara, Lieutenant, 236, 238-42, 244, 281
Olav, Crown Prince, 210, 263, 269
Olsen, Rudolf and Thomas, 200
Omaha Beach, 121
Omdahl, Oskar, 16, 20, 130, 131, 133, 136, 137
Operation Deep Freeze, 133
Operation Sonnie, 262, 264, 265
Operation Thule, 305
Operation Wet Nurse, 283
Orteig, Raymond, and Orteig Prize, 65, 89, 92, 94
Owen, Russell, 161, 177, 191

Pan American World Airways, 201, 202, 208, 216
Pangborn, Clyde, 91, 211
Paris; welcome for Byrd, 123-25
Parker, Alton, 145, 194
Parunak, Lieutenant, 231, 233
Pearl Harbor, 227
permafrost, Arctic, 234
Peterson, Carl, 165-67, 185, 194
Petterssen, Sverre, 299
Pleven, René, 210
Point Barrow, 37, 304
Polar Star (plane), 197
Pole, South. *See* Antarctica
Poles, Magnetic. *See* Magnetic
Post, Wiley, 145
Prince of Wales (Edward VIII; Duke of Windsor), 126

Prince Patrick Island, 299
Pritchard, Lieutenant, 240, 241
Purvis, Sir Arthur, 210

Queen Maud Range, 135, 163, 176, 182-84, 186, 188, 189, 191
Quesada, Pete, 213
Question Mark (plane), 213
Quiet Birdmen, 60, 195, 205, 212
Quisling, Vidkun, 250

radar, 306-08
radio, 110, 112, 114, 166-67, 275-76
Raeder, Grand Admiral, 260, 296
Rasmussen, Knud, *Across Arctic America*, 235
Raymond Orteig Prize. *See* Orteig
Rescue of O'Hara and others, 236-45
Richthofen, Manfred von, 60, 68
Rickenbacker, Eddie, 196
Riiser-Larsen, Hjalmar, 21, 38-40, 130, 199, 200, 210, 242, 269
Ritter, Lieutenant, 248, 249, 254
Rockefeller, John D., Jr., 169
Rockefeller Mountains, 169, 172
Ronne, Martin, 133, 162, 178
Roosevelt, Franklin D., 195, 201-02
Roosevelt Field, 91, 93, 94, 96, 99
Ross, Rod, 73, 74, 79, 80, 85
Ross Sea, 135, 149, 156, 159, 160, 162, 163
Ross Shelf, 148, 163, 165-69, 188
Royal Air Force, 211, 269, 278
Royal Norwegian Air Force, 20, 50, 64, 70, 110, 184
Russia. *See* Soviet Union

Sabine Bay, 251
Sabine Island, and bombing, 247-55
Samson (S.S.), 132, 133
sastrugi, 172, 181, 198, 246
Scandinavia, 309-10
  See also names of countries
Scandinavian Airlines System, 302, 310
Scharnhorst, 224
Schiller, Duke, 138-39, 141
Schmidt, Otto, 202-04, 304
Schreiner, Dave, 264, 265, 270, 283-85
Scoresby Sound, 235
Scott, Robert F., 153, 165

Scott's Nunatak, 169
Shackleton, Sir Ernest Henry, 165
Shcherbakov, Colonel General, 294-96
Singapore, 211
Sinkankas, Lieutenant, 21
skiing, 30, 35, 43-44
Skyward, by Byrd, 61
Sledge Patrol, 247, 248, 253, 255
Smith, Dean, 144-45, 177, 184, 194
snow compaction, 305, 306
Soederman, Harry, 266-68, 273, 280
Sognefjord Glacier, 264
South Pole, 17
    expedition, Byrd's, 125-28, 148-92
South Pole, The, by Amundsen, 127
Southern Cross (plane), 145
Soviet Union, 202-04, 302-05, 307-10
Spaatz, Carl, 60, 213-14, 261, 269, 277,
    281-82, 302
Spencer (aviator), 239, 241, 242, 244
Sperry Gyroscope Company, 209-10
Spirit of St. Louis, The (plane), 92, 98
Spitsbergen, 31-33
Stark, Howard, 95
Stars and Stripes (plane), 144
Stavangerfjord, 129
Stevenson, F. J., 74, 76, 77, 79-86
Stinson, Lieutenant, 230, 233
Stockholm, 265
Strategic Air Force, 261, 311
Stroem, Sverre, 153, 155, 179, 191
Strong, Harold, 245, 246
Super-Universal plane, 136
Sweden, 260-61, 265-68, 270, 288
Sweetzer, Doctor, 243, 244
Swope, Herbert Bayard, 139, 146
Symington, Stuart, 305

Tarascon (aviator), 92
tent, Balchen-Ronne, 178
Tenth Rescue Squadron, 303-04, 309
Tetley, Sergeant, 240-42, 244
Thule, Greenland, 235, 298, 300, 305-06
Tirpitz, 283

transatlantic air service, 201-02
Turner, Colonel, 256
Turner, "Pappy," 242, 251
Twining, Nathan, 303

Udet, Ernst, 60, 195, 205-06, 235, 267
United States Air Force, 212, 215-16
United States Coast Guard, 216, 235, 247

Ve Do Its, 269, 272, 274
Vetlesen, Georg Unger, 210-11, 258, 280-
    83
Virginia (plane), 144

Walden, Arthur, 162, 165, 179, 198, 219
Walker, Jimmy, 57, 128, 193
Wanamaker, Rodman, 88, 91, 93, 95, 96,
    99, 114, 123
Washington; reception for Byrd, 194
weather, Arctic, 228-29
Wedell (flight engineer), 241
Wellman, Walter, 32
Wergeland, Doctor, 292
Western Canadian Airways, 71, 73, 79,
    86
Whalen, Grover, 56-59, 97, 100, 220
whaling, 149, 156-59
"Where and When," 288
whirlybirds, 303
Wilbur, Curtis D., 128
Wilkins, Hubert, 37, 38, 46, 48, 145, 146
Williams, Al, 205
williwaws, Arctic, 237-38, 246, 305
Wimsatt, Colonel, 242, 246
Winant, John G., 258
wind, Antarctic, 173-76; Arctic, 228-29
Windsor, Duke of. *See* Prince of Wales
winter clothing, 226
World War II, 227; end of, 293
Wright Cyclone engine, 137
Wright Whirlwind engine, 66-67

Zeppelin, Count, 30
Zhukov, Marshal, 296, 297